SO YOU
TO KN

So You Want to Know?
(About Sex and Growing up)

AIDAN HERRON AND DOMINIC McGINLEY

POOLBEG

A Paperback Original
First published 1991 by
Poolbeg Press Ltd.,
Knocksedan House,
Swords, Co. Dublin, Ireland.

© Aidan Herron and Dominic McGinley 1991

ISBN 185371 155 I

All rights reserved. No part of this publication may be reproduced or transmitted in any form or by any means, electronic or mechanical, including photography, recording or any information storage or retrieval system, without permission in writing from the publisher. The book is sold subject to the condition that it shall not, by way of trade or otherwise, be lent, resold or otherwise circulated without the publisher's prior consent in any form of binding or cover other than that in which it is published and without a similar condition including this condition being imposed on the subsequent purchaser.

Cover design by Pomphrey Associates
Illustrations by Steven Hope
Typeset by The Set-Up
Printed by The Guernsey Press Ltd.,
Vale, Guernsey, Channel Islands

Contents

Part I So You Want To Know– About Sex and Growing Up?

1	The Growing Girl	1
2	The Growing Boy	16
3	Making Love–Pregnancy	24
4	New Life	32
5	Growing Up Healthy	40

Part II So You Want To Know More?

6	Introducing Me	51
7	Family Matters	59
8	School and You	72
9	Under Pressure	76
10	Your Emotional Life	87
11	Love and Sexual Attraction	97

12	**Marriage and Parenthood**	**104**
13	**Family Planning and Abortion**	**111**
14	**The Risk of Infection**	**122**
15	**The Moral Aspect**	**131**
16	**Ageing and Death**	**143**
	Before You Go	**153**
	Useful Addresses	**156**
	Index	**159**

Introduction

Perhaps you know a little already—about sex and growing up.

Perhaps you've heard some things you don't fully understand.

Perhaps you have questions you would like answered.

If so, then this book is for you.

We begin with the changes that happen to girls and boys during adolescence.

Part I

So You Want To Know About Sex And Growing Up?

1

The Growing Girl

Maturation

By the time most children are twelve they have started to show some of the signs of growing to adulthood. The changes in the body are called **puberty** and the time during which these changes take place is called **adolescence**.

For girls, these changes may have begun at ten years of age and will be complete by the age of sixteen. For boys they will normally have started by twelve and be complete by seventeen. No two people are the same! Even identical twins, whom it may be impossible to tell apart, may not develop at the same rate.

Reproduction

Reproduction is the way plants or animals of the same species produce new individuals. **Sexual reproduction** involves the male and female of the species. The term **sex** means the difference between male and female.

When the female ovum, or egg, is joined with the male sperm, or seed, then a new life begins. (See section on **Pregnancy**.)

Sex characteristics

The primary sex characteristics are the **genitals** or **private parts**. There are many popular and slang names for these but the correct names are as follows:-

Girls have a **vulva** and **vagina** and boys have a **penis** and **testicles**.

The secondary sex characteristics in girls are the breasts, hair under the arms (which some girls like to remove) and **pubic** hair.

In boys these are voice change, beard growth, hair under the arms (and sometimes on the chest and body) and pubic hair.

The female reproductive organs

The female reproductive organs are inside the body, while the male's are outside.

The **uterus** or womb, where babies grow before birth, is really quite small. It is about the same size and shape as a small pear, held upside down. During pregnancy the uterus expands as the baby develops.

The female reproductive organs

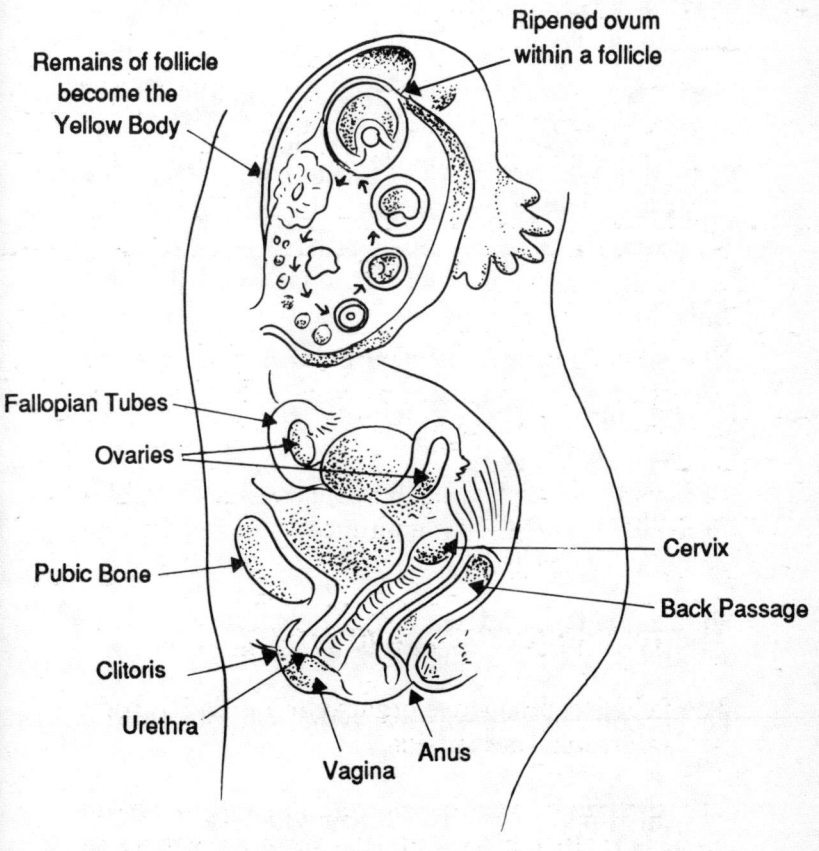

Above the uterus, on either side, are the **Fallopian tubes,** which lead to the **ovaries**. The ovaries are where the unripened eggs or **ova** are stored.

The neck of the uterus is called the **cervix**. The entrance of the cervix is very small and needs to open only when a baby is being born. The cervix leads to the vagina.

The vagina is a muscular passage which leads to the opening between a girl's legs. At the entrance to the vagina are two pairs of **labia** or lips. They are folds of skin. This area is called the **vulva**. When a girl matures, the outer lips will have pubic hair on them. The inner lips won't. Some girls find that the inner lips protrude slightly beyond the outer ones. This is normal and nothing to worry about.

Girls should know what their private parts look and feel like. However, it is not easy for a girl to get a clear view of her vulva from above, so a hand-mirror could prove useful.

A girl has three openings in this part of her body. The first is the **urethra**. This leads from the bladder and it's for urinating (peeing) through.

The second is the vagina, which leads to the uterus.

The third opening is the **anus** which leads from the back passage. This is for getting rid of body waste. Digested food is expelled from the bowels.

The vulva

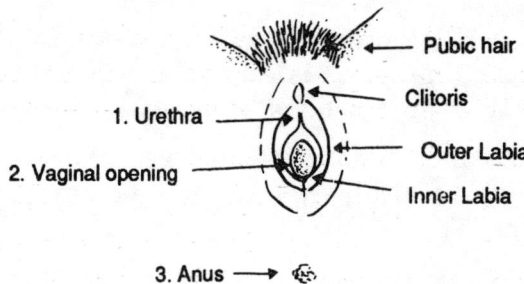

> The medical term for food waste is **faeces** or **excrement**. Many people pass a bowel motion at least once a day. Others may need to go only every second day. In the past people used to fear constipation and often took regular doses of laxatives to make their bowels move. This was not a very healthy practice and you should avoid taking laxatives unless you really need them. If you eat a well-balanced diet, with a reasonable amount of fibre in it and take regular exercise, you are unlikely to suffer from constipation.

The clitoris

The **clitoris** looks like a small bump just above the urethra. It's a part of a girl's body where she feels strong sexual pleasure. It is connected by nerves and tissues to the inner labia.

During sexual excitement it swells, rather like a

penis does, and afterwards goes back to its normal size. Above the clitoris is the pubic bone. This area is often called the **mons** and it is covered with pubic hair.

The hymen

Many girls, though not all, have a very thin membrane of skin which partly covers the entrance to the vagina. This is called the **hymen**. The hymen was once thought to be the only sign of virginity in girls. But girls who exercise or use tampons may cause the hymen to break without even noticing it. A virgin is a person (male or female) who has never had "intercourse".

Breasts

As a girl's breasts begin to grow they may feel tender and uncomfortable. This is normal and a comfortable, well-fitted bra will help. Many of the larger stores have specially-trained fitters, who can help girls choose a bra. A girl who is shy about this should ask her mother or older sister to help her.

Girls sometimes worry about the size of their breasts. They may think their breasts are too big or too small. One breast may be slightly larger than the other because the two sides of the body are not symmetrical. By the time a girl is fully grown her breasts will usually be the same size. Fashions change regularly. Sometimes big breasts are thought fashionable, while at other times the opposite is true. Whether a girl feels in or out of fashion, short of having expensive cosmetic surgery, there is not a lot she can do. Breast size does not affect a woman's ability to breastfeed her baby.

The female breast is a mass of tissue which contains special milk-producing glands. These become active during pregnancy to provide food for the baby. Milk comes out of the nipples. The area surrounding the nipple is called the **areola**. The nipples normally protrude and they react to excitement and the cold. Sometimes nipples are inverted, which means they turn inwards, but this need not affect the ability to breastfeed. Men have nipples too, but they have no function.

It is quite common for hairs to grow around the nipples. These are nothing to worry about and may be removed. Clip them with a nail scissors, rather than pluck them. Hair-removal cream can cause burning in this sensitive area, so it's best avoided.

Self examination
Girls should learn to examine their breasts and take note of any changes. The best time to do this is after menstruation. It is good to be familiar with your own body. Self-examination can be done lying down. If one arm is placed behind the head, the free hand can be used to check the breast; use the right hand for the left breast and vice versa. Any unusual lump in either breast or any unusual changes in the nipples should be examined by a doctor.

Menstruation

Menstruation is the medical term for the monthly flow of blood and small parts of lining from the uterus. The flow comes out through the vagina. Menstruation (or monthly periods) begins in puberty and usually occurs about every 28 days until a woman is in her late forties or early fifties. The length and heaviness of a period will vary from time to time. **Menarche** (pronounced "men-are-key") is the name given to the onset of the first period.

When a woman no longer menstruates, this is called the **menopause**. Periods are a part of the menstrual or fertile cycle.

Ova

When a girl is born her ovaries contain a vast number of immature **ova** (the singular is **ovum**). Very few of these ova ever fully mature. Like brain cells many of them fade away each day. Usually only one ovum ripens fully during each monthly cycle. During a woman's life only about five hundred ova will ripen.

In a four weekly cycle the first day of the first week is when the period begins.

In the second week the ovum ripens within a special group of cells called a **follicle**.

Around day fourteen or early in the third week the ovum is expelled from the ovary, caught by one of the

The menstrual cycle

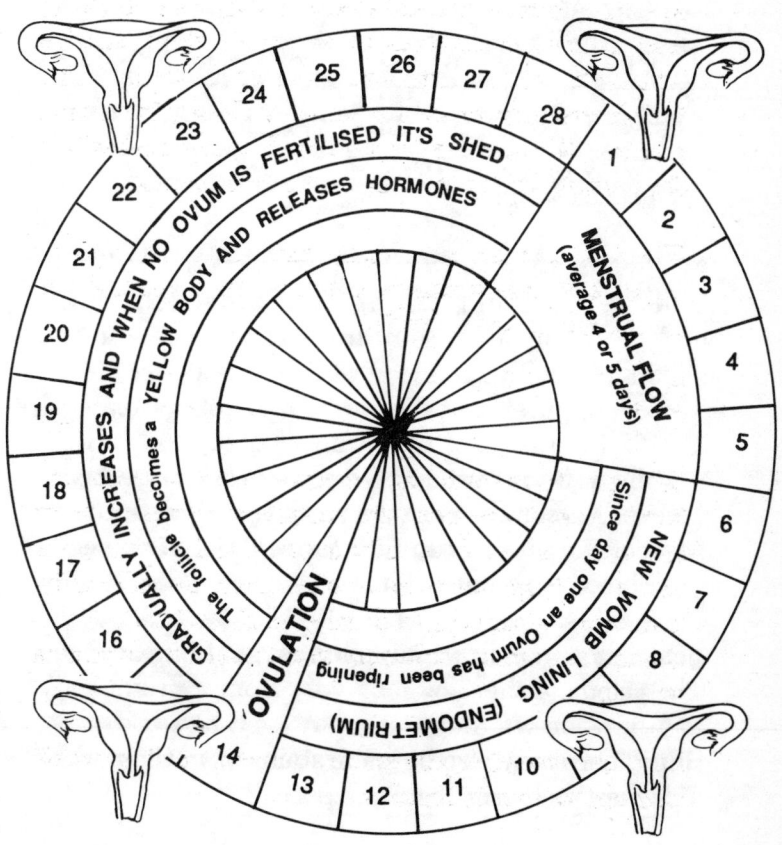

Fallopian tubes and directed down towards the uterus. (This is called **ovulation**.)

In the fourth week the womb-lining breaks and the flow begins.

The diagram shows how the cycle works:
The lining of the womb is called the **endometrium**. During each monthly cycle, it thickens and fills with rich blood cells. The endometrium will nurture a fertilised ovum as it embeds itself in the wall of the womb.

Most of the time, however, an ovum is not fertilised and so the womb lining is not needed. The endometrium breaks up into tiny pieces and is shed along with the blood cells as the period flow. The ovum passes out too, but this is not noticeable. The follicle in which the ovum ripened (now called a **yellow body**) produces and releases extra hormones. Although monthly periods are associated with bleeding and can last for several days, very little blood is actually lost.

Some days the flow may be heavier than others. The colour of the flow may vary from a bright red to a dark brown and there may even be some clotting. There may also be some staining on the pants a day or two before or after a period.

Sanitary protection

In the past, women and girls wore a piece of cloth between their legs to catch the flow from the vagina. This was washed out and kept for use during each period. Now, however, disposable pads are used. These pads are called **sanitary towels** and they come in various sizes and are designed to fit comfortably. They are made of absorbent material.

A **tampon**, which is a small wad of tightly packed cotton, may be used instead. It is placed inside the vagina and it fits very snugly, so snugly that the wearer doesn't even notice it! A tampon absorbs the flow and can easily be removed because it has a string firmly attached which remains outside the vagina.

For convenience and privacy, a girl will usually change her sanitary towel or tampon when she goes to the toilet. Small pads and tampons can be flushed away. Toilets in shops, hotels, schools and work-places usually have a special bin for used sanitary protection. Some tampons have a small cardboard applicator which cannot be flushed away. These should be put in the bin.

Pads and tampons are made in a range of sizes, including small sizes for girls who have just started having periods. You should talk to your mother or to someone you trust about what kind of pad or tampon to use. It is important to change the pad or tampon regularly.

Painful periods

Girls who suffer from painful periods may find that gentle tummy-stretching exercises help to ease their discomfort. Sitting with knees up for a while with a hot water bottle on the tummy or taking a warm bath or a rest in bed may also help. If none of these work, a mild painkiller may do the trick. In some severe cases a girl might need to visit her GP, who can prescribe medication.

It is unlikely that anyone will know that a girl has her period unless she tells them. Periods are nothing to be ashamed of. There is nothing dirty or nasty about them. In the past, a woman might have been considered unclean when she was menstruating. There were also many superstitions and "old wives' tales" about periods. This caused women and girls to think negatively about menstruation. Some even considered it a "curse".

It used to be said that it was harmful for a girl to have a bath, wash her hair or swim while she had her period. This is quite untrue. There is no reason why a girl cannot do any of these during her period, if that's what she wants.

Girls have different terms for describing their periods, like "having their friend." Remember: having periods is a sign that a girl is physically ready to have a baby. It is a good and positive part of growing up.

A girl who hasn't started her periods yet might worry, especially if her friends have. Talking to someone who knows about periods can relieve a lot of unnecessary anxiety.

The fertile cycle

Most girls quickly get to know their own cycle. They can usually tell when their period is due. They can feel that it is about to arrive.

It may take several months for a girl's menstrual cycle to settle down to a regular pattern. Many girls have irregular periods. Illness, shock, excitement and severe dieting can cause periods to stop. They also stop during pregnancy and after the **menopause.**

Discharge

For some months before a girl begins her first period, she may notice a whitish discharge from her vagina. This is normal. Some days or weeks before her first period, she may also notice slight staining on her pants.

After the onset of menstruation a girl will soon discover that there is a cycle of mucus from her vagina. This will be more noticeable at some times more than others.

Ovulation

During the middle of the cycle, about fourteen days after the period has started, or thereabouts, girls may notice a certain amount of stringy mucus. This looks and feels rather like a white of an egg. This mucus appears when ovulation occurs and may last for a day or two.

(Sometimes a slight pain accompanies ovulation). One month ovulation will occur in the right ovary. The next month it will occur in the left. Occasionally two ova ripen during the same monthly cycle.

Some days the vagina may feel slightly wet and other days rather dry. This is all a part of the normal menstrual cycle. But there are some vaginal discharges which are not normal. Sometimes the balance of friendly bacteria in this area is upset. This gives unfriendly bacteria a chance to take over.

Thrush

A fairly common vaginal infection is **candidiasis (thrush).** It can be caused by a lack of hygiene but antibiotics can also upset the balance of friendly bacteria and cause thrush.

Thrush causes a whitish discharge which may be smelly. It is usually accompanied by intense itching around the private parts. The good news is that it can be very easily treated with special creams prescribed by your doctor, or by homeopathic methods.

Some points to remember about vaginal mucus:-
- A certain amount of mucus discharge from the vagina is perfectly normal.
- Thrush (candidiasis) is a fairly common infection in women and can easily be treated. It can also affect babies, and men sometimes get it too.

- Thrush is **not** a sexually transmitted disease, although it can be passed on to a sexual partner.
- If you notice anything unusual about your vaginal discharge or your periods, or how you feel before, during or after your periods, e.g. an offensive smell, severe pain, depression —don't suffer or worry—Go To Your Doctor!
- If you are shy or embarrassed about talking to a male doctor, then make an appointment with a female doctor.

PMT

Pre-menstrual tension (or Pre-menstrual syndrome) is a condition now recognised by the medical profession. It is caused by the changes in the hormone balance in a woman's body.

It may cause moodiness or a feeling of being "out-of-sorts" around period time or at other times during the menstrual cycle. Some women find it helpful to cut down the amount of fluids they drink and lower their intake of salt by avoiding crisps, popcorn and other salty foods. In severe cases of PMT, vitamin supplements or medication may be prescribed. If you find you have problems with PMT, seek advice.

2

The Growing Boy

The male sex organs are mainly outside the body. When it comes to reproduction, however, some of the workings are internal also.

The **penis** is a tube-like organ. It is made of spongy tissues and contains the **urethra**—the tube which is connected to the bladder. It is for urinating or "peeing"—passing waste water from the body.

The urethra has another function which only begins after puberty. This is for passing **semen**, a combination of **sperm** and **seminal fluid**, from the body. The penis of a young boy is quite small, but at puberty it thickens and becomes longer. It also becomes darker.

Some boys and men have a fold of skin which covers the tip or **glans** of the penis. This piece of skin is called the **foreskin**.

Circumcision is the surgical removal of the foreskin. Some boys are circumcised. This may be for religious reasons—Jewish and Muslim boys are always circumcised. Boys of other religions may need to have their foreskin removed, when they are older, especially if the foreskin is tight and cannot be fully drawn back. There are no advantages or disadvantages to being circumcised.

Many men and boys worry about the size of their penis. It cannot be stressed often enough that the size of a man's penis has no effect on his ability to enjoy sex or father a baby. Some people say that when it comes to sex, bigger is better! This is simply **not** true! Myths and jokes about penis size make men and boys feel self-conscious and inadequate. The average penis is from about six to ten centimetres long when it is flaccid (not erect) and from about fourteen to seventeen centimetres when erect. Some may be larger, some smaller. A penis which is quite large when it is flaccid will not increase very much in size when erect. A penis that is small when flaccid will increase much more in size when erect.

Boys experience erections from infancy, but after puberty they may sometimes occur in the most embarrassing situations. An erection occurs when the spongy cells of the penis fill up with blood. This can be caused by pressure from a full bladder or when sitting in a moving vehicle. It can also be caused by sexual excitement.

The testicles

The testicles (often called the "balls" in slang) are

The male reproductive organs

1. Bladder
2. Seminal Vescicle
3. Prostrate gland
4. Cowpers gland
5. Urethra
6. Spongy tissue
7. Foreskin
8. Glans
9. Scrotum
10. Testicle
11. Epididymis
12. Vas deferens

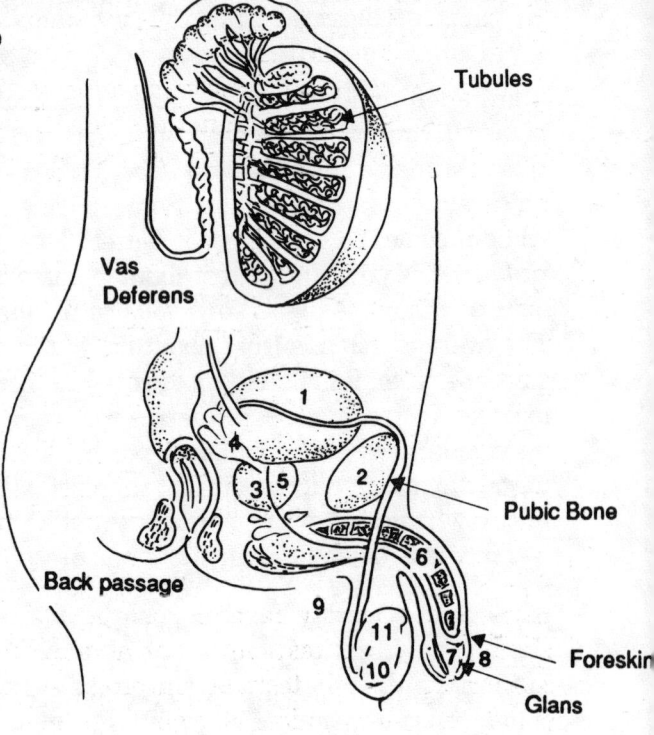

oval. They contain very tightly-coiled tubes. Each testicle is connected to the inside of the body by the **vas deferens.** This is the duct which carries sperm to the urethra.

About four weeks or so before a baby boy is born, his testicles descend from the abdomen into the **scrotum**. The scrotum is a bag of skin which is designed to keep the testicles away from the body. This is because sperm cannot develop at body temperature. The testicles are kept cooler, away from the body.

Boys realise that when they are cold or frightened, the scrotal sac tightens up, drawing the testicles closer to the body. In warm weather, the scrotum will expand, allowing the testicles to descend. Raising and lowering of the testicles is a reflex action, just like blinking, and you have no control over it. It is normal, however, for one testicle (usually the left one) to hang lower than the other.

A boy may be born with only one testicle. In rare cases, a testicle may have to be surgically removed. Having only one testicle is not a cause for great concern as a single testicle can produce more than enough sperm to make babies in later life.

Sometimes it happens that one or both testicles stay in the abdomen and do not descend. A minor operation will relieve the situation.

Every boy knows that a bang or kick in the testicles can be excruciatingly painful. It can also be quite dangerous, so you should never kick anyone there. Sportsmen should **always** wear proper protection during sports. A jock-strap or swimming-togs will hug the testicles close to the body. A "jock box" is a specially designed covering which can be worn during sports to support and protect the testicles.

> The Latin word **testis** means a witness. Nowadays, people swear on the Bible that they are telling the truth in court. Before there was a Bible to swear on, men who were called as witnesses in court had to swear an oath on their testicle. This meant that if they were not telling the truth, their testicle could be cut off—a rather painful punishment for perjury!

Self examination

Just as it is a good idea for girls to examine their breasts for unusual changes, boys should check their testicles regularly. This can be done when the scrotum is relaxed and the testicles are hanging away from the body. The ideal time to do this is after a bath or a shower. Both testicles should be carefully examined. Any unusual lump, whether painful or not, should be medically examined. It's far better to have a quick check-up and be reassured than to suffer in silence!

Sperm

When a boy reaches puberty, the testicles become larger and heavier and the sex hormones stimulate the making of sperm. Sperm are the male sex-cells. They are formed when cells near the surface of the testicles are drawn into the tubules. Thousands of sperm are made every day and mature sperm are stored in a part of the testicle called the **epidydimis**.

Sperm are so small that they cannot be seen without the aid of a powerful microscope. Each sperm contains twenty-three chromosomes and moves along by lashing its tail. It is often compared to a tadpole, but the shape is the only real similarity.

It is part of the normal working of an adolescent boy's body that from time to time, fully-developed sperm pass out through the penis, through the urethra. This is called **ejaculation**. Before sperm are ejaculated, an erection occurs. The sperm then travel along the vas deferens and mix with a special fluid which is called **seminal fluid.** This is formed by two glands called **Cowper's** gland and the **prostate** gland. When the sperm mix with seminal fluid, the mixture is called semen. Semen is a milky, whitish, sticky liquid.

Ejaculation is caused by contractions of the prostate gland. There are several of these contractions and there is usually a feeling of intense pleasure in the penis and around the genital area. This intense pleasure is called **orgasm**. The slang term for this is "coming."

Sometimes ejaculation occurs when a boy is asleep and it may be accompanied by a vivid sexual dream. When it occurs during sleep it is called a

nocturnal emission, or wet dream. The amount of fluid which comes out is about a teaspoonful. There are about five hundred million sperm in one ejaculation. Girls have sexual dreams too, which are sometimes accompanied by orgasm but they do not have an ejaculation.

Masturbation

It is necessary for people to handle their private parts from time to time, especially when washing or going to the toilet. Small children touch their private parts a lot. They are usually unselfconscious about it. As you get older, however, you realise that there are certain things which you do in private. It is not appropriate for us to handle our private parts in public, even through our clothes. Handling the private parts for pleasure is called **masturbation**. It was once thought that masturbation could be harmful, whether orgasm was achieved or not. This is simply **not** so and sadly many people suffered seriously from worry because of this misunderstanding. Masturbation does not cause any physical harm. Many boys and girls and adults masturbate from time to time. This does not affect a person's ability to have a sexual relationship or have children in later life.

Some people worry about masturbation because they feel guilty about what they are doing or about the fantasies they have while masturbating. People who masturbate a lot and who can't think of anything else may really have deeper worries than they realise. Excessive masturbation, like excessive eating or drinking, can be a sign that a person needs to talk out real problems with someone who can counsel them and give them good advice.

3

Making Love –Pregnancy

Intercourse

When a man and woman become sexually aroused, her vagina becomes moist and his penis becomes stiff and erect. If the penis is placed inside the vagina this is called **sexual intercourse**. The act of intercourse is also called "making love". This is usually sexually exciting for both partners. If this excitement continues it can lead to orgasm (or climax), commonly called "coming". The man's ejaculation will leave a pool of semen in the vagina close to the cervix. The millions of sperm which are then released, immediately begin the journey towards the Fallopian tube to find an ovum. It is a marathon race. Only a few hundred will manage to complete the journey, even though it is only a few centimetres. This is why there are so many sperm in each ejaculation.

Fertilisation

The sperm which do manage to reach the ovum

mill around it, trying to make their way inside. If the head of one sperm finally manages to penetrate the ovum, its tail breaks off. The ovum then self-seals so that no other sperm can get in. Fertilisation has occurred. The twenty-three chromosomes in the head of the sperm join with the twenty-three chromosomes in the ovum. Together the fourty-six chromosomes form a new cell, the beginning of a new human being.

Conception

If a couple have unprotected intercourse around the time of ovulation and a sperm fertilises an ovum, this is called **conception**. This usually occurs in the Fallopian tubes. The fertilised ovum travels down to the womb. If it embeds itself in the wall of the womb, then pregnancy has begun.

The date of pregnancy is calculated from the day on which the last menstrual period began. The average length of a pregnancy or gestation period in humans is 280 days (forty weeks), or just over nine months. Pregnancy is often divided into trimesters of three periods of three months.

Signs of pregnancy

One of the first signs of pregnancy is that the menstrual periods stop. There are many other changes which take place in a woman's body during pregnancy. It is common for a woman to experience nausea and vomiting during the first eight weeks of pregnancy. This is called "morning sickness"

From conception to birth

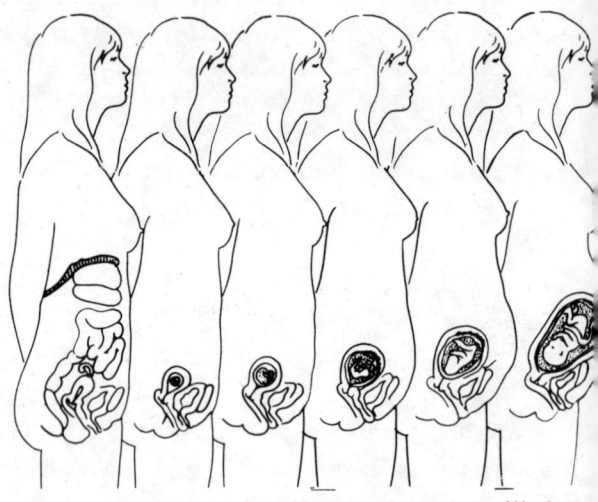

Conception   Week 4   Week 6   Week 10   Week 14   Week 18

although it can happen at any time—day or night.

A quick and simple urine test can be carried out to check for pregnancy. A sample of urine can be left into any maternity hospital or Family Planning Clinic to be checked. The results are usually available immediately.

Expectant mothers need proper ante-natal care and should attend their doctor or a maternity hospital as soon as possible after pregnancy has been confirmed.

Multiple births

A fertilised ovum may spilt into two, three or more

Week 22   Week 26   Week 30   Week 34   Week 40

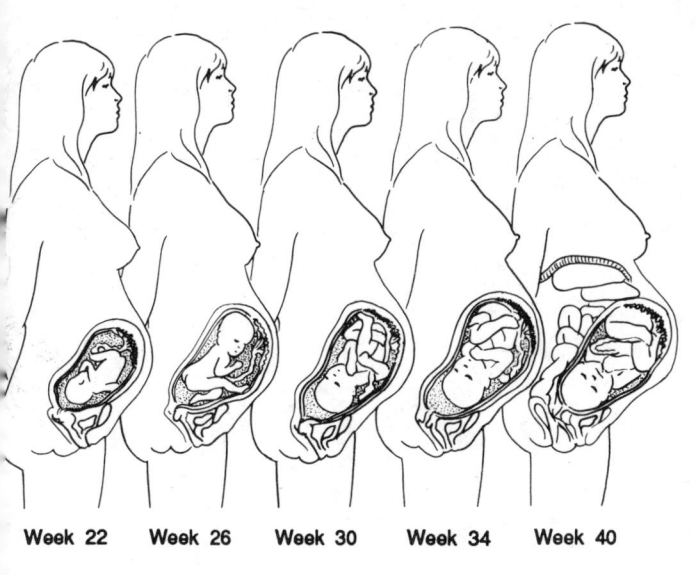

sections. If each section develops separately, more than one baby will be born (i.e. twins, triplets, quadruplets, quintuplets, or sextuplets). All of the babies will have the same sex and will look alike. They are said to be identical. Babies will not be identical if separate ova are fertilised. They may be of either sex and they are said to be fraternal.

Miscarriage and stillbirth

Miscarriage is when a baby fails to develop within the womb and is expelled. Doctors are usually uncertain why a woman miscarries. In general, women are delighted at the thought of being pregnant and look forward to the birth of their baby. Miscarriage can be very upsetting, as there is great

How identical twins develop

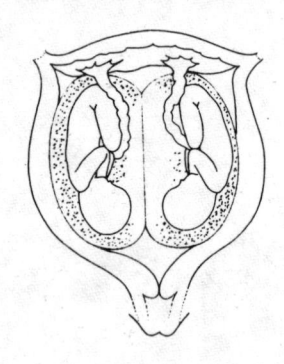

Identical (one - egg) twins

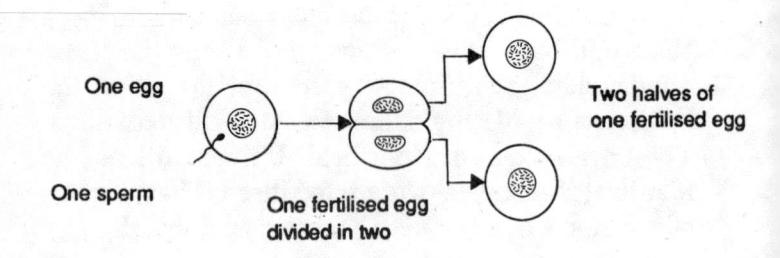

One egg

One sperm

One fertilised egg divided in two

Two halves of one fertilised egg

How fraternal twins develop

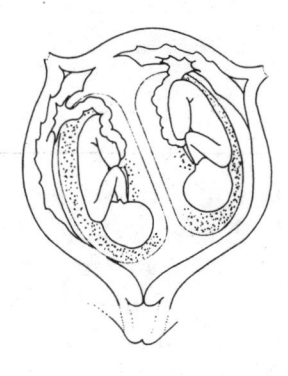

Fraternal (two - egg) twins

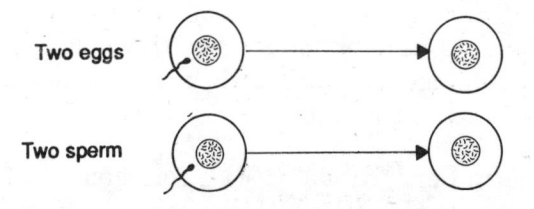

Two eggs

Two sperm

Two separate fertilised eggs

sadness and disappointment at the loss of a baby. Miscarriages generally occur within the first trimester (three months) of pregnancy. In some cases miscarriage occurs so early in the pregnancy that it is hardly noticed.

If a baby dies in the womb after the 28th week of pregnancy this is known as **stillbirth**.

Infertility

Most people presume that they are fertile and that they will be able to have children if they choose to. For some couples this does not happen. No matter how hard they try, they may be unable to have a baby. There are several different medical techniques which can be used to help infertile couples conceive. But the failure rate is high and some of the methods are controversial.

- Artificial Insemination is when the male sperm is placed inside the uterus by a doctor who uses a special syringe.

- In Vitro Fertilisation (IVF) is commonly called the test-tube method. Under laboratory conditions, some of the woman's ova are fertilised by sperm in a special glass dish. The fertilised ova are then placed in the Fallopian tubes in the hope that pregnancy will occur.

- Gamete Intra Fallopian Transfer (GIFT) is another method which can be tried. It involves taking ova from the ovaries and placing them in the Fallopian tubes along with sperm so that they can be fertilised naturally.

- Fertility drugs, which are high doses of hormones, have proven successful in some cases. It is common for a woman who has taken fertility drugs to have multiple births i.e. four, five, six or even more babies. In many cases like these, not all the babies born survive.

4

New Life

Giving birth is a very important time for the mother and the baby. Some mothers decide to have a home-birth. Generally though, the mother goes into a special hospital called a maternity hospital.

When the baby is ready to come into the world the mother goes into **labour**. At this time the mother gets cramps in her tummy. The cramps at first may be 20 or 30 minutes apart but gradually they get closer together and become stronger. These cramps are called **contractions**. Each contraction helps to push the baby downwards. First the cervix or neck of the uterus (womb) opens up enough to let the baby through. With each contraction, the cervix opens wider to allow the baby to pass into the vagina. The walls of the vagina can stretch and expand to allow this to happen. The baby now moves through the vagina or "birth canal." The muscles of the womb continue to push the baby through until it is born. Babies are usually born head first, then the rest of the body slips out easily.

The birth of a baby is called **childbirth** or **delivery**.

When the baby is born, it is still attached to the

mother's womb by the **umbilical cord**. The first thing the midwife does is clear the mucus from the baby's nose and mouth. The baby then begins to breathe air. When the mother and father have cuddled their baby for a little while, the midwife cuts the umbilical cord. This does not hurt the baby as the umbilical cord has no nerves. A small scab forms, which falls off after a few days leaving the belly-button or **navel**.

The baby is weighed, wrapped up warmly and given to the mother and father to hold. It is important for parents to have time to do this. They have waited for so long to see their baby and now is the time to start to get to know it.

Sometimes during childbirth, problems or difficulties may arise. The doctor may decide that the baby cannot be born through the vagina. When this happens an operation called a **Caesarian section** is carried out. The mother's tummy is cut and the baby lifted out. The wound is then stitched or clamped.

Babies need lots of love, care and attention. Newborn babies can do very little for themselves. They can cry, cough, sneeze and yawn. They can see, hear and can feel pain. They also have certain reflex actions like sucking.

Feeding

For the first few months of a baby's life, the only food it needs is **milk**. Breast milk is the food nature intended for the baby. Every woman's breasts contain cells that can produce milk. When a woman is pregnant, these cells become active. The milk is made from substances in the mother's blood, which are extracted as it passes through her breasts. The mother must eat well and stay healthy while she is feeding her baby. When it is time for the mother to stop breastfeeding, she gradually cuts down the length of time she allows the baby to suckle. At the same time she introduces bottle-feeding. Some babies are bottle-fed from the beginning. They are usually given powdered milk mixed with boiling water which is then cooled.

Most babies swallow air while feeding. To wind the baby, hold it upright and pat it on the back. Sometimes babies will bring up milk as well. Later on the baby will be able to take solid foods. But "solid foods" do not mean burgers and chips. Babies have no teeth so they cannot chew. Solids for baby mean mushy foods. Changing the baby from milk foods to solids is called **weaning**.

Babies learn from the very first day of their lives. At first they have very little control over their own bodies. That's why they need their parents to look after them. They can't walk, talk, chew food or clean themselves. They need to be cared for. Babies cry if they are hungry, thirsty, lonely, uncomfortable, cold, or unwell. Some babies just cry for attention. But all babies need love and care to help them to grow up strong and healthy.

Growing up

From the time of conception a baby's growth depends on how well it is fed. Until birth this food comes from the mother's body and passes through the placenta and the umbilical cord (see diagram).

After birth, a baby's growth depends on the food it eats. Good nourishment will mean good growth. Special body chemicals called **hormones** become active in the body as the child matures.

There are four main types of hormone in the body.

They are for

- Growth;

- Looking after blood and internal organs;

- Changing food into energy;

- Sexual reproduction (i.e. making babies).

Until they are about ten years old, boys and girls of the same age are roughly the same height. Many girls then grow taller than boys. It takes nearly two years for the boys to catch up, but then they usually pass the girls out and end up being quite a bit taller. (See Diagrams.)

By the time you have reached your fifteenth or sixteenth birthday you will probably have reached your full adult height although it is possible for you

The growing girl

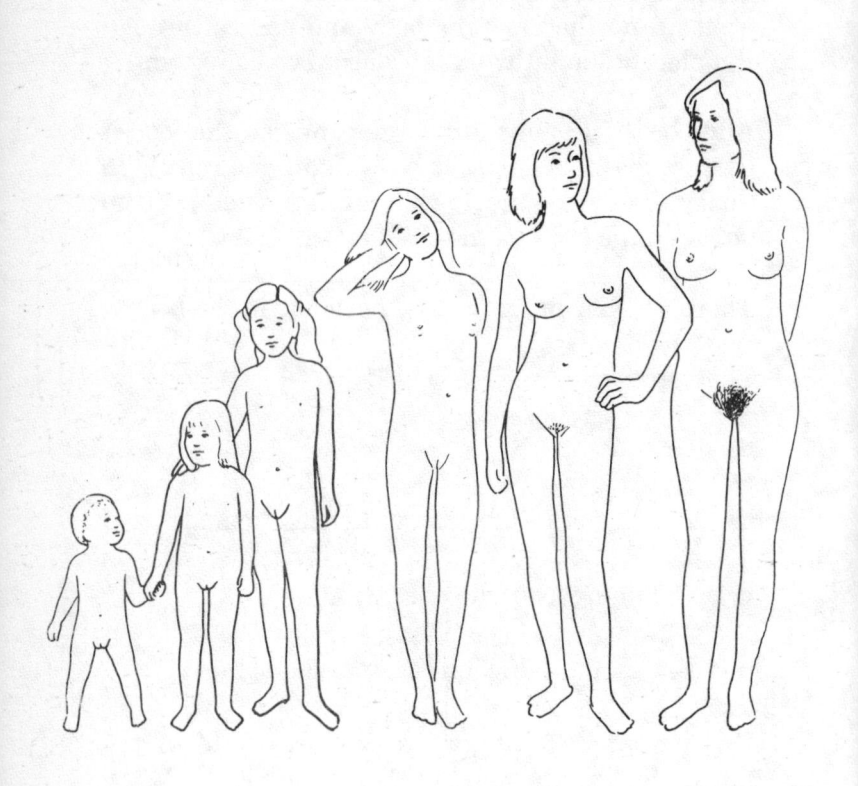

The growing boy

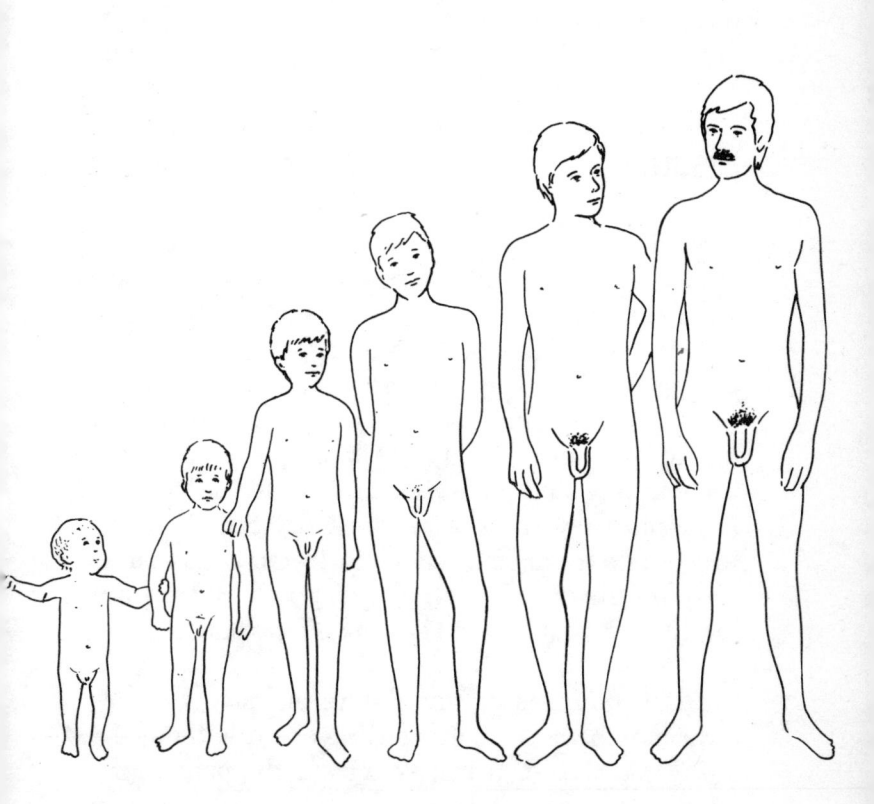

to continue growing until you are twenty years old. Your full adult height will depend on how much growth hormone your body secretes. Tall people simply make more of this hormone than small people. You may feel self-conscious about your height but it is one of those things over which you have no control.

Disability

A child may be born with a physical or mental disability. This is called a **congenital birth defect.** Some birth defects are the direct result of an infection (e.g. the **rubella** virus) caught by the mother during the early stages of pregnancy. Damage from rubella or German measles can be prevented by inoculating pre-teenage girls. Some people may become disabled as a result of an accident or an infection they themselves pick up. Poliomyelitis was once a common infection in Ireland but thanks to immunization, it is now very rare. There are many Irish people who bear the effects of polio.

A physical disability may reduce mobility. The sufferer may have difficulty getting about without the aid of crutches or a wheelchair. In the past, many people with a disability experienced educational discrimination, but happily this is not quite as common now. Special schools are provided and in more and more cases disabled children attend ordinary schools. Architects are required to take account of the needs of the disabled when they are designing new buildings. Most modern buildings have access for wheelchairs although much needs to be done to improve existing facilities.

Many able-bodied people find it very difficult to cope with those who are disabled. They may avoid talking to them or speak to them as if they are deaf. This is a source of great annoyance to disabled people.

A small percentage of the Irish population suffers from mental handicap. Down's Syndrome is the most common form. Special training centres and sheltered workshops can help those with mental disability to earn a living and lead a reasonably independent life.

5

Growing Up Healthy

As you grow up, it is important that you take good care of yourself. Good health involves:

- Exercising often.

- Eating good food.

- Keeping clean.

- Avoiding anything harmful to your health.

Exercising often

Young people need plenty of exercise and fresh air. Playing outdoor games and joining in sports is good for your body. It helps to develop your muscles, your heart, lungs and bones. Being fit means that you will be more likely to avoid certain illnesses when you get older, for example, heart disease. If you exercise regularly, your heart will work harder pumping blood around your body. This makes the heart stronger and more efficient. Exercise also keeps you supple and helps to keep you slim by burning up calories. Choose an exercise you like, such as walking, cycling, running, dancing or swimming.

Eating good food

When we look at "the ideal shape" in magazines and on T.V., it may be difficult not to feel cheated in some way, especially if we feel that we are overweight or underweight. However, there is no need to panic! Don't suddenly decide that you are "too fat" or "too thin." People of different builds put on weight and lose weight at different rates.

- What should you do if you think you are overweight?

    First of all, find out if that is so. Ask someone whose opinion you trust and believe them. Don't focus too much on the parts of your body with which you are not happy. If you become very worried about your weight and you want advice on a diet, then why not visit your family doctor? There is no need to be embarrassed or worried. The advice you get from your doctor will be professional and confidential. Make sure then to act on that advice.

- I can eat what I like!

    A hundred years ago many people suffered from the lack of essential nutrients. Today the problem is that of over-consumption. With the range of food available to us, it should be easy to eat healthily. Just cut down on fats, sugar and salt. If you can do without sweets and treats, then do so. Eat plenty of fresh fruit, vegetables and foods that contain fibre. Make sure to get plenty of variety in your food. As teeth are more vulnerable to decay in the teen years, replace sugary snacks with fruit or yogurt.

Dieting generally means following an eating plan to lose or control weight.

Diet is the total daily intake of food, especially the amount of nutrients that this food intake provides.

- I can always go on a diet!

    Treat all diet fads with a lot of suspicion. Cutting down or not taking essential foods is no solution to a weight problem. Your body needs a balanced supply of vitamins and minerals, especially as you develop through adolescence. If you do lose weight as a result of a "crash diet" you are likely to put that weight back on again when you finish the diet. Starving is not very sensible either. You can make yourself ill and possibly do long term damage to your health by starving or crash dieting.

- What is **anorexia**?

    Putting it simply, anorexia is "going too far with a diet." It is also called the "slimmer's disease." People who are anorexic starve themselves compulsively. It's not the type of disease that you can catch from other people but it can be very dangerous. It is a psychological illness and the victim may need to receive therapy and be hospitalised. Anorexia may be caused by lack of confidence or worries and anxieties of some kind, e.g. thinking that your appearance isn't very nice. Anorexia is always dangerous and can be fatal.

- What is **bulimia**?

    Bulimia is when you eat as much as you can and then vomit it all back up again before your body can digest it. People with bulimia are often compulsive eaters and go on food binges—i.e. they eat without knowing when to stop. They may also use laxatives to flush the food from their bodies. They get no benefit from their food and starve their bodies of the nutrients they need to grow strong and healthy. Like anorexia, bulimia is very dangerous and cannot be ignored.

Some useful tips about eating!

- Eat only at mealtimes or when you are hungry.

- If you feel hungry between meals, make sure to eat fruit.

- Take fruit every day. Fruit is good for all parts of your body—your skin, eyes, hair, teeth and so on.

- Be sensible about junk food. The odd Big Mac

or packet of crisps will not do you any harm, but don't make a habit of eating junk food.

- Cut out things like sweets and cakes (if you can). If not, try to keep them as treats. They are full of sugar which your body does not need. Examine the list of ingredients in sweets and candy bars. Does your body really need all those additives?

- Take the diet version of fizzy drinks. Better still, drink tap water. It's cheaper and it's better for your skin.

- Go for things marked **Low Fat, Diet, Reduced Sugar** or **No Added Salt.**

- Eat a proper breakfast. You will feel better during the day.

- If you want to check how much you eat during the day, make a list. Then see what is unnecessary and avoid this in future.

- A **balanced** diet is the key to good health.

How food helps

The nutrients in food consist of: **proteins, carbohydrates, fats, minerals** and **vitamins**.

- Protein: repairs damaged cells; helps us to grow; provides energy. Found in meat, fish, eggs, dairy produce, pulses.

- Carbohydrates: provide energy. Found in two

groups of food:
starch group—bread, rice, pasta, cereals;
sugar group—sugar, sweets, fizzy drinks, confectionery, fruit.

- Fats: major source of energy. Found in meat, dairy products, fried foods.

- Minerals and Vitamins: help to keep the body healthy and protect it from disease. Found in a wide range of foods. Each mineral and vitamin is important.

Eating a balanced diet ensures that you get sufficient nutrients to grow and develop in a healthy way.

A **vegetarian** is a person who does not eat meat. (**Vegans** avoid eating any animal products.) By eating a varied diet of cereals, pulses, eggs, nuts and dairy products, vegetarians get all the protein they need to remain healthy. In fact, a vegetarian diet is sometimes healthier. Getting sufficient vitamins is not a problem for most vegetarians, but if you are thinking of becoming vegetarian you should check with a doctor or dietician to see if you need to take a vitamin supplement.

Keeping clean—feeling comfortable

- The bowels and vagina are home for certain types of **bacteria**. After going to the toilet, girls should always wipe themselves from the front to the back to prevent the spread of unfriendly bacteria.

- In many males **smegma** gathers under the foreskin. This is a cheese-like fatty substance which is secreted from the sebaceous glands of the penis. In females a similar substance comes from the glands of the clitoris and the inner lips of the vulva. Smegma becomes smelly and can cause irritation if it is allowed to accumulate.

- Personal hygiene is very important. Daily washing of the bottom and the private parts is advisable.

- Don't forget to wash your feet and under your arms too!

- It's best not to use heavily-scented soap or perfumed spray around your private parts. They can cause irritation.

- Change your underwear and socks daily.

- Wear cotton underwear rather than artificial fibres. You'll feel better if you do because cotton allows air to circulate around your private parts, keeping you cool!

- During puberty the sebaceous glands of the face produce lot of oil. If pores are blocked the oil can build up and cause pimples, blackheads or acne. Severe acne can be relieved with special ointment or antibiotics. Milk is a very effective skin cleanser. Just dab it on with cotton wool. Wipe it off before it dries. A few drops of lemon-juice in water make an excellent skin toner.

- Greasy hair can also be a problem during adolescence. Washing your hair too often can increase the amount of oil but talcum powder is a very effective "dry" shampoo. Just shake it on and brush it out. It really does work!

- Dental hygiene is most important. Brush your teeth regularly and visit the dentist, especially if you have any problems with wisdom teeth. If you're short of a tooth-brush, then chew the end of a matchstick and rub your teeth with it. Many teenagers need dental appliances, such as braces, and may feel self-conscious. Braces are uncomfortable but the effort is well worth it in the end. If you look after your teeth they should last you your whole life long.

- If you keep yourself clean you'll feel good!

Avoid anything harmful to your health

Smoking, drinking, taking drugs or sniffing solvents can do very serious harm to young people. That is why it is necessary to talk about such things with your Mum and Dad. These substances are **addictive**. This means that if the body gets used to having them, it will not be able to do without them. Many people who are addicted to alcohol and nicotine develop serious illness. Certain drugs are extremely dangerous and can kill.

Perhaps somebody you know will try to get you to smoke or drink. Should you do it? Say "No" and stay healthy.

Part II

So You Want To Know More?

6

Introducing Me

When we meet people for the first time our first impressions are based on what they look like. But not for long. While these first impressions are significant, getting to know somebody better has nothing to do with looks. The type of person you are is much more important. Qualities like humour, friendliness and honesty are much more valued than looks alone. So the next time you look at yourself in the mirror and say "I'm ugly! Nobody will ever like me!", just think of the injustice you are doing yourself. Look again and see more than simply a reflection.

Do the bus-stop check next time you see a queue of people; take a good look. How many of them are really perfect? Would you change places with any one of them? Do a body check on the beach—weather permitting, of course. People come in all shapes and sizes, complete with blemishes and faults. No two people are alike. The word "person" comes from the Latin word *persona*, meaning "an actor's mask" or "a character in a play." Growing up is a time of change and development so you've time to experiment with different images and styles until you find one that suits your personality. Adopting a fashion helps to identify you as part of a group, or as an individual. Some styles are extreme, others are fun but they should never hide the real you. Has someone ever said, "I can't get through to you"? What they mean is that they find your image an obstacle, an impenetrable wall. In other words your image should not be a mask for disguising and covering up. People want to know what's behind the mask. They want to know **you**.

Confidence and self-image

When you were younger you probably did not attach much importance to having confidence. But now you are more aware of yourself and how you look and sound.

You are learning about yourself—about how your body and mind work. You learn about others too. All this learning can become very confusing sometimes, and you may wonder what sort of a person you will be. It's possible that you may not like a lot of things about yourself—you may even end up hating yourself sometimes. Most teenagers feel like this at some stage. If you know beforehand some of the things involved in growing up, it will help you to be ready for problems as they arise.

Having confidence in yourself is a good preparation for growing up. So how can you develop it if you feel you have none? The following hints are just suggestions. It's up to you to make them work.

- Take care of your appearance. Wear clothes that you feel good in. Keep hair, face, hands clean. Nails bitten back to the quick are most unattractive. Brush your teeth well. If you think you have bad breath, then use a mouth wash.

- Learn not to be too critical of your face or shape. Everybody has some flaw, so why dwell on yours? It's the **person** you are that's important and that's what others see. Concentrate on developing your personality.

- Don't worry about being shy or quiet. Not everybody is loud or brash. People sometimes hide their insecurity behind extrovert behaviour.

- Making lists can be useful to help sort out the things you worry about. Write down what you like and dislike about yourself. We tend to be very critical of ourselves, so concentrate on developing those qualities which are positive. But ignore the things you can do nothing about—like the shape of your nose or the fact that you have freckles—and get on with what matters i.e. changing the things you **can** do something about.

- Join a sports club or a hobby group. Get involved in activities which are stimulating and suited to your personality. Apart from the fun you'll have, it's an opportunity to get to know people.

- Don't think of yourself all the time to the exclusion of others. Be considerate towards your friends as well. They are probably going through the same difficulties as you. Sharing feelings and experiences is a valuable part of friendship.

- Growing up is hard work and not everything goes the way you would like it to. So give yourself a treat every now and then. You deserve it!

Moods and blues!

"Snap out of it."

This may not have been said to you yet but it probably will at some stage. Every now and then life gets us down. The blues set in and we can't seem to shake them off. Your moods and behaviour can be affected by your hormones. You may feel down without knowing why. However, once you realise that the "blues" are likely to strike, you will be at least prepared for them and will not allow them to defeat you.

Being taken **unawares** does not mean being taken **unprepared**.

- Learn to avoid situations where you know you will be likely to become short-tempered or impatient with others.

- Occupy yourself with something you enjoy doing.

- You must be prepared to make an effort to

cheer yourself up so don't wallow in the dumps making everyone else miserable as well.

- Expect at times to be hurt, let down, disappointed or rejected. Learning to cope is part of growing up. Letting things get to you is a recipe for unhappiness.

- Learn to negotiate and compromise. Talking things over and allowing for a bit of give and take is a more mature way of solving problems. Don't resort to selfish tantrums.

- Separate the big problems from the small ones. If necessary, make a list of them on a piece of paper to help you sort them out. Then **do** something about them! Otherwise they'll come back.

Out of proportion

There may be things about yourself that you find hard to accept. A lot of these problems are to do with the way you look. Legs, noses, ears and hair have been criticised for generations, but there's more to people than appearances. There's what's inside too!

Many young people discover that they need glasses or a brace, so you certainly won't be the first one. And you won't be the last! After a few weeks, nobody will care or notice that you've specs or a brace. They'll just see you as you are.

Perhaps you are conscious of your accent or you have a stammer. Maybe your name or nickname is a cause of embarrassment. Do you blush easily? Remember it is only you who sees these as flaws. Others may find these features attractive.

Whatever it is that bothers you, talk about it. Having a chat with a member of your family, a friend, or a teacher is a very useful way of "thinking out loud" and sorting out your feelings.

Criticism

Nobody escapes criticism. At times, you might feel that nobody loves you. This is probably not so, but it feels that way. It takes some people a lifetime to learn how to handle criticism. Some people never do.

Here are suggestions which you may find useful when someone criticises you. Try this four-point plan:

- Listen calmly to what your critic has to say.
- Decide if what they have to say is correct.
- If it is right, then do something about it!
- If you decide that their criticism is not valid, then say so calmly and dismiss what has been said.

The four-point plan can work for you when you feel that you're being put down all the time.

Most people react to criticism by becoming angry or

upset, or both. They often shout and become abusive, refusing to accept that they could be anything less than perfect. Many people find it **very** difficult to admit they are wrong.

People who are quick to point out the faults and weaknesses others often react badly when the tables are turned. They can give it, but they can't take it!

Just because everyone doesn't think the world of you doesn't mean that you are not a worthwhile person. You cannot expect to be loved all the time. Everyone has the right to their opinions even if you don't agree with them! We can all benefit from constructive criticism, but if you find that anyone (including your parents) deliberately embarrasses you, by criticising you in public, then you should talk to them privately about it and ask them not to do it again.

Giving and taking compliments

"Hey! Your hair is lovely!"—"Do you really think so?"

"Yeah! It really suits you!"—"You're not just saying that, are you?"

"No! It's really lovely!"—"I'm not so sure. Do you not think it's too big a change?"

"Look! I really like your hair, O.K?"—"But is it nicer than it was before?"

"I'm sorry I spoke!"

A great number of people find it very difficult to give or take compliments. Everyone needs to be reassured and to be appreciated but some people don't like giving compliments in case the person being complimented will get a "swelled head" and get ideas "above their station in life."

It's often said that Irish people are notorious for their begrudging attitude to those who do well. But if a compliment is deserved, it should be given and accepted graciously.

Be a compliment giver. Start today!

7

Family Matters

Part of the family

You are aware that home means more than just a roof over your head. Being part of a family involves relationships and responsibilities.

What does belonging to a family mean to you?

---
being loved   security   a hug
   company   having fun   a place to relax
a place to be yourself   a bit of comfort
being listened to   sharing   belonging
               they know me

What are the reasons for disagreements between teenagers and their parents?

---
clothes   friends   school and study
hairstyles   they think I'm lazy   nagging
   helping at home   keeping your room tidy
staying out late   TV and videos   boyfriends
girlfriends   staying in bed   being bored

Perhaps you can add a few reasons of your own.

Before you became a teenager, you probably did not think about staying out late or choosing your own clothes. But now you want to be more independent and decide some things for yourself. Your parents may need time to adjust to this so be patient with them. Part of the problem is that there are no formal stages through which you go in order to be considered "grown up." Mistakes can be made but love usually holds families together despite everything.

The parents' point of view

Let's look at it from your parents' point of view first. They have watched you grow since the time you were a baby. They know that you have to become more independent but they may still treat you the way they have always done. While they may still want to protect you, they can't do it the way they used to when you were younger. They have to trust the wisdom of their own decisions and your sense of responsibility.

How your parents treat you will affect your own growing-up period. Your parents may be strict, bossy, easygoing, over-protective or inquisitive. They may have changed as more children arrived in the family. Parents gain experience as their families get bigger. Since all children are different, they deal with them differently. Some are "handfuls" from the day they are born. Others sail through life without causing any bother at all. So allowances might have to be made. Parents and their children share a relationship. In your family, **you** influence how that relationship works so let's look at some common complaints that young people make.

The teenage point of view

- **My parents don't seem to care about me.**

    You may feel like a lodger in your own home if your parents don't communicate much with you. Some adults just find it hard to make a conversation. It doesn't necessarily mean that they don't care.

- **I have no privacy at home**.

    If you share a room, your scope for privacy is limited. So you have to be reasonable. Agree a fair division of drawer and wardrobe space with your brother/sister.

- **My parents don't like my friends.**

    Parents want to reassure themselves that the people whom you meet are fit friends for you. If at times they don't like the friends you are with, they might have good reason. Talk to them about it.

- **My parents expect too much of me**.

    Parents want their children to do well. While some young people need to be motivated, too much pressure is not helpful. Do your best and assure them that you are taking your work/studies seriously.

- **My parents are always fighting.**

    This is upsetting but raised voices do not mean the end of a marriage. Clearing the air is good in any relationship even if it's hard to listen to. Most marriages are happy ones in which arguments occur every now and then.

- **My parents never have any money like other parents.**

    They are probably deeply conscious that they can't give you all that you ask for. But do you really need all that you want? Your demands should be in line with what your parents can afford. Being jealous of others will only make you unhappy and dissatisfied.

- **My Mum/Dad's gone!**

    Many young people grow up in a one-parent family. Separation is painful but it may be the only solution to the terrible situations in which parents and families find themselves.

- **My parents are too hard on me**.

    Some parents over-react in certain situations. While they have a right and a duty to correct their children, violence and brutality have no place in family life. If they nag at you, have they justification for it?

- **My mother/father drinks a lot.**

    Unfortunately, if alcohol is a problem for a parent, then it affects all the family. It may be necessary to seek help.

- **My parents embarrass me.**

    Parents can embarrass you by what they say and do. But your friends shouldn't judge you by your parents nor should you judge your friends by their parents. A sense of humour and a thick skin are essential.

- **I'm going to leave home.**

    Some teenagers may feel that running away is a solution to their problems but runaways generally end up in worse situations than they leave. Many get into trouble. This need not happen if young people talk about their problems in time.

Talking sex

One difficulty that teenagers and parents share is a shyness about discussing sex with each other. Few parents today had an opportunity to talk to their parents about sex so you can see why it's a problem. They don't know what words to use. But it's important for everyone to make an effort to overcome that shyness so that you can get the information that you need.

Talking money

You must learn how to handle money prudently and live within your means. If you are always short of money, ask yourself:

- Do you buy on a whim?

- Do you buy what you don't need?

- Do you spend it all at one go?

- Do you spend it all as soon as you get it?

- Do you have a savings account?

- If not, why not?

- Have you tried baby-sitting?

- Have you looked for a part-time job?

- Can you create an opportunity to earn money?

- Can you sometimes do without money?

On the positive side for parents

There are things about having a teenage son or daughter that parents enjoy:

- You are able to join in adult conversation and activities.

- You are more of a **companion** now.

- You are more confident, mature and articulate.

- They can have pride in you and your achievements.

- You are more reliable and responsible.

- They can share a good laugh with you.

Looking at you, **they** experience a sense of achievement. No matter what rows occur, they remain proud of you.

How to survive your family

> 86 year-old: "I think children are great. I should know, I went to school with them."

- **Teasing** occurs in every family. The problems arise when it goes too far or if someone is tired and fed up. Know when to tease and when to stop.

- It's normal to feel **jealous** as well. But you don't have to moan every time your brother or sister gets something and you don't.

- At times it might seem as if your parents show **favouritism**. It's possible that your brother or sister needs a bit of confidence-building from your parents. Don't be left out. See if you can offer some support as well.

- Is there any **bullying** in your family? If you or another family member are being bullied, then your parents should be told and a stop put to it immediately. Nobody likes a bossy-boots either.

- When your little brother or sister annoy you by following you around or interrupting you when you're with your friends, explain to them that what they are doing is not fair and that you would like to be left in peace for a while. Then give them some of your time later on.

- If you have nobody else for company, brothers and sisters are a great stand-by. When you lose or change your friends, you still keep your family. As you all grow up, make sure to get to know them **as people**. Some day you will be glad to have them around.

I want to be independent

Although your parents may still want to know where you are going and who you are with, this is not unreasonable. After all, their responsibility towards you will last until you are fully adult. It's sensible and safer to tell them your plans.

- Being independent includes being responsible. Young people who behave irresponsibly are not able to handle the freedom they are allowed.

- Rules are absolutely necessary for us. They are not there to limit our freedom but to keep us safe. When we are not sure what to do, rules guide us.

- No matter how independent we would like to be, it's nice to know that we're part of a family.

How well do you get on with your parents?

You may realise by now that there are many things involved in a relationship with your parents that you did not think about before.

For instance:

- You have to consider **their** feelings at times, not just your own.

- You can't ask them about important things when they have something else on their mind. You must learn to judge when they are ready to listen.

- You must learn **how** to make requests; "I want…": "But I must have…:" "Everybody else has… except me." These forms of request (demands, really) may not get you what you want. Don't forget the magic words "Please" and "Thank you." Parents don't like to be taken for granted.

- Being thoughtful is important; parents appreciate little acts of kindness, e.g. a cup of tea, a magazine, or a chore completed.

- Your **tone of voice** is important; how do you speak to them? Cheery? Off hand? Sullen and surly? Do you shout?

- Relationships that you see on TV or in films are generally poor models for you, especially when so much time is spent focussing on problems and breakdowns. Most couples **work hard** at their relationships to stay together as they promised each other they would.

- You learn the **morals and values** that your parents have. In a world where young people come under so much pressure, you need them to talk to you about their value systems.

- Part of a relationship is **making mistakes**; it's unfortunate that parents and young people sometimes handle situations badly but forgiving and getting on with it are necessary in family life.

- You learn **tact and diplomacy**; just as parents have to make allowances for your moods, so you also must learn to respect **their** marriage.

- You now know that your parents can't answer every question or solve every problem. But they have always done their best for you and will continue to do so, even after you have left to make your own home.

Losing a parent

Nothing can prepare you for the death of a parent. Death is so final. If your mother or father died through illness, then perhaps you had some time to think about it beforehand. But many parents die through accidents. The loss is sudden and seems so unfair.

Memories of your parent are treasures to be kept for all of your life. Remembering things they said and did helps to keep them alive inside you. In that way you can keep them close to you. Don't forget that others around you are feeling bad too. So reach out to them and share your grief with them.

When someone dies, people go through a period of mourning. This can last a long time even for a year or two. If you know somebody whose mother or father has died, you can be of help. Your friend needs you now, perhaps to talk and certainly to listen. You must be there to hear what he/she has to say. Even if your friend is moody and irritable, be there to offer your support.

I'm an only child

What's it like not to have any brothers or sisters? Well, it has its good points and it has its bad points. On the one hand, your Mum and Dad can give you all their love and attention; you don't have to share your room or your things; you avoid silly arguments or bullying by brothers and sisters; most of your talk is with adults, so your attitudes should be fairly mature. On the other hand, you miss the company of a brother or sister; you won't get the benefit of their experience of growing up to guide you; bedtime can be lonely with no one your age to chat to; your parents might spoil you; and you might find it difficult to share or consider the needs of other people of your age. You will need to make as many friends as possible, especially, close friends. If you find the house a bit empty, then think about getting a pet. Apart from the company a pet offers, it will also help to make you more responsible.

A word about step-families

Getting used to a stepfather or stepmother can be difficult so you might find the following suggestions helpful:

- Nobody can ever take the place of your natural parent. Gaining a step-parent does not mean that you love your real parent any less.

- Your Mum or Dad has been alone for a while now and it's good for them to have companionship again. Be happy for them. You don't have to feel left out. Remember that you still matter to them.

- Take time sorting out your emotions. If you feel a twinge of jealously, it's quite normal. You might have had your Mum or Dad to yourself for some time now, so having to share a parent again does take a little getting used to.

- If there are step-brothers and step-sisters as

well, it might seem like an invasion. Don't rush into things. Take the time to get to know them. They are probably just as anxious about you, only you haven't thought about that yet. So don't worry.

- Look at the positive side of things. Your Mum or Dad is sharing a relationship again, you have gained a caring adult, and you are probably part of a wider family now.

8

School and You

What do you most like/dislike about school?

> teachers   the subjects   lessons
> the early start each morning
> exams   being bullied   not being liked
> the pressure others put you under
> sport   being called a swot
> failing / succeeding   the laughter
> seeing your friends   getting into trouble
> the uniform   the challenge

You can probably add a few more of your own. But what do you do if some aspect of school life becomes a problem for you?

Let's look at a few of them.

Teachers

Some teachers are more approachable than others. If you are having problems, there's bound to be at least one teacher with whom you can have a "chat." Don't confuse not liking the teacher with not liking the subject. While it's nice to be taught by someone you like, you can still learn from a teacher you dislike. Never be afraid to ask questions.

Working hard—getting nowhere

We all have different abilities when it comes to schoolwork. Some students try very hard and no matter how much they do, it still doesn't work out for them. School can give us a few hard knocks like that. It may be disheartening to see others who do well with little effort. Set yourself realistic targets. When you get frustrated with your progress, seek advice about better ways to study. But don't be too hard on yourself. Just do your best!

Being bored

If school is boring, it may be on account of the subjects you study. Perhaps you have difficulty with understanding what's being taught. Try putting an **extra effort** into your work and discuss your problems with the teacher. Perhaps you don't see the point of some of your lessons. **Motivation** is very important in school: you must see the relevance of what you are doing. Set ambitions for yourself and work towards them.

Being bullied

Being picked on is one of the hardest things to put

up with in school and it happens to quite a few young people. Don't, under any circumstance, give in to the bullying. It is a form of **abuse**, and you have a right to seek protection, if necessary, by making a formal complaint. Talk to your parents and teachers about it. After all, what **right** has a bully got to spoil your life? Don't suffer in silence!

If you bully or abuse others, then you should think carefully about the damage you do to your victims. Apart from the hurt and injustice which others have to endure because of what you do, bullying will also affect your life as you grow older. Bullying is a despicable activity which leaves many young people devastated. You have no right to make life miserable for others. Stop before you do any more harm!

Examinations

These can be worrying, even for those well prepared. Examinations are a means of measuring how successful you have been at mastering set courses of learning. The best preparation is to do a bit every day so that you don't end up having to do it all the day before the examination begins. Cramming is not a good idea. Do your work well in advance, then give it your best shot!

Having to study—helpful hints

- You can study alone or with a group, at home or at school. Some schools make special arrangements for their students.

- Working in a room with a TV or stereo going at full blast is not a good idea. Cut yourself off totally from distractions.

- Work for a period, then take a break. As you get used to studying, you will find that your concentration span will increase.

- Develop a method of study which suits your abilities, concentrating on the more difficult subjects first.

- If it's still a problem for you, find out how your friends study and try that out. Be sceptical if they say that they don't study at all.

- Talk to your teachers and seek their advice. But whatever you do, find a method that suits you, and use it.

- If others call you a "swot" it's probably because they're jealous. Don't change your attitude to your work because of someone else's problem.

A final word about study: There's no substitute for hard work. Don't forget the three Rs: **Read; Review; Revise.**

9

Under Pressure

Come on! Be part of the crowd

We all want to be accepted, to be part of the gang, to fit in. Being part of the group means joining in whatever the group does. So what happens if you're asked to do something that you don't want to do? While it may be easier to say "Yes" than to say "No," the important thing is whether you can stand on your own two feet! Pressure is something you **face**, not **give in to.**

The next few sections deal with **drugs**, so it is important for you to know what a drug is.

> A drug is a chemical which changes the way your body works, alters your feelings, or changes your behaviour.

Smoking

You've often been told by adults that you should not smoke because it's bad for your health. Yet those same adults may be smokers. So why don't they take their own advice?

It's all to do with the **choices** people make when they are young and the fact that smoking is **addictive** (habit-forming). People generally start smoking while still young and their first smoke was experienced in the company of friends. If you were offered a cigarette, would you have the confidence to say "No"? Or would you take it?

It's often easier to go along with the crowd, but you do have a choice, you know! You don't have to say "Yes" if you don't want to. So make your own decision and stick by it.

Is smoking really bad for you?

- Tobacco smoke contains numerous poisonous chemicals, including **nicotine** and **carbon monoxide**.

- Some of these chemicals remain in the lungs.

- Nicotine does not remain in the lungs. It's absorbed into the blood and takes about seven seconds to reach the brain. It is responsible for the addictive nature of smoking and for narrowing the arteries. Nicotine is a poison.

- Carbon monoxide is also absorbed into the blood. It replaces oxygen in the red blood cells so that less oxygen is available to the heart and organs.

- Tobacco smoke also contains **tar**. This tar makes the air passages in the body narrower. It gives rise to mucus in the lungs which leads to the phlegmy cough that smokers have. "Smoker's cough" is a symptom of bronchitis, a chest infection.

- Smoking is linked to: lung cancer, coronary heart disease, emphysema, bronchitis, cardio-vascular diseases, stroke and gangrene of the feet. Smoking also causes premature death.

- The health of others must be considered also. Anyone who lives or works in a smoky atmosphere is a passive smoker. They too suffer from smoking-related diseases.

- Smokers smell of stale tobacco.

- At present prices twenty cigarettes a day costs almost £800 in one year.

- Smoking affects unborn babies.

- Since smoking reduces the amount of oxygen the blood can carry, it affects performance in sport.

Giving up smoking

There is no easy way to give up smoking. You begin

with a firm decision to quit. Nobody else can do it for you. Stopping altogether is better than cutting down gradually. Once off, stay off.

> The best way to stop smoking is never to start.

What about alcohol?

- Alcohol is a depressant drug. While the first drink makes people feel relaxed and happy, the feeling doesn't last. As the brain slows down, reactions become sluggish and judgement and coordination are impaired.

- Alcohol does not affect everybody in the same way. For instance, because there is a difference in male and female body chemistry, a woman will generally become intoxicated more quickly than a man. Body-weight can be significant also.

- Inexperienced drinkers feel the effects of alcohol much more quickly than people who are used to drink.

- As alcoholic drinks are high in calories, regular drinkers may put on weight.

- Much of our social life hinges on drink. While most people drink sensibly, some have let it ruin their lives. It ruins family life as well. Drinking can easily get out of hand!

- Advertising shows the glamorous side of drinking. It does not show the problems and heartbreak it also causes. You know perfectly well why!

Why do young people drink? Is it because they are:

> mature   adult   tough   macho
> popular   looking for fun   confident
> convinced that it is sexy
> part of the gang   bored   insecure
> looking for thrills   anxious to impress

Although it might appear fun to be drunk, it's really downright stupid as you have no control over what you are doing. Many teenagers have allowed things to go too far while under the influence of drink. Afterwards their worry is not just about their headache but also what happened while they were drunk.

Quick tips for those of you who are old enough to take alcohol:

- Eat before you drink.

- You don't have to drink fast, just sip slowly.

- If you've been drinking, go home early.

- Never mix drink with other drugs.

- Treat drink with respect.

The law and alcohol

For young people under 18, it is an offence to:

- Buy any alcoholic drink.

- Drink any alcoholic beverage except in a private dwelling.

- Lie about your age in order to purchase alcohol.

- Be in an off-licence at any time.

For others, even those over 18, it is an offence to:

- Buy alcohol for anyone under 18 to drink.

- Give alcohol to anyone under 18, except in a private dwelling.

Other laws apply to publicans and licensed premises

- It is illegal to sell alcohol to anyone under 18 years.

- No publican can allow a person under 18 years to drink alcohol on the premises or allow anyone to serve a person under 18 years of age with alcohol on the premises.

- No publican can allow a person under 15 on the premises without a parent or guardian.

"Go on! Have a drink!"

How to say "No!" and get away with it:-

- Hangovers are a real pain.
- I want to keep my pledge.
- I want to wait until I'm older.
- I've a match tomorrow.
- No thanks! I'm on the bike.
- The last time I had a drink it made me sick.
- I can't stand the taste.
- I've had enough.
- My parents would kill me!
- Do you know what that stuff does to your liver?
- Be a pal! Don't push drink on me.
- Booze is a real downer.

> If your drinking causes you or anyone else problems, then **you have a drink problem!**
>
> If you **have** a drink problem—
> **Do Something About It!**

What about other drugs?

Young people are the target for illegal drugs simply because they are young and perhaps looking for a bit of excitement. They may experiment with whatever pills are in their own house first, then try other substances. Any drug can be harmful, even those in a medicine cabinet.

Cocaine and heroin are two of the better-known drugs on the illegal market. Both are highly addictive and are extremely dangerous. Sometimes, these drugs are mixed with other substances to "stretch" them. Taking them has proved fatal. Drug users suffer severe physical and psychological damage, and their stories are tragic. Marijuana, which is usually called "pot", is also harmful, though some people claim they can take it without ill-effect.

Drugs can be taken by smoking, sniffing, eating and injecting. All these methods are dangerous! But there is an added risk with injecting by syringe—the possibility of contracting AIDS.

Among the physical effects of drugs are the following:

vomiting	violence	fear and panic
hallucinations		confused speech
loss of appetite		loss of weight
runny nose	watery eyes	"dopiness"
lack of interest	irritability	crying
restlessness	deep sleeping	brain damage
loss of sanity		accidental death

- Death has resulted from inhaling vomit or overdosing.

- Using dirty, unsterilised needles can lead to hepatitis or AIDS.

- Financing a drug habit leads to crime and prostitution.

- For some, drug addiction has led to suicide.

Drug addiction affects whole families.

Solvent abuse

Solvent abuse is another dangerous practice. This is done by inhaling or "sniffing" substances which contain solvent chemicals. These include things like glues, sprays, markers, petrol, thinners and so on. Most of these products can be found in homes. Experimenting with them is very risky as they can have a rapid effect on the user. You could die!

Generally, fooling around with solvents occurs while young people are in groups and the pressure to join in can be great.

Try to avoid any drug unless it has been prescribed for you by a doctor.

Even then, follow the prescription carefully.

Pressure from ourselves

We often put ourselves under pressure—by trying to keep up with what others are allowed to do. No matter what freedom is given to you, there will always be someone else who can stay out longer or can go somewhere that no one else is allowed. Temper tantrums and scenes do little to show your parents that you are maturing into a responsible person. Rather it will have the opposite effect and you will find it takes much longer to achieve independence. Perhaps for the time being, missing something is better than finding yourself in a situation that you can't handle.

Vandalism

We are much more environment-conscious now than we used to be, so the effects of vandalism are more obvious to us now.

Broken trees, graffiti, damaged public property e.g. bus shelters, telephone kiosks, etc. ruin the appearance of an area. Most of the damage is done by young people and there is no excuse for it. Vandalism is sheer thuggery! If you come under pressure to join in acts of vandalism, then resist the temptation. Damaging and destroying the property of others is illegal and getting into trouble is just not worth it.

"Damn, blast and blazes!"

It is interesting to note that most of the "bad" language people use is related to sex and sexual activity. "Bad" language is often used in aggressive situations or when people want to express their anger, annoyance or frustration. It is easy to get into the habit of using swear words in conversation but not so easy to lose the habit. When boys and girls are together it is often seen as "grown-up" to use bad language. Sometimes people use swear words in conversation because they can't think of any better words to use.

Take the time to find out the real meaning of common swear-words and you'll see how silly they are. You'll also see how little they add to real conversation.

Try to find words which **really** mean something and use them instead. However, you must always remember that you will only be upset by someone else's "bad language" if you decide to let them upset you. Keep a sense of perspective. Words, after all, are only words! They will only cause offence if we choose to let them but common courtesy should tell us when "bad" language is just **not** appropriate.

Gambling

The enjoyment of computer and video games can easily lead to teenagers playing gambling machines. Arcade-style entertainment is costly and may become addictive.

10

Your Emotional Life

Strong feelings

Everyone experiences emotions like love, hate, anger, jealousy, grief and joy from time to time. As you get older you learn that showing certain emotions is more socially acceptable than others.

Love

Love has many different meanings. Maternal or paternal love is the good feeling parents have for their children. The love children have for their parents is called filial love.

Christian love is also called charity and is the positive feeling we have for God and our fellow human beings.

Sexual love is the intense feeling of desire to have a sexual relationship with someone.

You might love a friend very deeply and have a platonic or non-sexual relationship.

Love, friendship, commitment and loyalty are usually very closely linked.

You could love your country or your goldfish but you might also love to walk the dog. You could also love apple-pie and cream or music or art. These are all forms of love.

Love is something you choose.

If you choose to love someone, you do so because you see them as lovable. Your choice is not based on how they look, you love them for themselves or for what they can do.

Having a crush

Both boys and girls can have a crush on someone of the same sex. The object of their affections could be a teacher or a group leader. Feelings like this don't have to be acted upon and they don't necessarily mean that you are homosexual. The person whom you admire may not be aware of your feelings and that's probably just as well. You could seriously embarrass yourself by declaring your love for someone who has no idea how you feel.

Infatuation or true love

Infatuation is an unreasonable love which excludes everyone and everything except your loved one. True love includes sharing some of your time with others and allows your partner the freedom to do the same.

It is very easy to smother another person with your love. You must accept your partner as a person, an individual, who has the right to grow and develop. They have to have a life separate from you. If you really love someone, then you must give them the freedom to be themselves and they must do the same for you!

True love is about independence, not dependence.

As you mature, your understanding of true love should mature too and you won't be so overcome by your emotions.

Some young couples experience "real" love. Adults often under-rate and dismiss this, believing that "real" love is only for grown-ups.

Jealousy

Jealousy is a destructive emotion. If it is allowed to get out of hand, it can ruin relationships. Jealousy causes suspicion and mistrust and can lead to unhealthy rivalry and envy. Learn to control jealousy because there's so much to lose if you don't. Small children may feel that their parents are giving too much attention to someone else in the family. They soon learn that they can't keep their parents all to themselves.

Jealousy gets you nowhere. Like anger and bitterness, it can eat away at your peace of mind, leaving you feeling deeply unhappy. Just as you choose to love someone, you can choose to be jealous. You can also choose not to be jealous.

Jealousy is not a sign of love. It is a sign of mistrust:

"I saw you talking to him again!"—"That's right! He's my friend. We were in school together."

"Just a friend eh? Does that mean you want to go with him?"—"Of course I don't want to go with him. Don't you trust me?"

"It's not that I don't trust you. I just want to be with you!"—"What you really mean is that I shouldn't have any friends besides you! He's just a nice guy I know, okay?"

"Does that mean you like him more than you like me?"—"Oh, I give up!"

This cycle of jealousy does nothing to help a relationship.

They're jealous

A person may be jealous of another's property, appearance, possessions, skill, success, friends, personality or happiness. Jealous people may tell lies and spread gossip, simply to "get at" another person.

If you become the victim of jealousy, then simply accept that there are people who behave in this way. The problem is theirs, not yours—they're just jealous!

How to avoid being jealous

- Accept yourself as a worthwhile person.

- Accept that everyone has the right to have opinions and feelings and property.

- Accept that no two people are alike.

- Accept that everyone has different skills and talents.

Uncontrolled jealousy can lead to violence. Jealousy is often called the "little green-eyed monster." Don't allow yourself to be destroyed by this monster!

Hatred

A person might hate parsnips or bad weather. They might hate paying taxes but when it comes to hating people, the feeling is often based on **prejudice.**

Prejudice is when you decide you don't like someone before you meet them. You pre-judge them before knowing anything about them. Most prejudice comes from fear. Racial, social, sexual and religious prejudice cause discrimination.

Most people learn prejudice at home. But just as you learn prejudice, you can also unlearn it. A tolerant person is one who can accept that others have the right to be different from them.

It is very easy to acquire and keep the habit of being intolerant and prejudiced. Everyone has likes and dislikes. It is common for young people to go through phases of thinking that everyone else (especially teachers and parents) is a fool.

Dislike

Disliking someone is not the same as hating them. Dislike may grow a bit at a time. Once you begin to dislike someone you may find that everything about them annoys you. The person hasn't changed but your attitude towards them has. By continuing to nit-pick over silly things, your dislike of the person could turn to hatred unless you catch yourself on!

Anger

Everyone gets annoyed from time to time. You might get annoyed if you miss a bus or mislay something. Anger is a stronger feeling. Sometimes it might be directed at an object or at a person. You might lose your temper if a fiddly job goes wrong or if a friend lets you down.

Results of anger

Some people say and do things when they're angry that they wouldn't normally say or do. They may regret this later. If you find yourself in this situation, there's nothing for it but to apologise if you want to keep your friends.

"Hot-heads" allow their anger and temper to rule their actions. If you always react angrily when things go wrong, or when you don't get your own way, then you haven't outgrown the way you behaved as a small child.

Showing your feelings

A person who suppresses anger all the time can end up with serious problems. It is healthy to show your feelings if you have been wronged, or badly treated. Your anger is justified when it comes to defending yourself or ensuring your rights. Constant anger turns to bitterness. It is possible to become depressed if you always keep your anger to yourself and that can't be good for you! Anger and bitterness can make you a deeply unhappy person and bitter people are hard to like.

Some young people become hooked on uncontrolled anger. This is not as daft as it seems! When you get really angry, your blood-pressure rises, your breathing rate increases and adrenalin flows in your system. Anger can be very exciting but this kind of anger is usually directed at people or property and can be very destructive. When gangs become involved in vandalism and hooliganism it is because of uncontrolled anger. Do you think there is any connection between **anger** and **danger**?

Controlling anger

If you allow your anger to control your actions you may end up in serious trouble. There are ways of reducing your angry reactions. Here is a method you could try if you are a person whose anger often gets the better of you.

Think about the last time you were **really** angry.

- Did the situation merit an angry reaction?

- If you are inclined to "fly off the handle" all the time, there must be some reason for this. Can you honestly say what it is?

- A "short-tempered" person is usually intolerant of other people's mistakes. Do you set standards which are too high?

- If you think that things are more important than people, you may well find it difficult to accept the shortcomings of others. Do you put people first?

- If you get annoyed because others don't do things as you would, then you may be a short-tempered person. Do you feel that you are the only one who can do things right?

- The next time you feel ready to "explode" with temper, think about how your anger will add to the problem. "Blowing your top" will only make you feel better temporarily. What about the other person's feelings?

- Decide to avoid unnecessary anger. It's not good for you or for those around you. Give a thought to how other people feel.

- Taking a deep breath and counting to ten before reacting can help you cool down before you over-react!

"Be happy"

Everyone wants to "be happy" but circumstances don't always allow that. Everyone enjoys a laugh, but everything in life isn't funny. When you are happy within yourself, you find life easier to bear than when you are discontented. It is unreasonable to expect to be happy all the time.

Alcohol, drugs and promiscuity may "seem" to be very attractive. They even provide a temporary feeling of happiness but when people become addicted to anything they can end up hating the very thing they loved. Addiction is destructive. It destroys people and relationships.

No one chooses to become an alcoholic or junkie but since the beginning of time people have sought a recipe for perfect happiness. There is no such thing! Accepting this can help us towards being happy—some of the time!

Take a good look around and see what makes others really happy. As a general rule, those who put "people" before "things" tend to be happier than those who don't.

If you are a happy person you'll probably have a good idea why. If you're not, then what changes could you make in your life in order for you be happy?

Fear

Everyone is born with certain instincts, one of which is the "fight or flight" instinct. When we are confronted with danger, our bodies prepare either to face the danger or to run away from it. Our heart rate increases and adrenalin flows. The hairs on the back of the neck may stand up. When you get a sudden fright, you may feel sick in your stomach and get a strange taste in your mouth. The colour may drain from your face. These are all part of the same reaction. When you are nervous you might feel queasy and your palms will probably sweat.

Human beings are the only creatures on earth who will deliberately put themselves in a situation of fear. Some people enjoy the excitement of watching horror movies while others may love to scare themselves on a roller coaster.

Everyone in the world has something they are afraid of but a "phobia" is an irrational fear which may prevent a person living a normal life. People with severe phobias need understanding, not ridicule.

It is healthy to feel fear in the right circumstances but if you find that you have deep fears, which you cannot explain, then ask for help.

11

Love and Sexual Attraction

Sexual attraction is very difficult to explain. At first, it depends very much on what we see. If we like the look of someone, we will usually be attracted to them. We generally notice things about people's appearance without realising it.

What people find attractive varies from one culture to another. In most societies, it seems that the face is considered the most attractive feature. You know instinctively when someone fancies you. You'll have lots of eye contact. Holding a person's gaze is common to attraction and anger.

When a relationship develops, though, physical appearance does not matter as much as personality. If relationships are to last, then people need to be able to get on with each other.

Sometimes people choose a partner like themselves. Others may choose someone who is most unlike themselves. There are no particular rules for choosing a partner. You'll probably "know" when someone is right for you.

Attitudes to sex

Your attitude to sex has a lot to do with the way you were brought up, the time in which you were brought up and the way in which you found out about sex. It also has to do with what you have learned at home, in school, in religious education, with what ideas you have picked up from the media: radio, TV, newspapers, magazines, books, films and videos.

Human sexuality exists for the reproduction of the human race. There is no doubt that sex, as well as starting new life, helps to bond a couple together. For many, it is seen as a God-given gift which should only be used in the context of marriage.

Sexual images

A lot of advertising promotes the belief that certain products will make you happier, more beautiful and more attractive to the opposite sex i.e. if you have the right car, wear the right clothes, use the right deodorant, eat the right food or drink the right drink, you will be guaranteed happiness and you'll attract the perfect partner.

The message which comes across clearly from romantic stories, too, is that there is "someone" out there waiting for you, without whom your life will not be complete.

TV soap operas, films and "blue" movies do not reflect real life either. They tend to give the impression that what is shown on screen is what everyone does or ought to do.

In real life, sexual relationships are not so simple. Sex in real life involves real people with real feelings and real emotions. In romantic fiction and the movies these are only imaginary. Fact and fantasy are very different.

Showing love and affection

Really good relationships are based on friendship. Kissing and cuddling, hugging and holding hands are great ways of showing affection. Most people enjoy being hugged by people they care about. We all need tenderness and affection.

But kisses and cuddles don't have to mean intercourse. Some dating couples may well believe they are expected to behave in a sexual way. But you have the right not to be sexual if you chose. There's far more to relationships than sex.

Dating

If you're going to start dating you will need someone to go out with. How you meet this person may be a matter of where you live, the sort of things you like to do in your spare time or perhaps even the school you go to. There is no particular age at which you should be going out on dates, so don't allow yourself to be pressurised by either family or friends. It's up to you to decide!

If and when you see someone you fancy, who is available, you'll need to approach them. They won't know you're interested unless you speak to them. If you are naturally friendly this will show. Smiling is very important too. Be yourself and simply ask him or her if they would like to go out with you. Girls don't have to wait to be asked out on a date. There's no reason why a girl shouldn't ask a boy out.

It's normal to feel nervous or shy of making the first move. There's always the fear that the other person will say no to you. But don't allow fear of rejection to put you off. You won't know unless you ask, will you?

You'll want to look your best on your date and you'll probably make every effort to wear the kind of clothes you feel your partner will like. This will help you to feel good about yourself and will boost your confidence. Take no notice at all of anyone who teases you.

Going out can be expensive, but it doesn't **have** to be if you agree to share the cost. This can be decided very early on. Be honest! If you don't have the money to pay for your partner, then you really should say this in advance.

Going to the pictures is an old reliable. Bowling and skating are good too, but you don't have to spend a fortune to enjoy yourself! You might agree to meet each other at the disco or at the youth club and walk home together. This can cut down on expenses, but cheapskates are soon found out and no one likes to be known as a meany!

You can get to know someone really well by walking and talking with them. There may often be awkward silences—most people run out of things to say from time to time.

Don't be afraid to laugh at yourself if things don't work out as you dreamed they would. It doesn't help to take yourself too seriously.

Everyone suffers from **shyness** at some time or another. Some people try to cover up their shyness by being loud and brash, while underneath they're quite unsure of themselves. Very few people like a show-off or a know-all!

Don't expect to get on well with **everyone**. If you find that a date goes disastrously wrong you can expect to feel embarrassed. But that's all right! While you may feel uncomfortable you cannot actually die of embarrassment. If you find you have nothing in common, then it makes sense to cut your losses and not go out with that person again, unless you're a glutton for punishment!

Breaking up

If you have been going out together for some time, then you will know how your partner is likely to react to the news that it's all over. Show consideration for their feelings. Explain how you feel and why you should break up. You should be able to remain friends even though you're no longer going out together. It makes little sense to stay in a relationship because you feel sorry for someone.

If you are told that it's all over you may feel unhappy and disappointed but you may feel relieved. Some people are naturally shy of stating how they feel. You may feel heartbroken for a time but as you come to terms with your feelings you'll make a new relationship. Read the section on "Grieving" and you'll see how you might deal with your reactions to this kind of situation.

Some questions about dating

- If a couple are out together and the guy pays for everything—bus-fares, cinema tickets, sweets and chips and burgers on the way home, does that entitle him to have sex with the girl? (a)

- If they have been kissing and he begins to feel her breasts or private parts through her clothes, does she have to allow him? (b)

- If she says "No!" can he take it that she really means "Yes!" (c)

- Is it true that a "real" man should show his girlfriend who is boss? (d)

- Is it true that if a girl is sexually assaulted or raped, that it's probably her own fault? (e)

The answer to all of these questions is "No!"

Some comments on the questions:

- This situation can be avoided by both partners paying their own way. A partner who pays deserves thanks but that doesn't mean having sex. (a)

- No one has the right to force their attentions on you and you have the right to say so! (b)

- "N–O" spells No! (c)

- What's a "real" man—a bully? (d)

- The perpetrator of the crime is to blame—not the victim! (e)

Tell anyone who tries to take liberties to stop!

Tell them loudly and clearly.

Get angry if necessary!

Nobody has the right to force you into sexual activity!

If you are sexually assaulted, don't keep it a secret. Tell someone who can help you.

12

Marriage and Parenthood

Settling down

Dating couples usually see each other at their best. They enjoy each other's company and then go back to their separate homes. When they are living together things can be very different. They see each other at different times, when they may not be feeling or looking their best. Partners may not notice each other's annoying habits until they are living together. Each must learn to accept the other—"warts and all!"

When two people marry they should realise that life won't always be easy and that their commitment to each other means that they will have to live through good times and bad.

Marriage is a legally binding contract. Although a person can marry at sixteen years of age, most wait until they are older.

There are sound reasons for teenagers **not** to

marry. They have not seen very much of life and people's feelings change a lot during the teenage years. A couple who are "madly in love" at sixteen will grow and change.

Many teenage marriages cannot cope with these changes and a very high percentage end up in separation. That is not to say that teenage marriages never work out but the odds are against them.

A couple who decide to settle down together need a place of their own, where they can have peace and privacy. They may get a flat or, if they are lucky, a house. Everyone knows just how expensive things are and it's not an easy task for a couple to set up home.

When you live at home with your parents, you get a great deal for very little. If you are earning, you may have to hand up a certain amount of your money each week. This is only right, as you eat and sleep at home and have a lot done for you. But it's very different when you have to look after all the bills yourself.

Why do people marry?

- Because they love each other?

- So they can have sex?

- Because they think others will look down on them if they live together without being married?

- So they can have children?

- Because the girl is pregnant?

- Because they don't want to be alone or "left on the shelf"?

There are as many reasons for getting married as there are couples who marry. A person might choose marriage as a career; for security; for convenience; because everyone else does. Some people marry so they can "be" somebody i.e. someone's husband or wife.

Not just sex

A couple who marry simply for sex will quickly realise their mistake. Relationships cannot survive on sex alone. Sex is wonderful as **part** of an overall relationship. There are so many stresses and strains in ordinary, everyday life that sex can only take precedence for a very short time. The honeymoon period soon ends and life has a habit of becoming routine.

Having a family

Being a parent is often seen as an important aspect of marriage, but some couples cannot have children (See section on Infertility). If the couple still cannot conceive, they may be able to **adopt** a baby. If no babies are available for adoption, then they might **foster** a child. Both procedures involve counselling. Some couples choose not to have any children.

It is difficult being a parent. When you were born, your parents didn't get a degree in parenthood along with your birth certificate. Ask your parents about how it feels to be a parent and you will learn a little about what's in store for you, if you become a parent. Why not answer the questionnaire on **parenthood** on page 108.

In the past, most child-rearing was left to the mother. The majority of mothers stayed at home to mind the babies and be housewives. The term "housewife" is really rather a strange term, because no woman ever married a house. Some women still stay at home but they usually do so out of choice.

The roles of women and men have changed greatly. Fathers now tend to be much more involved in caring for and in bringing up children. This is a good thing! One of the main benefits is that men can understand just how difficult, yet rewarding, child-rearing is. The children benefit too! When the father and mother of a child both take responsibility for minding baby, they can help and support each other.

There is no exact set of rules that parents can follow to guarantee that they will be successful parents. No matter how good and kind they are, they cannot be sure how their children are going to turn out. There really is no such thing as the perfect parent, or perfect child, for that matter.

Listening

Children need to know that they are loved and cared for. Toys and gifts do not make up for parents' time and attention. Parents and children may talk a lot but they don't always listen to each other. Active listening takes time and effort. So how can you be a better listener?
Give, **Look** and **Take**.

- Give the person your undivided attention. This may mean turning off the TV or the radio.

- Look at the person you're listening to. Eye contact is very important in good relationships.

- Take the person seriously. Don't be tempted to dismiss them because you think they are too young or too old. If you dismiss them, you won't really listen to them.

Parenthood questionnaire

1. If you had the chance to choose your parents, would you choose someone like yourself?
   Yes / No   Why?

2. If you had the choice, whom would you choose to be the mother or father of your children?

3. What do you think makes a good parent?

4. What do you think is an ideal age for becoming a parent?   Teens? 20s? 30s? 40s?

5. Do you ever think about the job your parents have being parents?   Yes / No

6. Do you think being a parent is difficult?
Yes / No

7. What difficulties do you think parents face bringing up children today?

8. Are all these difficulties to do with money?
Yes / No

9. What do you think is the most difficult thing for parents?

10. What do you think parents worry most about when it comes to their children?

11. Do you think parents worry too much?
Yes / No

12. Do your parents worry about you? Yes / No

13. Are they right to worry?   Yes / No   Why?

14. Do you worry about them?   Yes / No   Why?

15. What do you like most about your parents?

16. What do you dislike most about them?

17. What sort of parent do you think you will be?

18. How could your parents improve things for you?

19. How could you improve things for yourself?

20. How could you improve things for your parents?

13

Family Planning and Abortion

Contraception is the avoiding of unwanted pregnancy by natural or artificial means. Contraception is also called family planning or birth control. There are many different methods of family planning. Some have been around for a long time. In ancient times unwanted babies were killed at birth or left out in the open to die of exposure or to be killed by wild animals.

The following is an outline of the various different methods of contraception. Specialist advice is necessary for their correct use.

Any method of contraception which does not involve the use of devices or medical intervention is called a **natural method.**

- The **withdrawal** method
  is the withdrawal of the penis from the vagina before ejaculation occurs. This is not at all reliable, because sperm can be released from the penis before ejaculation, resulting in pregnancy.

- The **temperature** method
  involves a woman taking her temperature every morning before she gets out of bed and charting the result. When she reaches ovulation, her body temperature will rise slightly, showing that this is the most likely time for her to conceive.

- The **ovulation** method
  involves observing the mucus which comes from the vagina. At ovulation there is a change in vaginal mucus, indicating that the woman is fertile.

- The **rhythm** or **calendar** method
  involves estimating the likely time of ovulation. This method is highly unreliable because it involves so much guesswork.

- The temperature and ovulation methods are often used together. In order for them to be used correctly, proper training is necessary. Couples using natural methods of family planning must avoid sexual intercourse for a certain part of every monthly cycle.

When contraceptive devices or medical intervention are used in preventing pregnancy these are called **artificial methods.**

The **barrier** methods of contraception prevent sperm from passing the cervix (neck of the womb).

- The **condom**, which is a rubber sheath, is placed over the erect penis and is designed to catch ejaculated semen. Condoms can burst. They can leak if they are not properly put on. They can also slip off during intercourse.

- The **Dutch cap** is a rubber ring which is inserted into the vagina to cover the cervix. (In the case of the cap and the sheath, special **spermicidal creams** must also be used. These are chemicals which kill off any sperm which might pass the barrier.) The rubber which makes up the Dutch cap can perish, so it must be replaced reasonably regularly.

- The **contraceptive sponge** is a foam sponge soaked in spermicide. It is believed by many doctors that the safest barrier methods are combinations of chemicals and rubber barriers.

- The **intra-uterine contraceptive device** or IUD (also called the **coil**) is placed inside the womb. It is made of moulded plastic with very thin copper wire strands attached. It is not fully understood how it works. It may be that it prevents a fertilised ovum from being implanted in the wall of the womb. It has to be inserted by a doctor.

  Many people have strong moral objections to the IUD because it may cause the abortion of a fertilised ovum. A woman may experience heavy periods as result of wearing the coil. The coil can become dislodged and come out of the womb and need to be replaced.

- The **oral contraceptive pill** is a specially made tablet containing artificial hormones. There are several different types of "Pill". They all have the effect of making the woman's body think that it is pregnant and so ovulation is suppressed.

The Pill must be taken exactly according to the instructions, otherwise it may not work. If a woman is taking the Pill, other medicines can sometimes prevent it from working properly.

- Recently, a **contraceptive injection** has been developed. Although it can work for up to three months, it is not very widely available.

- The "morning-after" Pill is a large dose of artificial hormones and is not generally used, except in cases of rape. It is considered controversial because it may cause an abortion.

Oral and injected contraceptives can cause side-effects. If a woman has a history of certain illnesses, then her doctor may not prescribe these contraceptives. Women who smoke and who are over thirty-five years of age can be especially at risk by taking the Pill.

Permanent methods

If a woman's Fallopian tubes are cut or blocked, this will stop a ripened ovum reaching the womb and prevent sperm from travelling up to meet it. This is called **tubal ligation**.

If a man has the vas deferens from each of his testicles cut or blocked then this will stop sperm from joining up with seminal fluid. This is called **vasec-**

tomy. The man still produces seminal fluid.

Both methods involve an operation and because they are permanent, the couple have to receive counselling. Men usually remain fertile for several weeks or even longer after a vasectomy.

In certain circumstances the operation can be reversed, but the chances of success cannot be guaranteed. Medical scientists are all the time looking for new and better methods of contraception. Among the artificial methods available, the most successful are also the most risky in terms of health.

The decision to use contraceptives is a very personal one and usually demands commitment and trust in a relationship. There are moral implications too!

The only way to be certain of avoiding pregnancy is to avoid sexual activity. All methods of contraception have advantages and disadvantages. It has been said that the word "No" is the best and most effective contraceptive there is.

Things to know

Some people engage in casual sexual activity without fully understanding the possible consequences. There are some strange and false notions about sex which need to be cleared up.

- A girl **can** become pregnant the first time she has sex. Young people are very fertile and you don't even have to have full intercourse to conceive a baby.

- If you have sex and don't become pregnant this does not mean that you are sterile.

- Having intercourse while you're standing up will not prevent pregnancy. Neither will jumping up and down afterwards. Some semen may come out of the vagina because of gravity but by the time the girl jumps up and down she may well be on the way to becoming pregnant, as hundreds of thousands of sperm will already be swimming towards her cervix. They swim at a speed of about half a centimetre per minute and all it takes is one sperm joining an ovum to achieve pregnancy.

- A girl does not have to have an orgasm before she can become pregnant. Many women who have had several children may never have experienced an orgasm during sexual intercourse.

- A girl **can** become pregnant by having sexual intercourse during her menstrual period. Some women ovulate very early in their menstrual cycle.

- Washing the vulva after sex will not prevent pregnancy. Although some sperm may be killed off by soap and water, sperm are very good swimmers.

- A girl should not believe a guy when he says he'll "be careful", meaning that he'll withdraw his penis before he "comes". This is no way to avoid pregnancy. Even if the penis is withdrawn before ejaculation, sperm in the fluid from Cowper's gland can fertilise an ovum.

- Mouth to mouth kissing—even deep or French kissing cannot cause pregnancy.

  Kissing can be great fun. Some couples kiss for long periods of time, especially when their relationship is in its early stages. Kissing is very enjoyable, but it can also be deeply arousing. The important thing to remember is that kissing does not have to lead to anything else.

- Condoms, used correctly, can reduce the spread of AIDS and sexually transmitted diseases (STDs).

  Anyone who engages in casual sex and who does not use a condom is totally irresponsible. STDs are very widespread and AIDS is increasingly being diagnosed among heterosexual men and women. While condoms do reduce the risk of infection they cannot guarantee absolute safety from pregnancy or disease.

- A person does **not** suffer any physical harm whatsoever, if they become aroused and do not have an orgasm.

The average age for reaching sexual maturity in girls is thirteen. For boys it is fourteen. This means that by these ages most young people are capable of "making a baby". Even younger girls have become mothers.

The decision to have a sexual relationship is a very serious one and should not be taken lightly. A couple who really care for each other will be responsible about whether or not to be sexually active.

> Casual Sex is risky sex—Avoid it!

Old enough?

The legal age for girls and boys to have sex is seventeen and there are many sensible reasons for this, mostly to do with physical and emotional maturity. If you feel pressure to have sexual intercourse with your boyfriend or girlfriend, or if you are not sure, then that's a clear sign that you are **not ready**, so don't. If you do decide to become sexually active, seek advice and remember the possible consequences of your actions. Babies are great when you are in a position to care for them properly. They are not a good idea when you're sixteen and still at school. Babies mean work, twenty-four hour care, money, commitment—things that you are not ready to give just yet. So wait until you are ready.

I think I'm pregnant

But what if the unthinkable happens? Suppose your period's late after unprotected sex with your boyfriend, what then? Well, you have a lot of thinking to do and some serious decisions to make, e.g.

- Telling the father of the baby. His feelings matter too. He has to help you face up to your joint responsibilities.

- Telling your parents. They will find out sooner or later and it's better to get their support as early as possible after they get over the initial shock.

- Doing a pregnancy test. This is quite a simple one which your local doctor can carry out for you and it only takes a short while.

- Attending a pre-natal clinic. The first few months after conception are crucial for the baby's health. You too will need proper pre-natal care.

- Deciding on the baby's future. You both will have to decide whether to keep the baby or allow the baby to be adopted. There might not be sufficient room in your parents' houses for a small infant.

- Telling others, including wider family and friends.

My girlfriend is pregnant

Your girlfriend is carrying your baby. You have responsibilities towards both of them. The things which she has to face will have to be faced by you also. Telling your respective parents is something you might consider doing together. Also you should support her through all of her visits to doctors and pre-natal clinics. You should give financial assistance if you are in a position to do so. After all, babies are expensive!

Important points:

- Was the pregnancy a result of sex on a first date, a regular relationship, incest or rape?

Obviously legal questions arise here especially concerning the age of the girl.

- The possibility of marriage could be discussed if the boy and girl are old enough, but it makes no sense to rush into it.

- Confiding in friends first might not be wise. Suppose they let it out and word got around? Tell your parents first.

Whether you decide to keep and raise your baby or give it for adoption, the consequences will last for the rest of your life. It's not just teenage girls who become pregnant. Many older women, both single and married, become pregnant and they also have decisions and sacrifices to make. So if you both have decided to keep the baby, do all in your power to give it the start in life that all babies should get.

Abortion

Abortion is an issue about which people have very strong feelings because it involves the taking of life. Abortion has existed since the earliest times so it is not something new. It's not enough to consider the physical aspects only. There are profound moral issues also, involving the right to life of the unborn. Most of the world's major religions consider life to be a gift from God and are strictly opposed to abortion. In Ireland it is illegal to give advice leading to abortion.

- What is an abortion? If a pregnant woman does not want to have a baby, she may decide to have an abortion. This is an operation to have the foetus removed from her womb. (This is not the same as a miscarriage, which happens by accident. An abortion is the deliberate termination of a pregnancy.) It would generally be carried out before the end of the third month of pregnancy, but can be done later.

- There are different methods of carrying out an abortion, depending on the length of pregnancy. Up to twelve weeks, the operation generally involves sucking the embryo out of the womb. For later abortions, the operation is more complicated. It is sometimes carried out in a hospital but an abortion can also be done in special private clinics. There are no such clinics in Ireland because abortion is illegal here.

Note: Abortion is not a method of birth control. It's an action designed to put an end to a pregnancy.

14

The Risk of Infection

Running the risks of infection

By now, you have read a good deal about sex and about relationships. You know a lot about what happens during puberty and adolescence and about choices you will have to make as you grow up. Just as you learn to take care of other parts of your body, you should also treat your genital area with respect. Because the sex organs are quite delicate, it is easy for them to get bruised or injured or to be exposed to infection.

All of the fluids that our bodies produce, e.g. semen, menstrual blood, urine, are in themselves clean. But once they leave the body, they are prone to bacteria. So daily washing of the genitals is very important for personal hygiene.

Bacteria can also enter the body through the openings in the vagina or penis. The resulting infection can cause discharge, irritation, inflammation or pain when passing urine. Tell your mother or father if you discover that you have a problem in this area. It might clear up of its own accord, but it's safer not to wait.

The immune system

Every day we come in contact with organisms, some of which can cause illness and disease. But before they can harm us, they have to get past the body's first line of defence called the **immune system**.

- Skin, a waterproof covering over most of the body, is part of the immune system. Sebum which is secreted on to the skin contains a substance which kills bacteria and viruses. The openings of the body also have their own special defences.

- Bacteria which are inhaled may be trapped by hair-like cilia before they get to the lungs.

- Bacteria which are swallowed may be killed by juices in the stomach.

- In both men and women, passing urine tends to wash out any invading organism. White blood cells made in the bone marrow are one of the most important parts of the defence system. Others include the thymus gland in the neck (where the white cells mature into **T-helper** cells), the tonsils, the spleen and the lymph nodes. Once activated, the white cells multiply and try to recognise and overcome the attacking bacteria or virus.

Some of these T-cells stay in the body for life. If the same bacteria or virus attacks again, the T-cells rapidly respond. This is how **immunisation** works. A **vaccine** consisting of a small dose of the bacteria stimulates the body's immune system to respond.

Sexually transmitted diseases

Personal hygiene is very important in guarding against infection. Some bacteria and viruses are transmitted by direct contact. If a person has a sexual infection this can be passed on by intimate sexual contact. These infections are known as Sexually Transmitted Diseases or STDs for short.

- Who can get sexually transmitted diseases and how are they spread?

  Anyone who engages in unprotected, casual sex is open to infection. In some cases they can spread in a non-sexual way e.g. by sharing a bath-towel with an infected person. Some can be picked up from dirty toilet-seats. Babies can be infected at birth if the mother has an infection.

- What are the most common STDs?

  Gonorrhea, syphilis, chlamydia, genital herpes, genital warts, pubic lice and scabies can all be sexually transmitted. AIDS can also be passed on sexually.

- Can they be cured?

Most can now be cured by medical treatment. People who think they may be infected are recommended to go to their doctor as soon as possible. Sometimes, because of shame and embarrassment, an infected person will not go immediately for treatment. The danger then is that the infection will be passed on to somebody else by sexual contact. To be effective, anybody with whom the infected person had sexual contact should be treated as well. Being cured once is no protection against being infected again.

> There is no cure for AIDS yet. AIDS is a fatal disease.

- Are STDs dangerous?

    Again the answer is yes, if they are left untreated. The symptoms of STDs are many and painful—sores, itching, discharges, swelling, rashes, blisters, inflammation, etc. Some can cause long-term illnesses, damage to the heart and the central nervous system, leading to eventual death, if ignored and untreated. In the case of pregnant women, STDs can cross the placenta and cause very serious problems for the unborn baby. So early treatment is essential to avoid serious complications.

- How do you know if you have an STD?

    The symptoms vary from disease to disease. They include the list given in the previous answer—and more. What makes it really difficult is that sometimes there may not be any symptoms at all, especially in women. So, it's possible for an infection to be passed from person to person, without anyone realising they are carriers.

- Can STDs be avoided?

  Yes! Most definitely! If you are careful and responsible when it comes to sexual contact, then you should be safe. If you avoid sexual contact until you are old enough to commit yourself faithfully to an uninfected partner who is faithful to you then you have no need at all to worry about sexually transmitted diseases. **Be sensible! Be safe!**

AIDS

Since AIDS is such a big threat, you need to know more about it.

- AIDS stands for Acquired Immune Deficiency Syndrome.

  Acquired—you catch it from someone or something;
  Immune Deficiency—your immune system is not able to protect you;
  Syndrome—the particular characteristics of the illness you get as a result.
  AIDS is not a separate disease—it is the destruction of the body's ability to fight off other infections that cause disease. The body

is thus helpless in the face of serious illness.

- AIDS is caused by a virus called HIV (Human Immunodeficiency Virus). It was first diagnosed in the USA in 1981 but the name HIV was not agreed upon until 1986. The first case of AIDS in Ireland was diagnosed in 1982. There are different theories as to where AIDS came from but, so far, no conclusive proof is available.

- The HIV virus attacks the immune system itself by destroying the white blood cells. The person is then left with no defence against any follow-up infection or disease.

- The virus may remain dormant for months or even years. Having HIV is not the same as having AIDS, but the virus can be passed on from person to person. It is estimated that at present about 50%-70% of those who are infected with HIV will go on to develop AIDS.

- No person with what is called full-blown AIDS has been cured. It is a fatal disease.

- The virus lives in a number of body fluids, e.g. blood or semen. So any activity involving blood or semen includes the possibility of transmitting the virus.

There are four ways in which the AIDS virus can be transmitted:

- By intimate sexual contact, either heterosexual or homosexual, with a person who is carrying the HIV. The virus is passed from one person to the other in the semen (male), in the vaginal fluids (female), or through blood. A person could be sexually active for years without realising that they are carrying the virus. So the spread of the disease is very difficult to control. People who now have AIDS were infected years ago.

- AIDS infection has resulted from blood transfusion—this is how so many haemophiliacs contracted AIDS. They were given blood which was infected with the virus. All blood is now screened for HIV before use in hospitals, so there is no risk of being infected.

- Drug users who share syringes (injection needles) are open to infection. Even minute quantities of blood on the needle or syringe can carry the virus, so one injection alone with a shared needle could be a death sentence.

- A pregnant woman who is carrying the virus may infect her baby during pregnancy or at birth. There is no way of knowing how many of these babies will develop AIDS as they get older.

How can AIDS be avoided?

- By abstaining from sexual activity altogether.

- By remaining faithful to one uninfected sexual partner who also remains faithful to you.

- By avoiding drugs where needles are used or shared.

More information about AIDS

Many people are confused about how AIDS is passed on. They do not realise that the virus can only survive a short while outside the body so there is no risk in using everyday things. You cannot get AIDS by kissing, hugging, sitting beside or shaking hands with an infected person. Nor can the virus be contracted by contact with cups, telephones, toilet seats, etc. Swimming pools are safe because the chlorine in the water kills the virus. Although the virus can survive in saliva, there is no evidence that it has been transmitted by this means. But, obviously, sharing toothbrushes, razors, or anything that punctures the skin is unhygienic, risky and should be avoided. Equipment used in ear-piercing, tattooing or acupuncture must be absolutely sterile before use.

AIDS is not confined to homosexuals and drug addicts. It is now in the heterosexual community, but it is impossible to know how widespread it is since the only way of checking for infection is to be tested in a clinic. The more sexual partners a person has, the greater the risk of infection. Using a condom reduces the risk but does not eliminate it.

Giving blood

Giving a blood donation is entirely safe. New needles are always used for each donor, and blood is screened for HIV before it is given to a patient in need of a transfusion. Giving blood and carrying a donor card are things that you should consider doing as soon as you are old enough.

Testing for AIDS?

A small number of hospitals (in Dublin, Cork, Belfast, Galway, Limerick and Waterford) have STD Clinics in which tests are carried out for the HIV virus. If a person tests positive for HIV, it means that while they are infected with the virus, it is not inevitable that they will go on to develop full-blown AIDS. But they can pass the virus on. All testing is confidential.

Tread carefully

The list of STD symptoms does not make pleasant reading, but it is important for you to know what happens when people are careless or irresponsible in their sexual behaviour. Saying "It'll never happen to me" is not smart. It could! The decision to be sexually active is a most serious one, and you should not make it lightly. So be careful!

15

The Moral Aspect

Morality

Morality is the most important aspect of all behaviour (including sexual behaviour). You have the right to make your own decisions but with every right you have, you also have a duty. Your duty is to be responsible in your decisions. A truly moral person will do the right thing simply because it is the right thing to do and not because they are afraid of what other people might think, or that they might get into trouble.

If you cycle or drive a motorbike or a car, then you are bound to obey the Rules of the Road. If you do not then there are legal penalties. When it comes to sexuality, however, although there are some civil laws, the main laws are moral laws.

There have always been people who messed around with alcohol, tobacco, illegal drugs, solvents and sexuality. There will always be irresponsible people who think only of themselves and there will always be casualties too. Addiction, unwanted pregnancy, disease and death can happen to people who believe it will never happen to them.

When it comes to sex, you must be extremely responsible because it involves such powerful emotions. You have a brain and a conscience to guide you. Reckless sexual behaviour can have very serious consequences.

If sexual intercourse becomes a casual feature of relationships then it will be treated casually. It then loses its meaning as a sign of total commitment to another person. Lasting relationships and marriages are based on total commitment. This demands courage.

Religion

Young children ask many questions and most of them are simple. Adults ask questions also and many of them are difficult—questions about suffering, disease and war. They ask about life and death and about life after death. Most people find the answers to these questions in religion. Believing in God helps to make sense of what happens to people while they are in the world. They lead good lives because they want to please God by following his rules. They pass on their beliefs to their children by what they say and do. They look forward to life after death in the presence of God.

Religion means the beliefs that people have and the way that they worship God. There are many different religions in the world but most of them accept that there is only one God. Religion fills a need in people's lives. Christians go to their local church every Sunday to pray at mass or attend service. Other religions have their holy places to which worshippers go.

Religion teaches us how to live together with our neighbours and is there to help us at difficult times in our lives, like, for example, when someone belonging to us dies.

Religion is important for most people. We must then respect other people's right to follow their own religion in their own way just as we would like them to respect ours. It's good when people come together to pray to God. But if someone introduces themselves in order to invite you to join a small group of young people who pray in private, be very careful. Seek advice before you do anything which they suggest.

In Ireland, the majority of people belong to the Roman Catholic and other Christian churches but there are other denominations as well.

Sexual orientation

Most people are sexually attracted to the opposite sex (i.e. male to female or female to male). They are said to be **heterosexual**, while those who are sexually attracted to the same sex are said to be **homosexual**. Females who are homosexual are known as **lesbians** and homosexual males are called **gays**.

A very small percentage of people are sexually attracted to both sexes. These people are **bisexual** or **ambisexual**.

During adolescence young people may feel strongly attracted to someone of their own sex. They may engage in sex-play and later feel guilt and anxiety about this, leading to the fear that they are homosexual. Not everyone who engages in homosexual activity during adolescence is actually homosexual. A small percentage are.

- Young people who find that they continue to be attracted to their own sex, may suffer a great sense of confusion. This is often called an **identity crisis**.

- Many crude expressions and jibes are used to describe homosexual people. These are based on ignorance and prejudice. This does nothing to help those who are worried about their feelings.

- People troubled by their sexual identity may become afraid for their future because they know that homosexual people can be subjected to prejudice and hostility.

- They themselves may even be prejudiced against homosexuals, yet still have homosexual feelings.

- What they need at this stage is wise counselling.

- There is no law which says that you have to date by a certain age. Just because a person has no interest in dating does not mean that they have a problem with their sexuality.

- Homosexuality is not a mental illness or a psychological disturbance which can be "cured."

- Homosexual orientation is not something people choose. Nor can you "catch" it. People are either homosexual or they are not.

- Homosexual people are to be found in every section of society. They look and act like "ordinary people" because they *are* "ordinary people."

- It was believed for a long time that if homosexual people had enough will-power they could change the way they feel. Truly homosexual people do not want to change the way they feel in the same way as truly heterosexual people do not want to change the way they feel!

- Homosexual stereotypes seen on TV do not represent the vast majority of homosexual people. These images are unfair and generally inaccurate.

- Homosexual and heterosexual people are equally capable of wanting and loving children.

- Some homosexual people marry, believing that they may outgrow their feelings. This can result in marital breakdown.

- A person's sexual orientation is no-one else's business, unless they choose to tell. Many homosexual people never announce how they feel. Everyone has the right to privacy.

- Homosexual orientation is not a criminal offence but homosexual activity, even between consenting male adults, is at present a criminal offence in this country; the law may change in the future. Female homosexual activity is not a criminal offence as it is not defined by law.

- Homosexual people may form a stable, loving relationship with a partner, just as heterosexual people do. The health risks involved in being promiscuous are great, regardless of a person's sexual orientation. There are moral implications too!

- In many parts of Europe homosexual activity between consenting male adults over twenty one years of age is no longer a crime.

- A person who is sexually abused is far more likely to be abused by a heterosexual person than by a homosexual person.

- **Trans-sexuals** are people of one sex who feel they ought to be a member of the opposite sex. A man may feel that he should be a woman and a woman may feel that she should be a man. In some cases, surgical operations can be carried out to help this process.

- A **transvestite** is also known as a "cross-dresser." Transvestites are usually men who like to dress as women. They may be completely heterosexual in their orientation but are simply attracted to wearing the clothes of the opposite sex.

Violence

Most people do not like to be hurt, especially by those whom they know and care about. Parents may occasionally smack their children for misbehaviour. But some children suffer a lot of physical abuse from their parents or from brothers or sisters. There are those who need the protection of the law if this becomes too serious.

People who abuse others physically may have suffered from the same abuse when they were children, although not always. This does not make it right for them to mistreat others.

Not the only way

Some children are brought up to believe that the *only* way to solve problems is with their fists. This of course is not true. Violence creates far more problems than it solves!

Kicking and thumping are not signs of affection or respect. People who care for each other do not hurt each other. If you are involved in a violent relationship, or if you see the potential for violence, then get out in time. You're on to a loser if you think that you'll change your partner's behaviour. If you accept violence, then that's what you'll get!

Aggression

Young boys are often brought up to be tough and

aggressive in the way they deal with others, while the opposite is generally true for girls.

Aggression means being first in to attack. Sometimes it is necessary to be aggressive—especially when you need to make a point or get your rights. But this does not mean that you have to use violence to make a point.

Sexual violence

Indecent assault is when a person touches or fondles another person in a sexual way, without their consent. It also applies to an adult who touches a child sexually.

Sexual assault is when one person forces another into sexual activity by threats or physical force or both.

Rape is defined as unlawful sexual intercourse i.e. penetration of the vagina by the penis, without the woman's consent. Rape now also includes oral sex, anal sex and vaginal penetration with an object when consent is withheld.

Indecent assault, sexual assault and rape are all serious crimes.

Aggression, hostility, anger and power are all features of sexual assault and boys are just as much at risk from this as girls. In most cases the victim knows the assailant and in most cases the crime was planned in advance (pre-meditated).

A woman has the right to dress as she likes and walk where she likes without feeling under threat from men. Just because a girl or woman dresses up for a night out this should not be seen as an invitation to sexual advances.

Incest

People who love each other show their feelings by holding hands, hugging and kissing. This happens in families as well, especially with smaller children. However, **incest** is different. Incest involves close sexual contact between members of the same family or relatives, (i.e. blood relations). Sometimes, children and young people do not realise what is happening to them if a person in the family tries to make them behave in a sexual way. They may become actively involved without understanding what is really going on. They may feel that it is an extra way of getting attention or of "being loved." But of course, this is not true! **Nobody** has the right to make you behave in a sexual way if you don't want to.

If this happens to you, then you **must tell**. It is not the young person's fault. The fault lies with the person who takes advantage. Sometimes threats are used to frighten a boy or girl into remaining silent; threats of punishment, separation, trouble etc. You must ignore these threats! The only way to put a permanent stop to what is happening is to **tell**. Keep on telling until someone listens.

Exploitation

Anyone who uses someone else for personal gain exploits them. There are many forms of exploitation but one form which is very upsetting is **sexual exploitation.** This is when someone uses another person sexually for selfish reasons. Prostitution and pornography are examples of sexual exploitation.

A prostitute is a person who trades sex for money. Prostitution is often called the world's oldest profession. It is not against the law, in this country, to be a prostitute. But it is against the law for a prostitute to publicly encourage, or solicit, someone to use their services.

A brothel is a place where prostitutes work. It is against the law to run a brothel. A pimp is a person, usually a man, who lives off the earnings of a prostitute. This is also a criminal offence.

In spite of legal penalties, prostitution exists in Ireland. Male and female prostitutes are to be found in all of the big cities and in many towns throughout the country.

In some countries prostitution is legal and there are special areas known as "red light districts" in which prostitutes work.

Many prostitutes become victims of violence. They are open to sexually transmitted diseases, including AIDS, and they are looked down upon by society.

The clients of prostitutes want sexual activity without any emotional attachment.

Some movies show prostitutes as happy people who just happen to have sex with others for money. This gives the impression that it is an easy comfortable life which guarantees a big income. The truth is very different.

Many lonely, frightened and poor people become involved in prostitution because they feel there is nothing else for them. A very large number of prostitutes, both male and female, were sexually abused as children. Many become alcoholic or addicted to drugs. They may end up with no feeling of self-worth and may feel that what they do is all they're good for.

Staying safe—tips for teenagers

The right to be safe is one of the fundamental rights that we have. But young people sometimes have this right taken away from them, mostly by bullies. It's vital for you then to have some idea of how to keep yourself out of potentially dangerous situations. Remember that not all assault on young people involves sex (bullying, for instance, seldom does). Staying safe does not mean being paranoid or seeing danger everywhere. It simply means being sensible and aware.

The following tips might be of some use to you.

- Learn to recognise situations where you put

yourself at risk.

- Agree certain limits with your parents e.g. places where you can go, what time to be back at, etc.

- Let your friends know these ground rules. Rules protect you rather than restrict you.

- Trust your intuition! It's seldom wrong.

- Know the facts about sexual assault (see p. 138) Tell if anything happens to you.

- Always have a fall-back plan agreed if you can't keep the original arrangement.

- Always have "panic money" in your pocket. It's reassuring to know that you can find your own way home independently if you have to.

- Stand up for yourself. Bullies are generally cowards who do not like people to stand up to them. But don't fight them. You might get hurt.

- Try not to keep secrets from your parents. You may have to tell them someday. Better sooner than later!

16

Ageing and Death

Getting old

When you are young you can hardly wait to be grown up. When you are old you may wish to be young again. The idea of living to a good age appeals to most people.

There have always been stories about the secret of eternal youth, but how long do you think you will live? Old people expect to die but most of them do not dwell on this. If you know any elderly people you should not be at all surprised to hear them talking about their own death, often in a good-humoured way.

People may talk of making a will, deciding who should inherit their property or money after they are dead. People who die without making a will are said to be **intestate**. This can cause serious legal problems for those left behind.

Talking about death or making a will does not bring death any closer. So don't be frightened by this. It is a sensible precaution to make a will if you have money or property.

Sexism is when people are discriminated against because of their sex. **Ageism** is when they suffer discrimination because of their age. In many different parts of the world the "elders" of the tribe are valued for their wisdom and their experience and their insight. Some societies do not treat their elderly with the respect and dignity they deserve.

In developed countries, people are expected to retire at a certain age, whether they want to or not, and planning for retirement is common. Many people now argue that those who have reached "retirement age" should not be forced to retire. Some people who retire from work become so active in their retirement that they may wonder how they ever had time to go to work.

The elderly are a cross-section of society which means that they are to be found in all social classes. They have different talents and skills, just as younger people do. Many young people believe that old age and loneliness go together but young people can be lonely too.

"You're as young as you feel!" is one of many sayings associated with age and many elderly people do not **feel old**. Most adults, whatever their ages, are happy to be the age they are.

Don't be tempted to dismiss the elderly as "old

fogies." You will expect to be treated well when you yourself are old. Be prepared to listen to and talk with your grandparents and parents. Age has given them wisdom and experience from which you can learn.

Mental health

It has long been known that physical health contributes to mental health. We often take both physical and mental health for granted, but they need to be worked at.

There is a lot of prejudice against people who are mentally ill. That prejudice is based on ignorance and fear. Seriously mentally ill people may need to be hospitalised but modern medicine can help the mentally ill to live useful lives outside mental institutions. Schizophrenia (split personality) and manic depression (extreme mood swings) and profound depression are common forms of mental illness.

Some stress is useful. However, sometimes people become so stressed that they need tranquillisers which slow down brain activity. But problems are not solved by taking tranquillisers, which are addictive. Tranquillisers are very useful but they should only be used for short terms, under strict medical supervision. Those addicted to drugs or alcohol can be so severely mentally affected that they need special treatment.

Suicide

Sadly some people find their problems so great that

they have not got the courage to continue living and decide to take their own lives. People who attempt suicide may not really intend to kill themselves. What they hope is that somebody will find them and look after them. In other words it is a cry for help and they need great sympathy.

Help

When people die by their own hand, their relations and friends are deeply disturbed. They feel desperately sad that the dead person did not feel able to confide in them. They feel guilty and blame themselves that they didn't notice there was a problem. They themselves may need counselling.

There are voluntary organisations set up to help and listen. Check the list of helping agencies at the back of this book, if you need them.

Death

Death is a fact of life! Every living thing must die. People can live to a ripe old age of one hundred years or more. It is more usual, though, for men to live to about seventy-two and for women to live to about seventy-six. These are average ages.

Some babies die before birth, through miscarriage or stillbirth. Babies may die soon after birth because of illness or for some other reason. **Cot death** is the name given to sudden infant death, where the cause is unknown.

Families are always deeply saddened by the death of a baby or young person. This is because, in developed countries, we do not expect people to die so young.

In underdeveloped countries many babies do not live beyond their second year because of disease, famine or lack of hygiene. This is called **infant mortality.** At the turn of the century this was the case in Ireland. Nowadays infant mortality in this country is very low indeed.

Accidents

Every year, hundreds of Irish people, many quite young, die in accidents. Accidents can occur anywhere—on the road, at home, by the sea, in the air. Many accidents are preventable; they often occur because of foolishness or carelessness. They may also be caused by people who are out of control through the misuse of alcohol, drugs or other substances. If you endanger your own life or another's you could be held legally responsible.

Young people love excitement. Sometimes, though, excitement leads to danger. Think first.

Grief

Everyone feels down from time to time but when something profoundly sad happens we suffer grief. When someone close to us dies we may feel shock and disbelief. We may deny that anything bad has happened. We may even feel angry with the person for dying on us or guilty if we failed to make up a recent disagreement. We might also feel afraid that someone else close to us, or that we ourselves, might die.

It may take months or even years before we regain our sense of well-being and happiness.

Adults may not recognise that young people grieve. They may feel that the young should recover more quickly than adults, which is not so.

How to cope with your own grief

- First of all you must allow yourself to feel sad. Crying can be a good release.

- Talk to someone about how you feel.

- Avoid moping, if you can, because self-pity is destructive.

- Try to continue you normal daily activities.

- Don't forget that others in your family may be sad too.

- In time, you will accept what has happened although you may still feel sad occasionally.

- Be nice to yourself!

Dealing with other people's grief

- Accept that the person is grieving. They have

not become different people. They just feel differently about life, at the moment.

- Acknowledge their sadness. You can do this by saying that you are sorry for their trouble. This may sound like a meaningless phrase but it is not. When you are expressing your condolences and are not sure what to say, then tell them that you don't know what to say. The fact that you are there and ready to listen means more than you will know.

- Let them tell you their story. People who are grieving need to tell their story.

- Don't be embarrassed if they start to cry. Crying is often seen as something to be ashamed about. But crying is a very healthy way to relieve pent-up emotions. Everyone can benefit from a good cry now and then. Tears don't harm at all!

Disgrace

If you have been disgraced by something you have done or something a member of your family has done, you may also feel a sense of grief and shame. You may feel that everyone is watching you and that everything they say is about you. You must accept that people soon forget. Unfortunately, if the disgrace has been made public, it may appear in the newspapers or on TV. This can be particularly embarrassing.

Your friends, if they are true friends, will be compassionate and understanding. This will help to heal your wounded pride. For most people time does heal all wounds.

Proverbs

It is interesting to note how many old sayings and proverbs really do have some grain of truth in them. The saying, "Laugh and the whole world laughs with you, cry and you cry alone" is often found to be true. Give a thought to your own feelings when you are sad and try to relate what you are going through to others. Recognise that when people are sad they need friends just as much, if not more, than when they are happy!

A word about counselling

Some people feel that they can solve all of their own problems. And maybe they can! But most find themselves in need of a little bit of help every now and then. This help may consist of money, advice, information, or simply lending a hand.

What if the problem is personal, confidential or embarrassing; something to do with the family, or an individual member of the family? At times like this, it is reassuring to know that there are people to whom we can turn; people who will respect our need for privacy and confidentiality; people who are on our side; people who can listen when nobody else will.

Perhaps this person is a teacher, somebody who

knows you and your family background well, yet can be objective in dealing with your problem.

A priest or clergyman is ideally suited to offer a friendly ear. They are trained in people-skills and are well experienced in problem-solving. You should know one personally.

Doctors have to deal with many problems that are of a non-medical nature. Prescriptions cannot always cure the illnesses that they diagnose. A good doctor is also a good listener.

Or perhaps you would think of non-medical counsellors. More and more people seek the services of psychologists, psychiatrists and psychotherapists. They deal with all sorts of mental problems. For some the healing process lasts a long time.

Finally, there are people at the other end of a confidential telephone line, offering a listening and advice service to those in need. Groups like the Samaritans exist because there is a need for their services. The lonely and desperate turn to them because they do not know where else to turn.

If you have a problem, something which really troubles you, to whom would you turn? Is it wise to let the problem gnaw away at you until you are really desperate? You will find a list of helpful agencies at the back of this book. But, hopefully, if you have a problem, you will have spoken to someone you know and trust before you need to look for a telephone number.

> Don't let problems grow! That way, they get out of control. Get help when you need it!

Before You Go

Taking care of the world

You have probably realised by now that there is far more to the facts of life than information about sex. Your sexuality is a part of your personality rather than something "apart" from it. You will also realise that physical maturity is achieved far more quickly than emotional maturity. As you go through life you will never stop learning or maturing. "You live and you learn."

As you grow, your responsibilities towards yourself and others increase. You'll become more self-reliant and independent. Most young people go through a stage where they want to "change the world." This is good as many of those who feel this way actually "do" something to make the world a better place for themselves and others.

Many of you who read this book will become parents of a new generation. One of the responsibilities which many parents take on is to make life as comfortable as possible for their children. You, in your turn, will probably want to do the same for your children.

By being a friend of the earth you can become aware of your responsibilities as a citizen and future parent. Be environmentally friendly by taking an interest in "green" issues and by avoiding anything which will damage the world. Some people say that there's little point in doing this as one person's efforts will not amount to much. But change occurs when individuals agree to work together.

To a great extent, the future of the world is in your hands. It's up to you to show that you can do a better job than your parents have done. You only get one chance at life. This is not a rehearsal. It's the real thing! Make the most of it!

Finally

If you've read all of the chapters so far, then you have a pretty good idea of what is in store for you as you grow towards adulthood. Of course you'll make mistakes and do the wrong thing from time to time. But it's part of learning about ourselves, about others and about life itself.

Adolescence is a time for growing into a new person. With a strong supportive family behind you, you will get to know and like the adult that you will become.

The urges and feelings you experience during your

teenage years are very strong and may seem difficult to control. Because of this, adults are often concerned about teenagers. But, in spite of their fears, many adults don't take sufficient time to talk and explain mainly because they don't know what to say. Maybe now, you will know what to say to them.

We hope you've learned a lot from reading this book. We have included a list of useful telephone numbers for you. Use them if you have to, but try not to let your problems grow to such a degree that you have no alternative.

So now you know it all?

Wanna bet?

Useful Addresses

- AIDS Helpline,
  60 Eccles Street,
  Dublin 1.
  Tel: 307888

- AL-ANON/ALATEEN
  INFORMATION CENTRE,
  19/20 Fleet Street,
  Dublin 2.
  Tel: 774195.

- ALCOHOLICS ANONYMOUS (AA),
  109 Sth. Circular Road,
  Dublin 8.
  Tel: 538998. Also 6795967.

- CHILDLINE,
  Freephone 1-800-666666.

- CATHOLIC MARRIAGE ADVISORY
  COUNCIL,
  Central Office,
  All Hallows,
  Drumcondra,
  Dublin 9.
  Tel: 375649.

- CURA (Pregnant and Worried?),
  30 Sth. Anne Street,
  Dublin 2.
  Tel: 710598.

(Regional telephone numbers available in directory)

- **DRUG ADDICTION TREATMENT CENTRE,**
  Trinity Court,
  30 Pearse Street,
  Dublin 2.
  Tel: 771122.

- **FOCUS POINT** (Housing Advice Centre),
  14a Eustace Street,
  Dublin 2.
  Tel: 712555.

- **FRIENDS OF THE EARTH,**
  26/28 Underwood Street,
  London N1 7JQ

- **GAMBLERS ANONYMOUS**
  Answering Service
  Tel: 721133

- **IRISH FAMILY PLANNING ASSOCIATION,**
  Cathal Brugha Street,
  Dublin 1.
  Tel: 727276.

  Other regional Family Planning Clinic numbers available in directory.

- **IRISH SOCIETY FOR THE PREVENTION OF CRUELTY TO CHILDREN,**
  20 Molesworth Street,
  Dublin 2.
  Tel: 6794944.

- NATIONAL ASSOC. OVULATION METHOD IRELAND,
  16 Nth Great Georges Street,
  Dublin 1.
  Tel: 786156
  Cork (021) 272213.

- RAPE CRISIS CENTRE,
  70 Lr. Leeson Street,
  Dublin 2.
  Tel: 614911.

- SAMARITANS,
  112 Marlborough Street,
  Dublin 1.
  Tel: 727700.

(Numbers outside Dublin available in local directories)

For telephone numbers outside Dublin (01) area, please check your local directory.

Index

Abortion 120-121
Accepting compliments 57
Acne 46
Adolescence 1
Adoption 106
Advertising 95
AIDS 80, 84; 117, 124, 125, 126-130; AIDS testing 130; and prostitution 140; AIDS Helpline 156
Alcohol 79-82
Alcoholics Anonymous and related organisations 156
Anorexia 42
Ante-natal care 26
Anus 4; 45
Areola 7
Aritificial insemination 30

Baby milk; breast-feeding 33-34
Bacteria 45, 122-123
Bereavement 69; 147-149
Bi(ambi)sexuality 134
Breasts 6-7, self examination of breasts 7
Bulimia 4
Bullying 66, 73-74

Caesarian section 33
Catholic Marriage Advisory Council 156
Cervix 4
Childbirth 32-33
Childline 156
Chlamydia 124
Chromosomes 25
Circumcision 16
Clitoris 5, 46
Cocaine 83
Conception 25
Condoms 112-113, 117
Congenital birth defect 38
Contraceptive injection 114
Contraceptive sponge 113
Contractions in labour 32
Cowper's gland 21
CURA 156

Dealing with criticism 56
Dieting 42
Disability 38
Discharge (vaginal) 13
Down's syndrome 39
Drugs 76-84
Drug Addiction Treatment Centre 157
Dutch cap 113

Eating habits 42-44
Ecology 153-154
Ejaculation 21-22, 24
Endometrium 10
Epididymis 21
Exercise 40

Faeces 5
Fallopian tubes 4, 24
Family planning clinic 26
Feeding for baby 33-34
Fertilisation of ovum 24-25
Fertility 13
Fertility drugs 31
Focus Point 157
Follicle 8
Foreskin 16, 46
Fostering 106
Fraternal twins 29
Friends of the Earth 157

Gamblers Anonymous 157
Gamete Intra Fallopian Transfer (GIFT) 30
Gays 134
Genital herpes 124
Genital warts 124
Glans (of penis) 16
Gonorrhea 124
Growth 35-37

Hepatitis 84
Heroin 83
Heterosexuality 133-135
HIV (Human Immunodeficiency Virus) 127-130
Homosexuality 133-135
Hormones 35
Hymen 5

Identical twins 28
Immune system 123-124, 126-127
In Vitro (Test tube) Fertilisation 30
Incest 139
Index
Infections 122-124
Infertility 30
Irish Family Planning Association 157
ISPCC 157
IUD (intra-uterine device) 113

Labia 4
Labour 32
Lesbianism 133

Making love 24 and *passim*
Marijuana 83
Masturbation 22-23
Menarche 8
Menopause 8
Menstruation 8; menstrual cycle 9-10; fertile cycle 13; painful periods 11; PMT 15
Mental handicap 39
Miscarriage 27, 30
Mons 5
Morning after pill 114
Morning sickness 25
Multiple births 26-27

National Association Ovulation Method of Ireland 157
Navel 33
Nocturnal emission (wet dream) 22

Nutrients in food 44-45
Nutrition 44

Orgasm 21, 24, 117
Ova (ovum) 4, 24; ovulation 10, 13; fertilisation of ovum 8-9, 24-25, 26-27
Ovaries 4
Ovulation method 112

Penis 2, 16-17
Periods *see* menstruation
Personal hygiene 45-46
Pill (contraceptive) 113-114
Poliomyelitis 38
Pregnancy 25-26, 115-116, 118-120 and *passim*
Private parts (genitals) 2; hygiene of 45-46
Prostate gland 21
Prostitutes 140-141
Puberty 1
Pubic hair 2
Pubic lice 124

Rape 138
Rape Crisis Centre 158
Rhythm method of contraception 112
Rubella 38

Samaritans 158
Sanitary protection 10-11; sanitary towels 11; tampons 11
Scabies 124
Scrotum 19
Sebaceous glands 46
Self-confidence 52-53
Semen 16, 24
Seminal fluid 16, 21, 115

Sexual intercourse 24, 132 and *passim*
Sexual reproduction 1 and *passim*
Sexual violence 138
Smegma 46
Smoking 77-79
Solvent abuse 84
Sperm 16, 20-21, 24
STDs (sexually transmitted diseases) 117, 124-126
Stillbirth 27, 30
Syphilis 124

Temperature method of contraception 112
Test-tube fertilisation 30
Testicles 2, 17-20; self examination of testicles 20
Thrush (candidiasis) 14
Trans-sexuality 136
Transvestism 136
Tubal ligation 114

Umbilical cord 33
Underwear 46
Urethra 4, 16
Uterus 2, 32

Vagina 2
Vas deferens 19, 114
Vasectomy 114-115
Vegetarianism 45
Virgin 6
Vulva 2, 4, 5, 46

Weaning 34
Weight problems 41-43

Land of Milk and Honey

The Story of Traditional Irish Food and Drink

by

Bríd Mahon

With an introduction and recipes by Kathleen Watkins

When our first settlers streamed across the land bridge from mainland Europe they found a country rich and bountiful, flowing with milk and honey. And so it should have remained but for the bitter accident of history. Bríd Mahon's authoritative and mouth-watering account of Irish foods throughout the centuries and their special associations with wakes, weddings and the calendar feasts of the year is a calorie-rich reminder of how sound Ireland's worldwide reputation for prodigal hospitality is. It also underlines how horribly wrong and avoidable the years of famine were. Milk and honey, meat and drink, bread and cheese—their Irish stories are told with great readability and historical accuracy.

POOLBEG

Prisoners

The Civil War Letters of Ernie O"Malley

edited by
Richard English and Cormac O'Malley

Ernie O'Malley (1897-1957) was one of the most charismatic figures to emerge from the 1916-1923 revolution in Ireland. He was converted to Republicanism during the 1916 Rising and remained an influential member of the IRA during both the Anglo-Irish War and the Civil War. *On Another Man's Wound* and *The Singing Flame*, his autobiographical accounts of the period, are classics.

These previously uncollected letters, written while Ernie O'Malley was imprisoned in 1923 and 1924, illuminate this important period in modern Irish history.

POOLBEG

Children's Poolbeg Books

Author	Title	ISBN	Price
Banville Vincent	Hennessy	1 85371 132 2	£3.99
Beckett Mary	Orla was Six	1 85371 047 4	£2.99
Beckett Mary	Orla at School	1 85371 157 8	£2.99
Comyns Michael	The Trouble with Marrows	1 85371 117 9	£2.99
Considine June	When the Luvenders came to Merrick Town	1 85371 055 5	£4.50
Considine June	Luvenders at the Old Mill	1 85371 115 2	£4.50
Considine June	Island of Luvenders	1 85371 149 7	£4.50
Corcoran Clodagh ed.	Baker's Dozen	1 85371 050 4	£3.50
Corcoran Clodagh ed.	Discoveries	1 85371 019 9	£4.99
Cruickshank Margrit	SKUNK and the Ozone Conspiracy	1 85371 067 9	£3.99
Cruickshank Margrit	SKUNK and the Splitting Earth	1 85371 119 5	£3.99
Daly Ita	Candy on the DART	1 85371 057 1	£2.99
Daly Ita	Candy and Sharon Olé	1 85371 159 4	£3.50
Dillon Eilís	The Seekers	1 85371 152 7	£3.50
Dillon Eilís	The Singing Cave	1 85371 153 5	£3.99
Duffy Robert	Children's Quizbook No.1	1 85371 020 2	£2.99
Duffy Robert	Children's Quizbook No.2	1 85371 052 0	£2.99
Duffy Robert	Children's Quizbook No.3	1 85371 099 7	£2.99
Duffy Robert	The Euroquiz Book	1 85371 151 9	£3.50
Ellis Brendan	Santa and the King of Starless Nights	1 85371 114 4	£2.99
Henning Ann	The Connemara Whirlwind	1 85371 079 2	£3.99
Henning Ann	The Connemara Stallion	1 85371 158 6	£3.99
Hickey Tony	Blanketland	1 85371 043 1	£2.99
Hickey Tony	Foodland	1 85371 075 X	£2.99
Hickey Tony	Legendland	1 85371 122 5	£3.50
Hickey Tony	Where is Joe?	1 85371 045 8	£3.99
Hickey Tony	Joe in the Middle	1 85371 021 0	£3.99
Hickey Tony	Joe on Holiday	1 85371 145 4	£3.50
Hickey Tony	Spike & the Professor	1 85371 039 3	£2.99
Hickey Tony	Spike and the Professor and Doreen at the Races	1 85371 089 X	£3.50
Hickey Tony	Spike, the Professor and Doreen in London	1 85371 130 6	£3.99
Kelly Eamon	The Bridge of Feathers	1 85371 053 9	£2.99
Lavin Mary	A Likely Story	1 85371 104 7	£2.99
Lynch Patricia	Brogeen and the Green Shoes	1 85371 051 2	£3.50
Lynch Patricia	Brogeen follows the Magic Tune	1 85371 022 9	£2.99
Lynch Patricia	Sally from Cork	1 85371 070 9	£3.99
Lynch Patricia	The Turfcutter's Donkey	1 85371 016 4	£3.99
MacMahon Bryan	Patsy-O	1 85371 036 9	£3.50
McCann Sean	Growing Things	1 85371 029 6	£2.99
McMahon Sean	The Poolbeg Book of Children's Verse	1 85371 080 6	£4.99
McMahon Sean	Shoes and Ships and Sealing Wax	1 85371 046 6	£2.99
McMahon Sean	The Light on Illancrone	1 85371 083 0	£3.50
McMahon Sean	The Three Seals	1 85371 148 9	£3.99
Mullen Michael	The Viking Princess	1 85371 015 6	£2.99
Mullen Michael	The Caravan	1 85371 074 1	£2.99
Mullen Michael	The Little Drummer Boy	1 85371 035 0	£2.99
Mullen Michael	The Long March	1 85371 109 8	£3.50
Mullen Michael	The Flight of the Earls	1 85371 146 2	£3.99
Ní Dhuibhne Eilís	The Uncommon Cormorant	1 85371 111 X	£2.99

Author	Title	ISBN	Price
Ní Dhuibhne Eilís	*Hugo and the Sunshine Girl*	1 85371 160 8	£3.50
Ó hEithir Breandán	*An Nollaig Thiar*	1 85371 044 X	£2.99
Ó Faoláin Eileen	*The Little Black Hen*	1 85371 049 0	£2.99
Ó Faoláin Eileen	*Children of the Salmon*	1 85371 003 2	£3.99
Ó Faoláin Eileen	*Irish Sagas and Folk Tales*	0 90516 971 9	£3.95
Quarton Marjorie	*The Cow Watched the Battle*	1 85371 084 9	£2.99
Quarton Marjorie	*The Other Side of the Island*	1 85371 161 6	£3.50
Quinn John	*The Summer of Lily and Esme*	1 85371 162 4	£3.99
Ross Gaby	*Damien the Dragon*	1 85371 078 4	£2.99
Schulman Anne	*Children's Book of Puzzles*	1 85371 133 0	£3.99
Snell Gordon	*Cruncher Sparrow High Flier*	1 85371 100 4	£2.99
Snell Gordon	*Cruncher Sparrow's Flying School*	1 85371 163 2	£2.99
Stanley-Higel Mary	*Poolbeg Book of Children's Crosswords 1*	1 85371 098 9	£2.99
Stanley-Higel Mary	*Poolbeg Book of Children's Crosswords 2*	1 85371 150 0	£3.50
Swift Carolyn	*Bugsy Goes to Cork*	1 85371 071 7	£3.50
Swift Carolyn	*Bugsy Goes to Limerick*	1 85371 014 8	£3.50
Swift Carolyn	*Bugsy Goes to Galway*	1 85371 147 0	£3.99
Swift Carolyn	*Irish Myths and Tales*	1 85371 103 9	£2.99
Swift Carolyn	*Robbers on TV*	1 85371 033 4	£2.99
Swift Carolyn	*Robbers on the Streets*	1 85371 113 6	£3.50
Traynor Shaun	*A Little Man in England*	1 85371 032 6	£2.99
Traynor Shaun	*Hugo O'Huge*	1 85371 048 2	£2.99
Traynor Shaun	*The Giants' Olympics*	1 85371 088 1	£2.99
Traynor Shaun	*The Lost City of Belfast*	1 85371 164 0	£3.50
	The Ultimate Children's Joke Book	1 85371 168 3	£2.99

While every effort is made to keep prices low, it is sometimes necessary to increase prices at short notice. Poolbeg Press Ltd reserves the right to show new retail prices on covers which may differ from those previously advertised in the text or elsewhere.

All Poolbeg books are available at your bookshop or newsagent or can be ordered from:

**Poolbeg Press Knocksedan House
Forrest Great Swords Co Dublin
Tel: 01 407433 Fax: 01 403753**

Please send a cheque or postal order (no currency) made payable to Poolbeg Press Ltd.

Allow 80p for postage for the first book, plus 50p for each additional book ordered.

To the small band of p[...]
Rocky Mountains in t[...]
meeting with Major D[...]
a fateful encounter. [...]
ham, it is especially [...]
Mormons, she is still unable to accept their faith, though she willingly accompanies them on their trek. The Major intrigues her—for he too is a misfit.

But Dart has vowed never again to become involved with a woman. So why, instead of enjoying the pleasures of St Louis, does he find himself shepherding a small company of women, children, oxen, goats and hens across the icy wastes in pursuit of an ideal?

By the same author in Masquerade

LION OF LANGUEDOC

Pioneer Girl
Margaret Pemberton

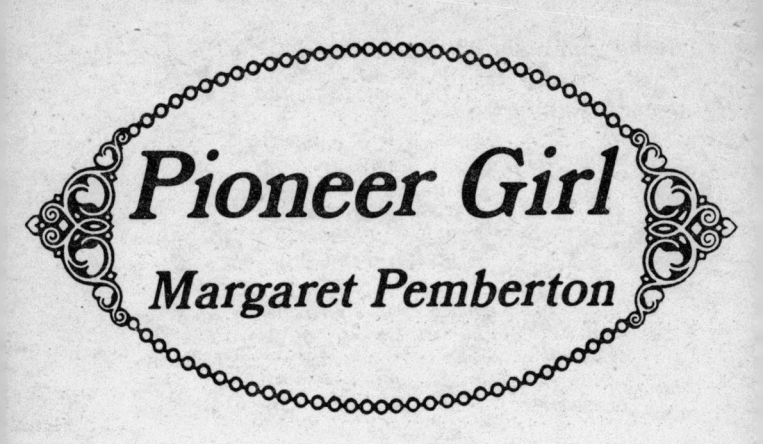

MILLS & BOON LIMITED
London · Sydney · Toronto

*First published in Great Britain 1982
by Mills & Boon Limited, 15–16 Brook's Mews,
London W1A 1DR*

© Margaret Pemberton 1982

*Australian copyright 1982
Philippine copyright 1982*

ISBN 0 263 73822 1

The text of this publication or any part thereof may not be reproduced or transmitted in any form or by any means, electronic or mechanical, including photocopying, recording, storage in an information retrieval system, or otherwise, without the written permission of the publisher.

This book is sold subject to the condition that it shall not, by way of trade or otherwise, be lent, resold, hired out or otherwise circulated without the prior consent of the publisher in any form of binding or cover other than that in which it is published and without a similar condition including this condition being imposed on the subsequent purchaser.

04/0482/

Set in 10 on 11½pt Times Roman

*Photoset by Rowland Phototypesetting Ltd
Bury St Edmunds, Suffolk
Made and printed in Great Britain by
Cox & Wyman Ltd, Reading*

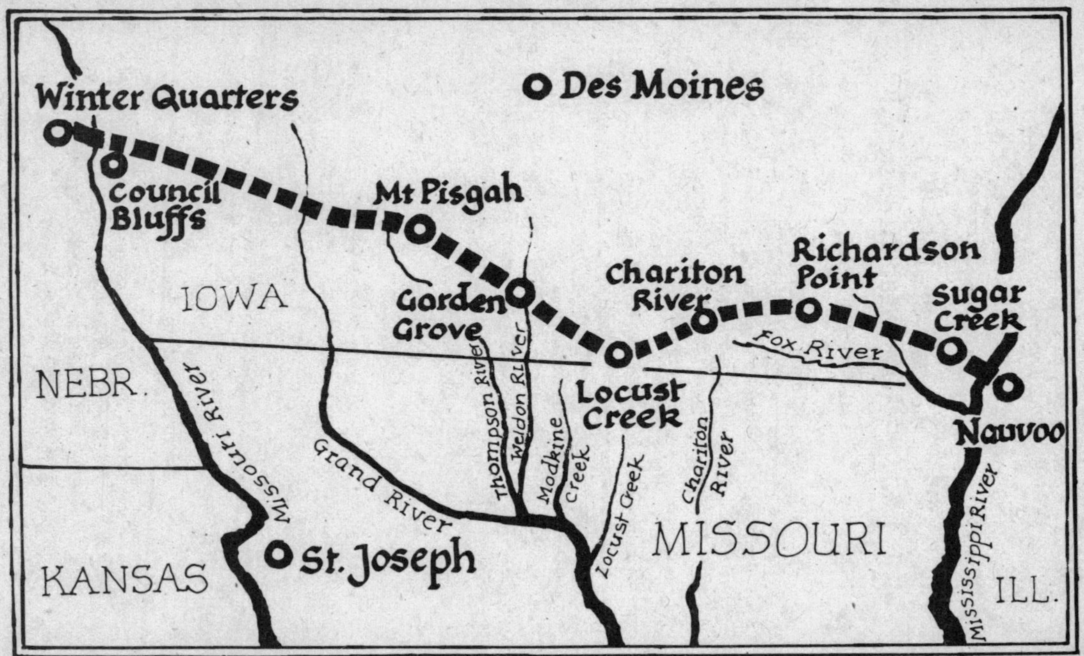
Winter Quarters
Des Moines
Council Bluffs
Mt Pisgah
IOWA
Garden Grove
Chariton River
Richardson Point
Sugar Creek
Fox River
NEBR.
Locust Creek
Nauvoo
Missouri River
Grand River
Thompson River
Weldon River
Modkine Creek
Locust Creek
Chariton River
Mississippi River
MISSOURI
KANSAS
St. Joseph
ILL.

For John and Catherine Wilkins,
true Latter-day Saints and true friends.

CHAPTER ONE

POLLY KIRKHAM sang as the thick fall of snow crackled beneath her feet. It was winter and though she had only a thick shawl over her plain cambric dress, she was oblivious of the sharp cold. Over her arm was a large basket, full of fresh brown eggs from Sister Fielding of Dallow Farm, some four miles from Nauvoo and Polly's own home. The eggs had been bartered for a carefully stitched skirt of heavy wool. Sister Fielding had provided Polly with the material, for her eyes were too feeble for stitching and sewing. Polly had obliged cheerfully. A skirt for eggs; a ham for a sack of freshly ground wheat. Money rarely passed hands in Nauvoo. Every neighbour helped the other and it never occurred to Polly that people should live differently.

She shielded her eyes against the sinking sun as she stepped from the last of the beech trees. Nauvoo lay curled in a bend of the great Mississippi. A small town; a new town; a beautiful town. Joseph Smith, the man who had brought them there and built Nauvoo from the deserted swampland had told his followers that Nauvoo meant 'Beautiful Place'.

Polly hurried her steps. It would soon be dark and Lucy Marriot would be waiting for the eggs to make supper.

Polly was only eighteen, but she could well remember her first sight of Nauvoo. Her parents had been alive then, and though not converted to Joseph Smith's revealed restoration of the Gospel, had cast in their lot with the Mormons, for they, too, were outcasts and friendless. They had lived all their lives alongside the Smith family and when the Mormons, or 'Saints' as they were called locally, had decided to move to avoid persecution, the Kirkhams had moved with them.

Nauvoo had been a few miles from Quincy: a deserted, swamp-infested place that no one wanted and Polly's young heart had quaked at the sight of it. She had been twelve then, and with her own hands had helped her parents and Joseph's followers build a generous city of wide streets and evenly-spaced sturdy homesteads. The river marshes had been drained. Trees and shrubs had been planted at every turn. Nauvoo had truly become the beautiful place that Joseph had prophesied.

The Mississippi shimmered under its coating of ice and Polly's usually happy heart felt almost as cold as she paused momentarily in her quick stride. Many had died while Nauvoo was built. The cholera had come and the old and the weak had succumbed. Her mother had died first: a pretty woman with Polly's corn-coloured hair and startling blue eyes. She had recently given birth to a baby that had been still-born, and, weakened by the hard labour, had fallen an easy victim to the dreaded disease. The next few months had been spent in a haze of misery that Polly had thought nothing could equal. Then, six months later, her father had contracted the disease and joined his beloved wife in the grave.

Lucy and Tom Marriot had taken her in. Devout Mormons, they had given her shelter and love and had waited patiently for her to embrace their faith. She had never done so.

The dark came suddenly and she closed her mind

against memories of the past and broke into a run. Lucy would be worrying about her and maybe sending her son Jared in search of her. Not, Polly thought, as she placed the basket of eggs carefully on the far side of a fence and vaulted it in an unladylike manner, that she would mind Jared's company for the rest of the way into Nauvoo, but he had work enough to do and no time to be treating her as if she were an Eastern miss made of bone china.

'Polly! Polly!' Jared Marriot raced along the track towards her, as her crisp white bonnet shone like a lantern in the dark.

She was about to break into a run to greet him, but, remembering the eggs, she continued at a more sedate pace until he reached her breathlessly and said:

'I was feared something had happened to you.'

Polly laughed, allowing him to take the heavy basket from her arm.

'At Sister Fielding's? The worse that could happen there is that the goats eat the hem of my gown, as they did last time I visited.'

His usually smiling mouth was grim. 'There's been trouble again. Our Illinois neighbours descended on the Spencers and forced them from their home with musket shot.'

'Was anyone hurt?' Polly's heart seemed almost to cease beating. She was accustomed to the hatred that the Saints seemed to arouse wherever they went, and attacks on out-lying farms and homesteads were nothing new. If it wasn't Indians, it was the respectable citizens of Illinois, demanding that the 'damned Mormons' be moved from their doorsteps.

'No, though it's only thanks to the Lord that they weren't. Brother Spencer was all for going straight back, but father persuaded him to allow his family to spend the night with us. Sister Spencer was badly frightened and the little girls half terrified out of their lives.'

'Why do they do it, Jared?' she asked, as they entered the broad street that led to the Marriot's sturdy, stone-built house. A house built with their own hands, with care and love, just as the Spencer home had been.

'They don't understand,' Jared said bitterly. 'They can't accept us because they can't understand us.'

His frank open countenance, normally one that laughed and smiled so easily, was set in sombre lines.

'You'd think, after what they did to Brother Joseph, that they would leave us in peace,' Polly said tentatively. She knew how a mention of Joseph Smith's death caused Jared such pain that at first it had frightened her. It was not to cause him more pain that she mentioned it now. Only to try and understand. Although she was not a Mormon, she had always been treated with love and kindness by them. Every Mormon she knew was quite prepared to live cordially alongside his non-believing neighbours. But the non-believers would have none of it. They wanted them away.

Only two weeks ago Brigham Young had led over 2,000 of Nauvoo's inhabitants over the frozen Mississippi and West to the far distant Rocky Mountains. Their houses had been evacuated, their belongings packed tightly in the covered wagons that would be their homes for many months. Only the old and sick had remained, believing in the governor's promise that they would be protected. The promise had proved impossible to keep and now Tom and Jared, who had stayed behind in consideration for Lucy's health, were already regretting their decision. But it was unthinkable that Lucy should give up her home, and though she had not told Tom or Jared, Polly knew that the older woman suffered pains in her side that sometimes left her prostrate.

'They thought Joseph's death would be an end to our faith,' Jared said as they approached the welcoming lamplight of their home. 'They were mistaken. His murder achieved nothing. We have Brother Brigham to lead us now and we still have our faith. Nothing can take that from us.'

They paused at the gate and his hand touched hers, his eyes pleading.

'If only you would make it your faith too, Polly. Accept the Gospel . . .'

His touch on her hand was warm and comforting. Accept the restored Gospel and become a Mormon—and Jared Marriot's wife.

She felt suddenly too old for her eighteen years. For as long as she could remember, she and her family had lived among Latter-day Saints, for Mormons was only a nickname, but her parents had never accepted Joseph Smith's faith and Polly could not either. Not even to become Jared's wife—and Jared would never marry a woman who did not share his faith. He was too totally committed to Joseph Smith's teachings. He wanted marriage not just for this life, but for the next. Latter-day Saints believed that marriage was for eternity. Polly hoped sincerely that it was: not just for them but for everyone who truly loved.

She said, 'I'm tired, Jared. There'll be many beds to make up if the Spencers are with us, and extra cooking.'

'I love you, Polly,' he said as she moved away from him. 'I want you to be my wife.'

She stood still, gazing at the sturdy homestead with its welcoming lamplight in the windows. If she married Jared she would have a home of her own, children. She said tentatively:

'Then marry me as I am, Jared.' Even in the darkness she could see the sadness in his eyes.

'I cannot, Polly. I cannot marry you until you share my faith.'

She had wanted him to say that he could not live without her: that he loved her so much the difference in their faiths could be overcome. Her heart felt heavy in her breast, for at that moment she was faced with the painful truth. Her love for Jared was not great enough. If it had been, she too, would have overcome the obstacles that lay between them. Memories of her mother flooded back. 'Rebel' was the word the Latter-day sisters had used to describe her. It was a word that Polly knew they often used about herself. As a little girl she had laughed at such a description of her sweet-faced mother. Now she understood. Like Mary Ellen Kirkham she did not fit into the tight-knit community in which she lived.

Her mother had come from a good-class Philadelphia family. Her parents had arranged a most suitable match and their headstrong daughter had refused it adamantly and had eloped with Harry Kirkham, a man with no skills but those of a farm boy. It had, to say the least, been disastrous as far as the Jamesons were concerned. No doubt they still talked about it. Polly did not know: she had never met any of her Jameson relations and had no desire to do so.

Lucy Marriot flung open the door. 'Thank goodness you're safe, child,' she exclaimed gratefully. 'The Spencers have been driven from house and home and Susannah Spencer is half-demented with the shock.'

Polly hurried after Lucy, knowing there would be many household tasks to accomplish. Food to prepare, beds to make. Jared crossed to the large, scrubbed kitchen table where his father and Nephi Spencer sat, shoulders hunched. For a brief second, before she hurried into the kitchen, Polly's eyes lingered on his slim-built figure. He was a good man and an honourable one. His hair was nearly as fair as her own, and his deep grey eyes caused many a young girl to gaze after him wistfully and wait hopefully at dances for his attention. There were not many young men in Nauvoo as handsome as Jared Marriot. Polly knew she was envied by many of the local girls, for Jared had made no secret of the fact that he wished to marry her.

They had lived under the same roof for over five years. She knew that she loved him, but she also knew that her love was not strong enough—it was not the love a woman should feel for the man she is to marry. Rather it was the love of a sister for a brother.

Once again she thought of her mother who had defied convention because she loved so deeply. She had exchanged a life of comfort and ease for one of hardship and unremitting happiness. Her daughter did not care about convention either. She, too, wanted to love as her mother had done. But such a love was not one-sided. Harry Kirkham had worshipped his wife. There was nothing he would not have done or given up for her. Polly wanted to be loved like that. She wanted Jared to love her so much that he would not care whether she shared his faith or not.

She gave herself a mental shake. There was no time to be dreaming of a love that would sweep her off her feet. Lucy Marriot had the whole Spencer family to feed as well as her own.

She put bacon and beans in a pan and then warmed milk and took it into the parlour where the Spencer children huddled on a rag rug before a roaring log fire, their eyes huge in their white faces. As she hurried off to find fresh linen and make up extra beds, other neighbours arrived to comfort the evicted family.

Eliza Cowley looked nearly as frightened as Susannah Spencer. City-bred, she was a timid woman and terrified that the disaster that had befallen her friend would befall her. Sister Schulster, a tart-voiced widow rumoured to be well in her eighties, had arrived with her and shortly afterwards Lydia Lyman, a capable and formidable spinster, stamped the snow off her boots and entered the parlour, immediately taking one of the children on her lap. Polly handed out the warm drinks and was rewarded by a grateful smile from Lucy.

'Bless you, child. What I'd do without you I can't think.'

Sister Spencer hugged herself, crying ceaselessly, ignoring the proffered milk.

Sister Schulster clicked her tongue impatiently. 'Do stop wailing like that, Susannah. It's a house you've lost, not a child.'

Sister Spencer continued to sob. Three times in her married life she had been forced to flee her home: first in Kirtland, then in Quincy, now in Nauvoo. She had lost everything; their heavy, hand-embroidered bedspread, left to them by her mother; the pretty rosewood mirror Nephi had given to her on their tenth wedding anniversary; the samplers the children had sewn when they were learning to stitch.

Eliza Cowley put a comforting arm around her and Jared's eyes lifted, meeting Polly's briefly before she returned to the kitchen. His face was grim. He had never wanted to remain behind in Nauvoo and Polly guessed that he was doing his best to persuade his father to leave.

'Fetch a pitcher of milk,' Lucy said breathlessly as she joined her at the stove. 'There's enough bread made, thank the Lord, and plenty of blankets. We'll none of us be cold tonight.'

Through the open door the men's voices carried clearly.

'What hope is there for us here when the Governor never even brought Joseph's murderers to justice?' Brother Spencer asked, so savagely that Polly spilled the hot barley-water she was pouring for Sister Schulster.

'The stronger we grow, the more we are hated.' Tom Marriot's voice was weary. 'It happened in Kirtland and now it's happening here.'

'We should have gone West with Brother Brigham.' It was Jared's voice and there was the sound of his fist slamming on the table. 'We have the wagons and the provisions!'

Eliza and Susannah looked at each other. Another uprooting. Another town to build in the wilds and the wastelands. Lucy began to cry softly and returned to the parlour and her husband's side.

'We'll have no more such talk tonight, Jared,' Tom Marriot said, putting his arm around his wife. 'Tomorrow will be soon enough for any decisions that have to be made. Let's eat now. Sister Spencer and the babes need hot food and the comfort of warm beds.'

Polly settled the children at the table with plates of beans, a knot of excitement deepening within her. Were they really going to leave? When Brigham Young's convoy of wagons had rolled through Nauvoo's streets and over the frozen river, her heart had ached with longing to be among them. They were setting off on a great adventure, and she wanted to be part of it. Her love for Lucy was the only thing that had prevented her from joining the hymn-singing pioneers as they set off on a trek fraught with unimaginable dangers: a trek to land where they could live in peace.

She headed back into the kitchen for more plates and then dropped them on the stone floor as a volley of shots rang out and there came the sound of galloping hooves and shouts and blasphemies. Through the window horsemen could be seen clearly, masked faces ghastly in the light of burning brands. With a sob of fear Polly dropped the heavy wooden bar into place against the door and raced into the parlour.

Tom and Jared had already seized their pistols and Nephi Spencer was busily loading his rifle.

'No! No!' his wife pleaded, grabbing his arm. 'You cannot shoot at them, husband! Vengeance is the Lord's prerogative! We cannot become murderers because they are!'

Nephi Spencer paid her no heed. He had been forced to flee once that night and he knew he would rather be dead than flee again.

Stones smashed the windows, one of them hitting Sister Schulster on the temple and sending her reeling, blood pouring down her face.

Polly rushed across to her and as she did so musket fire splintered Lucy's piano and rained on the walls. The women screamed, huddling for safety behind the sofa, shielding the terrified children with their bodies.

'Shoot high!' Tom Marriot was shouting to his son. 'Don't shoot to kill! Shoot high!'

Susannah Spencer was praying, her eyes tightly closed. Lucy was clutching her heart. Eliza Cowley was half insensible with fear and the children cried piteously as the noise and shots increased. As Polly tended Sister Schulster, a burly figure leapt through the shattered kitchen window, and rushed into the room behind her. With a cry of pain and terror, her arms were wrenched behind her back and she was dragged to the far side of the room as her captor shouted.

'One more shot and I'll blow her brains out!'

She had a dazed recollection of Nephi and Tom turning in horror and dropping their pistols. Of Jared's face, white and contorted with helpless rage.

There was the sound of breaking wood as the door was forced and then the mob poured into the little parlour, laughing and jeering, smashing all they could lay their hands on while Tom and Jared and Nephi were herded outside, muskets at their backs.

With her arms held cruelly high behind her Polly watched, appalled, as crockery and books, mirrors and pictures, began to fly through the open windows and smash on the hard-packed snow.

'Oh no! Please God, no!' she protested, her heart feeling as if it would burst.

Lucy was pathetically reaching restraining hands to an oaf who was ripping down her carefully-stitched curtains. Sister Cowley was lying prostrate on the floor. Sister Schulster, oblivious of her injury, was vainly attacking a man who had lascivious hold of Lydia Lyman. Sister Spencer was clutching the Marriot Bible to her breast, her eyes wild, her sobbing children clinging to her skirts. As Polly watched, grimy hands forced the children aside and wrenched the Bible from her grasp. Furiously, Polly writhed free of her captor and hurled herself forward, grabbing the Bible, drumming booted feet into rock-like legs, overcome with a rage that was murderous.

There was a crescendo of fresh screams and a rushing, roaring sound as burning brands were tossed into the middle of the parlour. A sheet of flame leapt across the room, its heat searing her face. Lydia Lyman broke loose from her captor and seized Sister Cowley, hurling her from the room. Polly grabbed Lucy, sparks catching at her hair and skirt. Outside their tormentors whooped and cheered, feeding the flames with anything they could lay hands on.

'Heathens! Infidels!' Susannah Spencer sobbed, clutching her children in her arms.

Tom Marriot had fallen to his knees in prayer. His son stood, his fury that of a man demented as he was held by the mob and forced to watch as his home was devoured by flames. Lucy's sobs were uncontrollable.

'What shall we do? Where shall we go?' she cried pathetically.

Polly felt the rage inside her grow cold and hard. She knew what they would do and where they would go. They would travel West. Far away from the thugs who burned and looted for the sheer sport of it.

'Fetch the tar bucket, boys,' cried the brute who had half wrenched her arms from their sockets. 'There's a feather tick saved and t'would be fool to waste it.'

Polly felt her face drain of blood. Sister Spencer screamed and kept on screaming. Lydia Lyman threw herself physically at the ringleader and was rewarded by a blow that sent her reeling to the frozen ground.

The men laughed and one said regretfully, 'We'd best content ourselves with one of them. These flames will bring the militia down on us within the hour!'

With pistols at their heads, Tom and Nephi were forced to watch impotently as Jared's shirt was stripped from his back and despite his crazed struggles he was bound hand and foot.

The older women turned their heads away, weeping, as the feather tick was ripped open and a rag was thrust in Jared's mouth. Lucy gave a low moan and collapsed insensible on to the snow. Polly gathered the crying children around her, feeling as if she had been transported to hell as she pressed their faces to her skirt, and Jared Marriot was tarred and feathered by the light of his burning home.

CHAPTER TWO

It was noon the following day before the combined ministrations of the women had removed the blistering tar and the feathers. Jared's skin was inflamed and burned, his eyes red-rimmed and bloodshot. Only the rag in his mouth had prevented the tar choking him to death.

'Heathens and ruffians!' Sister Schulster said vehemently as she applied salve to Jared's raw skin. 'Not one more day will I stay! I'll leave for the West and the Promised Land if I have to leave alone!'

'I doubt you'll be alone, Sister,' Tom Marriot said wearily. 'There can be no future for us here.'

'We should have gone with Brother Brigham,' Susannah Spencer said tearfully. 'I told Nephi that we should have gone with the others, but he urged that we wait till spring. Now see what has happened! We have no home! No shelter!'

'We had the Governor's promise,' Tom Marriot said gently. 'Brigham Young would not have left one single soul behind if he had thought that harm would come to them.'

'The Governor cannot control the thugs of St Louis,' Lydia Lyman said flatly. 'Sister Schulster is right. We must go, and the quicker the better.' Sister Lyman was a formidable woman of forty years or more. She had made her own wagon with the help of a neighbour, and was a lady of such awesome capability that it wouldn't have surprised Polly if she had felled the very timber for it herself.

Jared eased his shirt on gingerly, his expression frightening. 'We go, but not until I have exacted revenge.'

The jug in Lucy's hand clattered to the floor. 'What do you mean, son? There can be no revenge against men who are mad and will stop at nothing, not even murder.'

Jared seized his pistol and rammed it down his belt. 'I'm riding for St Louis. I'll find that mob if it's the last thing I do!'

Lucy's face was grey. 'No, Jared! Wait!' She clutched his arm restrainingly.

'Revenge is not the way,' Tom Marriot said quietly.

'Then what is?' Jared's eyes blazed with frustration. 'Are we women, to stand by while our homes are burned and looted?'

'We are Christians,' his father said. 'We defend our own whenever possible, but we do not seek revenge. It is not the Lord's way. Put down your pistol, son, and help us make plans for joining Brother Brigham.'

Their eyes held for a long, silent moment and then Jared's shoulders sagged and he removed his pistol from his belt.

Lucy gave a cry of relief and her husband looked across at her queryingly. 'Do we go too, wife?'

Lucy nodded. She had pleaded with Tom that they stay behind when their friends and neighbours had left. The prospect of the hazards of the journey West had daunted her. Now she had no more doubts. Anything would be preferable to seeing her son hanged for murder.

All that day and through the next night, by lamplight and candlelight, houses were evacuated and wagons loaded.

Sister Schulster was to travel with the Spencers. Sister Lyman would be travelling alone. The Marriot wagon was furnished with bedding from neighbours and Lucy thanked her maker that her store of grain and preserves had been locked in the storehouse and had been kept safe from the flames.

Sister Schulster's friend, the elderly Sister Fielding, insisted that she, too, accompanied them and it was arranged that she would travel with the Cowleys.

'Where are we going, young man?' she asked the white-haired Tom Marriot.

'Across the Great Plains to the Rocky Mountains. There, at least, no one will follow us.'

'Except Indians,' Eliza Cowley said, fighting back tears. 'We'll be travelling deep in Indian country and how a small party like ours will survive, the Lord alone knows.'

'The Lord will be with us,' her husband said firmly, 'and He's more than a match for any Indian. Come, wife, there's work to do.'

Jared, young and strong, had recovered from his ordeal with amazing resilience. Despite his mother's pleas that he rest, he worked with the others, packing their sturdy, home-built wagon to the brim with provisions. As Polly handed him an armful of preserves, he halted in his task and took her hands in his.

'Let's travel West as man and wife, Polly. Brother Spencer can baptise you and we can be married before sundown.'

His eyes were pleading and Polly felt her resolve weakening. Jared's suffering at the hands of the mob still burned in her mind like a red-hot brand. Perhaps she was foolish waiting for a love that she could barely imagine. Perhaps she should marry Jared with his quiet devotion and steadfast loyalty.

'I . . .' she began and got no further.

'Come along you two,' Sister Schulster said briskly. 'There's work to be done and no time to be tarrying in idle chatter.'

With an agonised expression in his eyes Jared released her hand and Polly returned once more to the storehouse. She had nearly said yes to his proposal of marriage. Why then did she feel no elation? No disappointment at Sister Schulster's intervention?

The Saints' anger had changed first to despair and then to optimism. Despair that they had tried to live amicably with their neighbours and failed. Optimism for the new life that lay ahead of them.

Tom Marriot began to hum a hymn, and then to sing, and gradually his companions joined in and their spirits lifted. By the time dawn broke their desolation had turned to zest.

'Will there be Indians?' little Serena Spencer asked as her mother wrapped her up in blankets and lifted her aboard.

'None that we can't deal with,' her father said confidently.

'And buffalo?' little Jamie Spencer asked. 'Will there be buffalo?'

'Buffalo in plenty, son. Now you stay quiet while we finish loading up. The ground is frozen and we'll have only the nourishment we can take with us.'

'That's the last,' Tom Marriot said with relief as he heaved a sack of grain into the back of his wagon. 'What isn't loaded now will have to be left behind. There's not room for so much as an extra tinderbox.'

Polly, struggling to wedge in a final jar of preserves, agreed fervently, not knowing how she and Lucy were going to find room to sit once they set off. Tom had already harnessed up his four finest horses. Two oxen and two goats were tied complainingly at the rear, and a coop, full of hens scattering feathers left and right, was perched precariously on top of the baggage.

'How long will it take us to catch up with Brother Brigham?' Lydia Lyman asked, as the Cowley wagon, driven by oxen, creaked ponderously towards them.

'Only a matter of days if we drive hard,' Tom replied optimistically. 'Brother Brigham is making for Council Bluffs and then continuing West on the north side of the River Platte. If we follow the same route we should have no trouble catching them up.'

The snow that had fallen intermittently all through the night now fell with fresh vengeance, whipping into their faces and freezing their hands.

'How many miles do you reckon we can cover in a day, young Jared?' Lydia Lyman asked as he climbed into the teamster seat, his buckskins tucked tight into his boots, a heavy cape around his shoulders and a gleaming clasp knife in his broad leather belt.

'In this weather, seven or eight miles,' he shouted, the wind whipping his words away.

'And how far is it to the Rocky Mountains and the Promised Land?' Sister Schulster asked from the interior of the Cowleys' wagon.

'A thousand,' Brother Cowley said, his face grim as Tom Marriot yelled:

'*Are we ready to roll, then?*'

There came a roar of assent. With a whoop of exultation, Jared flicked the reins and led the way through the deserted, snow-clad streets.

Tom Marriot wore his brown felt hat at a jaunty angle and began to sing lustily as the little caravan of wagons and livestock teetered precariously down the banks of the still-frozen river.

'I hope the ice holds,' little Serena Spencer said anxiously to Polly. For lack of room in her own family wagon she was travelling with the Marriots.

'The ice will hold, never fear,' Polly said, holding her hand as she joined in the singing.

They were off on a great expedition and her adventurous heart was revelling in it. She wished she could sit up front, but there was only room for Tom and Jared and she had to remain inside with Lucy and Serena. The jolting of the wagon was uncomfortable; the cold—despite their warm clothing and blankets hugged around their knees—piercing. Eventually Serena fell asleep, her hand held tightly in Polly's, and even Tom Marriot ceased to sing as the raw wind froze his breath.

It was a long, hard day with everybody suffering from lack of sleep. By the time dusk fell and they made camp at Sugar Creek, it took all of Polly's strength to help Jared shovel away snow with numbed fingers, so that they could light a campfire. The older women huddled around the fire, grateful for hot food and drink, and then buried themselves deep beneath their blankets and their respective wagons and tried not to think too longingly of the comfortable homes and soft beds a day's travelling behind them.

'Could we not stay here awhile and let the women rest?' Tom Marriot asked Josiah Cowley as they lingered around the heat of the fire.

The other man shook his mane of white hair. 'It would be senseless, Tom. We must keep going. Keep moving.

Tomorrow we'll start off for Richardson Point, following the Fox River.'

Sister Lyman trudged wearily across to them, her high-buttoned boots sinking heavily into the snow. Her heavy woollen cloak was clutched tightly beneath her chin.

'I have a loose axle, Brother Cowley. I've been struggling with it this last hour, but my hands are frozen.'

Polly rushed to her side, her face horrified at the sight of the bloodless, swollen hands.

'You shouldn't have done so, Sister Lyman! You'll never hold the reins tomorrow!' Quickly she hurried her into the Marriots' wagon and began feverishly rubbing the lifeless hands as Sister Lyman gritted her teeth and winced with pain.

'Careful man!' Tom Marriot's shout was panic-stricken.

There was an horrendous creaking and a loud cry. Lucy Marriot clutched her bedclothes around her and thrust her head out of the wagon and into the night.

'What is it, Tom? Are you all right?'

Polly dropped Sister Lyman's hands and sprang to the snow-covered ground, running with Jared to where Sister Lyman's wagon lay at an ugly angle.

Brother Cowley was lying in the snow, clutching his shoulder, groaning with pain. Tom Marriot was breathing harshly, half dead from the effort of holding up the weight of the wagon so that his friend could roll free. Behind her, Polly could hear Lucy and Sister Lyman praying aloud. Jared had swiftly opened Brother Cowley's coat and was feeling his shoulder and arm, saying grimly.

'Tis broken all right. Help me get him under cover.'

And then, questioningly to Polly, 'Will you be able to fix it?'

She nodded. She was known for her skill at setting broken bones, but she had never had to do so in such terrible conditions.

It was two in the morning before Josiah Cowley lay, pale-faced in his bed, his broken arm strapped in splints and an exhausted Polly was almost fainting with weariness and cold.

'Who will drive us?' Sister Cowley whispered, gazing from Tom to Jared with a helpless expression. 'I cannot manage the oxen on my own.'

Tom sighed. Of all women to be without a fit man, Sister Cowley was the most vulnerable. She had been city bred and farm life had never come easy to her. She had still not mastered skills that girls of fourteen took for granted.

'I'll drive you,' he said, patting her shoulder reassuringly. 'Now get you some sleep. We've a hard day ahead of us.'

'Should we turn back?' Lucy asked her husband tentatively when he returned to their wagon. 'Brother Cowley's arm will take weeks to mend and there's seven women and five children to take care of.'

'We go on, wife,' Tom said gently. 'I doubt if we could return now, even if we wanted to.'

He had no need to say more. At the thought of strangers invading her beautifully-kept parlour and cheery kitchen, Lucy turned her face away and prayed for strength. They had a thousand miles to travel and had travelled only seven. The expedition that seemed so viable when they had planned it around their kitchen table now seemed more and more impossible. She wanted to cry but would not, for Tom's sake.

'Don't worry,' Polly said comfortingly as she slid at last beneath her blankets. 'It was a bad start, but the morning will be better.'

It wasn't: it was worse. It nearly quenched even Polly's optimism. First, it took several hours of struggling in the snow to mend Sister Lyman's wheel and then Tom Marriot began to shake with a chill and Jared had to replace him at the reins of the Cowley wagon, leaving Polly to handle their own team. For hour after hour they journeyed through trackless wilds of snow, the bleak north-west wind blowing in their faces with a keenness that almost took the skin from their cheeks.

Serena began to cry because of the cold and as dusk approached there was still nowhere suitable to make camp. Wherever they stopped they would be exposed to the merciless wind. It was then, when their spirits were at their lowest, that Nephi shouted;

'A rider! Do you see?'

Polly strained her eyes into the distance. The small blur became a definite shape; a rider and horse were galloping at full speed towards them.

'The Lord be praised!' Lucy Marriott said. 'Can you see who it is? Is it one of the Kimball boys or the Romneys?'

'It's neither,' Nephi said with a trace of disappointment. 'It's an army man.'

'No doubt he'll be able to tell us where to camp,' Lucy Marriot said, and to Polly's astonishment, Lydia Lyman said musingly:

'I always think a man looks well in uniform.'

The one approaching them certainly did. Despite the snow his knee-high boots gleamed, his trousers tucked into them with none of the untidiness of Jared's buckskins. His dark blue jacket, lavishly embellished with gold braid, fitted perfectly across broad shoulders and he rode his black stallion with insolent ease.

'Welcome!' Nephi Spencer called out, reining-in his team as the horseman approached.

There was no sign of welcome on the dark, almost savage features of the rider as the horse wheeled in a flurry of snow.

'Where the devil do you think you're going?' he snapped at Brother Spencer.

'To Richardson Point,' Brother Spencer said genially, well used to turning the other cheek.

'The hell you are!'

'We are Latter-day Saints, sir, and do not take kindly to oaths and bad language,' Lucy Marriot remonstrated.

'I don't care if you're angels from heaven! You'll turn this team around immediately and return from whence you came.'

'No sir. We will not be doing that,' Brother Spencer replied composedly. 'I wish you good day and am sorry for taking up your time.'

He urged his horses into movement, but the stranger leaned across and seized the reins from his grasp with a gauntletted hand.

'You will go nowhere without my authority!'

Polly watched the altercation with interest. The stranger had a face so different from those she was accustomed to seeing that it was almost alien. For a start, his skin was much darker than that of any men she had previously seen, save Indians. It was swarthy, almost olive in tone. Beneath the broad-brimmed hat with its narrow circle of gold ribbon she could see that his hair was jet black and straight, worn longer than was normal among military men. Winged eyebrows met in a savage frown and beneath them Polly could see equally dark eyes slanting above high cheekbones. It was an interesting face. His mouth was drawn in a tight line of anger, but it was a well-shaped mouth and one that held her attention.

'And what authority is that, sir?' Nephi asked, blandly ignoring the Major's insignia.

'That of a Major in the United States Army,' the stranger replied tersely. 'Now get this rabble turned around. There's nothing ahead of you but wilderness.'

Jared's wagon had been in the rear, now he ran up to them, knee-deep in snow, his face furious.

'Apologise at once for that remark!' he shouted up at the seated horseman.

The Major, still with Nephi's reins in his hands, turned and looked down at Jared. For a brief second Polly thought she saw amusement flicker in the depths of the black eyes, but then she knew she had been mistaken for he said in a voice that sent a shiver of fear down her spine.

'Back to your wagon, boy.'

'Why, you . . .' Jared lunged furiously at him, but the Major caught his wrist, imprisoning him in a hold of steel.

'If you want to make a fool of yourself in front of your womenfolk I'll be only too happy to oblige, but it will be dark within minutes. Now turn your team around and I will accompany you back towards the Mississippi.'

Jared, face burning with anger, wrenched his wrist away but made no further attempt to unseat the arrogant stranger. To do so would only have been to make himself look ridiculous.

'We crossed the Mississippi only yesterday morning,' Nephi replied equably. 'We have no intention of repeating the experience.'

The Major's eyes flicked from one wagon to another. When they came to Polly's they rested on her, studying her face and then moving slowly, admiringly downwards. Polly's cheeks flushed at his impertinence as he turned once more to Nephi.

'Where are your men?'

'Brother Marriot has the fever,' Lydia Lyman replied briskly. 'Brother Cowley broke his arm in an accident late last evening. Brother Spencer and Jared Marriot you have already met. We are,' she added unnecessarily, 'a small party.' She sat straight-backed and gazed defiantly at him.

It was at this moment that Serena began to cry again. The Major lost his fierce composure.

'Good God! Are there children with you too?'

'Five, and as Sister Marriot has pointed out, we do not approve of the Lord's name being taken in vain.'

Polly could see comprehension dawn on the Major's handsome dark face.

'I might have known it,' he said exasperatedly. 'Mormons!'

'Then you've met up with those ahead of us?' Nephi asked eagerly as Susannah and his children crowded around his shoulders to stare at the stranger.

Polly thought she saw the Major flinch at the sight of the five pairs of large eyes fixed unblinkingly on him.

'Tell him begone if he cannot be civil,' Sister Fielding called from the inside of her wagon in a wavering, high-pitched voice.

Dark brows flew upwards.

'An elderly sister,' Lydia Lyman explained unnecessarily.

'How elderly?' The black eyes were suspicious.

Unfortunately lying did not accord with Sister Lyman's faith. She tried to sound suitably vague. 'Seventy or thereabouts.'

'*Seventy?*'

Polly thought the Major would fall off his horse. The full force of his fury was directed at Nephi.

'You bring a gaggle of babes and an old woman out into a wilderness twelve degrees below zero and expect me to treat you as a sane man?'

'Two old women,' Polly corrected, unable to keep silent any longer.

He swivelled to look at her and she wished she had kept silent. He looked distinctly forbidding.

'Two?' he asked through clenched teeth.

'Sister Schulster is in her seventies as well,' Polly explained, wishing she sounded as sure of herself as Sister Lyman had done and aware that beneath his piercing gaze an unwelcome blush was tingeing her cheeks.

'Eighty-four!' came a sprightly voice from inside the wagon and Nephi and Jared groaned simultaneously.

'Of all the half-baked, half-witted, idiotic, irresponsible, senseless . . .'

'You didn't answer my question, sir,' Nephi said with maddening politeness. 'Have you met with those ahead of us?'

'Yes, I have, and compared to you they're on the borders of sanity!'

'Praise the Lord!' Nephi said joyously. 'Do you hear that, Tom? The Saints are only a little way ahead of us. We'll be with them soon.'

'Not if I have anything to do with it,' the Major said crushingly. 'They are way ahead of you at Richardson Point. You stand no chance of catching them up. Also, come another few months, there won't be many there to catch up with.'

'What do you mean?' Tom Marriot had dragged himself up beside Nephi, wrapped in a thick woollen blanket and shivering convulsively. 'Is there sickness there?'

'No, but the army wants the men to fight in the war against Mexico. I'm on my way to St Louis on leave, but on my return my orders are to raise a battalion. There isn't much action yet, but there will be come the summer.'

'We are travelling West to find a home in which to worship in peace, not to fight a war,' Lydia Lyman said tartly.

'Maybe, but if you're loyal subjects of the United States you'll have no objection to fighting in her cause, will you?'

'I hope you're not referring to me personally, Major,' Lydia retorted with a flash in her eyes.

The Major threw back his head and roared with laughter, his whole countenance changing.

'By God, you Mormons may be mad, but you breed remarkable women!'

Lydia Lyman tried to look affronted and failed. Polly wished his attention would return to her once more. She was the one who should have been making him laugh. Not Lydia Lyman who had grey hair and was an old maid.

His laughter did not last long. Darkness had fallen while they had been talking.

He said with a return of his bad temper, 'It's too late now to go either forwards or back. We'll have to camp here for the night.'

'You're staying with us, sir?' Nephi asked with

pleasure as Jared glowered.
 'I'm staying,' the Major said, slipping agilely from his horse. 'I'm staying because I'm going to personally escort the lot of you back across the Mississippi come daylight!'

CHAPTER THREE

THE presence of the Major sparked up everybody's spirits but Jared's. Despite his curtness and unaffability he had encountered their friends on the trail. That fact alone was enough to put fresh heart into them.

Tom Marriot's fever had increased and he was unable to join them around the camp fire. Lucy tended him anxiously, surrounding him with stone jars filled with heated, melted snow and staying at his side, his hand in hers. Brother Cowley sat uncomfortably for a few minutes with them, but soon returned to his bed. His arm was paining him and the bitter cold only increased his discomfort.

Jared had turned as surly as the Major. While Polly cooked beans and tried to make the dried salt pork as palatable as possible, he remained silent and taciturn, the very opposite of his usual self. Polly knew why and sympathised. The Major had emasculated him by calling him a boy and Jared had been in no position to retaliate.

'Were they well?' Nephi asked, spooning beans into his mouth with relish.

The Major eyed Nephi silently for a few minutes and poked a rolling log on to the fire with the toe of his boot.

'Some of them,' he replied non-committally.

Polly found it very hard to take her eyes away from him. When she had served him with his plate of dinner, he had not looked up at her, but her arm had brushed his and she had been aware of an undercurrent of excitement she had never experienced before. There was nothing tame about Major Dart Richards. Nephi, with patient questioning, had finally elicited his name from him.

Dart. It was a strange name. Almost an Indian name, and it was one that suited him well.

Lydia Lyman's eyes sharpened. 'Only some of them, Major. What of the others?'

Polly noticed that beneath her heavy cloak a fichu of lace peeped at her throat. Sister Lyman had never been known for feminine fripperies. Polly wondered if it was the Major's presence that had prompted her to unearth her finery.

She could well understand why, if it was so. He was a man who, with one brief glance, could make a woman feel wholly feminine.

The hard lines around his mouth had softened slightly as he ate and Polly found herself wondering what it would be like to be kissed by such a man. Certainly it would be a very different experience from being kissed by Jared or any other of the local boys. At the realisation of her thoughts she blushed scarlet and dropped her spoon in confusion. She was becoming as lewd as Letty Cummings, who had been disfellowshipped some months ago for behaviour that no one had satisfactorily explained to her.

Major Richards' eyes held Sister Lyman's unflinchingly. 'Some have chills and fever, as the brother in the wagon has. Some have died of the cholera and all are suffering from lack of suitable nourishment.'

'Cholera!' Polly blanched.

His disturbing eyes rested on her and he said with an edge of sarcasm, 'Why yes, Miss Kirkham, sickness will be a part of your great trek, or hadn't you realised that when you so hare-brainedly set off on your idiotic venture?'

'Sister Kirkham's parents both died of the cholera,' Nephi said quietly. 'She is an orphan and has no one in the world but the Marriot's who took pity on her and gave her a home.'

'I am sorry.' The sarcasm was gone. His eyes held hers and there was something in their depths that unnerved her even more than the accidental touching of his arm had done.

'Have there been many deaths, sir?' Susannah Spencer asked anxiously.

'Enough. You would see the graves on the trailside if you were to continue.'

'We *are* continuing, Major.' Susannah Spencer's voice was as authoritative as his.

Something like respect flashed in his eyes and disappeared.

'You will not,' he said abruptly, 'for you have no comprehension of the hardships ahead of you. A small band such as yours would never survive. Even now two of your men are incapacitated and you are left with only . . .'

For a heart-stopping moment Polly thought he was going to say 'One man and a boy' but instead he said, 'Two fit men.'

'We can overcome whatever hardships lie ahead of us,' Lydia Lyman said firmly.

'Hunger and cold, yes. But you cannot overcome the elements.'

They looked at him questioningly and he said irritably, as if he were addressing children, 'Another week and the snow will melt and the rain will come.'

'A little rain never hurt anybody,' Susannah Spencer said defiantly.

'A *little* rain?' the Major expostulated. 'Good God, woman! It rains in torrents out there on the plain!'

His anger was so intense that Susannah did not even remonstrate with him for taking the Lord's name in vain.

'It pours down as if from buckets! The ground is reduced to mud so deep that the wheels of your wagons will sink completely. Planks of timber will be needed to try and roll them from the quagmire. That sort of effort requires scores of strong, fit men. Not women and children. To save weight in the wagons you will have to walk ankle-deep and sometimes knee-deep in the mud and water. Then at night the mud will freeze and that will not end your troubles, for the track will become even more impassable. Wagons will overturn on the uneven surface, children will be crushed beneath the wheels.'

Polly gasped, her face paling.

'Oh yes,' he said harshly, turning to her once more. 'Already one child has lost its life beneath the wheels of its family's wagon.'

Even Nephi remained silent. Major Richards continued mercilessly, 'The rain will flood the streams. Your way lies along the River Fox and it has many tributaries—the only way of fording them is to swim. Could your two elderly sisters and children swim the rushing, freezing currents of the Locust and Modkine Creeks?'

There was silence. Then Nephi said stubbornly: 'We go on.'

'God's teeth!' The Major sprang to his feet in a fury. 'Never, in all my life, have I met such pig-headed, stubborn, intractable people as you!'

'Never before have you met Mormons,' Lydia Lyman retorted.

'Never do I want to meet more! Your are the most unreasoning, eccentric . . .'

Lydia Lyman cut him short as she rose to her feet. 'The prophet Joseph called us a peculiar people,' she said as she nodded her goodnights.

'Then prophet or not, I cannot but agree with him,' Major Richards said, and marched off into the darkness. His fists were clenched, the set of his shoulders indicating that if he had stayed a moment longer his anger would have risen far above blasphemy.

'Do you think what he says is true,' Susannah Spencer asked her husband anxiously as the Major's forbidding figure disappeared in the darkness.

'Aye, the man's no liar. I'd stake my life on that.'

'He is a blasphemer and a heathen!' Jared said through clenched teeth. 'The sooner we see the back of him the better.'

'I've a feeling that will be no easy task,' Nephi said drily.

'But if there are floods . . .' Susannah began.

Nephi took her hand in his. 'The others survived, wife, why should not we? Come, let's have a hymn before we go to bed. The Major may have given us much-needed information, but he has lowered our spirits and taken our mind from the Lord.'

They began to sing and from the nearby wagons, Sister Fielding and Sister Schulster, the Cowleys and Marriot's, joined in with them. Fifty yards away in the darkness, Major Richards heard them and swore volubly. They were fanatics and as illogical as all fanatics. Despite all he had said there was no way he could force them to return East against their wishes, and the alternative was to allow them to continue to certain death. Even as they sang he heard the cry of a wolf. He swore again. They had spirit and courage, but no sense. One of them had something else too. Golden curls peeping from the hood of her cloak and eyes the colour of summer gentians. He grinned suddenly to himself in the darkness. Trust the first passable female he met in months of celibate soldiering to be a Mormon!

All single Mormon women were virgins, he had learnt that from bitter experience back at Richardson Point where the main party under their leader, Brigham Young, had established a temporary camp. If one wanted to live, one did not tamper with the chastity of a Mormon girl. Which was a pity, as the one who had sat opposite him across the camp fire had been uncommonly pretty. Beautiful even. He shrugged his broad shoulders. There would be women enough when he reached St Louis.

Nephi put more wood on the fire to keep it burning through the night and then they all retired, more sombre even than the previous evening. Major Richards' words had given them all a lot to think about.

Tom Marriot had fallen into an uneasy sleep and Polly helped Lucy to bed and then snuggled beneath her own blankets, removing only her cape. By the time they reached Richardson Point they would have fleas and lice to contend with, as well as cold. Washing, other than face and hands with melted snow, was an impossibility, and the sub-zero temperatures saw to it that not even the most fastidious removed more than damp cloaks when they retired. Lucy and Lydia's thoughts were of the floods ahead of them. Polly's were of Major Richards.

In the firelight his black hair had taken on a blue sheen and there had been a moment when he had spoken to her when his eyes had lingered on her mouth and she had felt a little pulse begin to beat in her throat. Then he had ignored her as if she no longer existed, and the rest of his attention had been given to the Spencers and Sister Lyman.

Jared had not spoken a word to him all night and the Major had not bothered to make amends for referring to him as a boy. Polly doubted if Major Richards made amends for anything. Jared's fury was wasted where that gentleman was concerned.

Tired though she was, sleep would not come. She found herself debating as to whether the Major was a gentleman or not. Surely his rank denoted that he was? Yet his behaviour belied it. She giggled when she remembered his expletive of 'God's teeth'. It was one she hadn't heard since her father had died, and then only rarely.

Tom Marriot groaned and began to thrash in his blankets. Polly reluctantly left the warmth of her bedding and crossed to him. His forehead was burning, his hands cold. She felt the stone jars and they too had lost their heat. She fumbled with her cloak, not wanting to light a lamp and disturb the sleeping Lucy and Serena, and with a stone jar beneath each arm faced the freezing cold to return to the still-burning fire.

He was sitting on an upturned box, a military cloak around his shoulders, his feet wide apart, his hands between his knees as he gazed into the flames.

As she drew nearer she saw the silver of a flask at his side. Shock flooded through her. Her father had not been a Mormon but neither had he been a drinking man. But then he had not been a soldier and the Major had at least had the good manners not to offend by drinking openly in front of them.

He swung around at her step, his black eyes narrowing.

'I have come to heat the stone jars for Brother Marriot.'

His muscles, which had immediately stiffened at her approach, relaxed.

With sudden nervousness Polly shovelled snow into a pan and set it on the fire, remaining as far away from the overpowering figure as possible.

If he had briefly thought she had come to seek his company he was disabused of it. The girl had no intention of flirting with him. Her errand in the depths of night was one of mercy, not of pleasure. Nevertheless, he found her a pleasant sight to watch as she shook the handle of the pan, swirling the snow around as it hissed and melted.

She couldn't be a day over eighteen, but her body was that of a woman. She had come out hurriedly and her cloak was only fastened loosely at the throat, falling open as she leaned over the fire. He could see the soft swell of her breasts and the tantalising curve of her hips.

The pan handle grew hot and she gasped.

'Here, let me.' He crossed to her side, leather-gloved hands removing the pan and pouring the steaming water into the wide necks of the jars.

They were so near that beneath the brim of his hat she could see tiny flecks of gold near his pupils and was acutely aware of the undefinable smell of his maleness and the granite-hard muscles barely contained by his immaculately-cut uniform.

For his part, Dart noticed that near to, her beauty was not only fancy but fact. Her skin had not yet been weathered by the harsh winds of the plains and was as soft as that of a peach. Her hands too, instead of being rough and chapped, were soft and smooth and carefully tended. His eyes were no longer uninterested. They were bold and black and frankly appraising.

'Thank you, Major,' she said, hoping that he could not detect the tremor in her voice. If only he would finish pouring in the water and let her escape!

Her mouth, as he had seen at a distance, was soft and inviting. He wondered what it would be like to kiss and dismissed the temptation. He would only have an hysterical female on his hands and Nephi Spencer firing his six-shooter in all directions.

At last the water was poured and she began to screw the corks in with difficulty. Silently he took the jars from her and accomplished the task with two firm twists of his wrist.

'Thank you.' Her voice was low and well-modulated, but there was steel there, and sense. Probably more sense than was shown by her companions. He said suddenly,

'Are the women of your party of the same determination as the men? Do they intend to continue West?'

She nodded.

'Even the elderly ones?'

'Yes.' The jars burned against her cloak. 'We have nothing to return to. The Marriot's home was razed to the ground by a mob and the Spencer home pillaged and looted. Even Sister Schulster was terrified by vandals as she sat in her own parlour.'

'Is Sister Schulster the sharp-voiced octogenarian?'

Polly wasn't sure what the long word meant, but assumed he had guessed correctly.

'Yes.'

The lines around his mouth tightened. 'Take the hot jars to the brother who needs them and then return and tell me more.' It wasn't a request, but a command.

'Yes,' she said again, scurrying back to her wagon, her heart throbbing painfully.

To sit out late at night, unchaperoned, with the devastating Major was an impropriety that not even the kindly Tom Marriot would easily forgive her, yet the temptation was too strong to be resisted.

When she returned, he had kicked a box close to his own, and wrapping her cloak tightly around her, she sat where she was bid.

'The Mormons I met at Richardson Point spoke of persecution and intolerance. I had not realised it was of such magnitude.'

'It has been unspeakable,' Polly said quietly. 'When I was ten I lived with my parents on a farm near Shoal Creek. It was a sunny day and I was playing with lots of other children on the bank of the creek. One of them was a boy my own age, Sardius Smith. I did not know it, of course, but for weeks the surrounding townspeople had been insisting that all Mormons gave up their faith or leave the district.' She was silent for a minute or two. 'At tea-time we went to our homes and I was standing with my mother in the parlour when I saw a large body of armed men on horses, heading towards the blacksmith's shop and mill. Their intentions were obvious and we heard one of our neighbours cry "Peace", but he was shot down as we looked and then the riders chased our neighbours into the shop and all we could hear was gunfire and screams.'

She stared broodingly into the flames. 'Sardius was so frightened he had crowled under the bellows of the forge, but a Mr Glaze of Carrol County found him and shot him through the head. Eighteen people died that afternoon. My father had been away buying livestock.

When he returned he said he was ashamed to live among men who were murderers, and that although he was not a Mormon he would go with them and not remain behind. It was then that we moved to Kirtland.'

A dark brow rose queryingly. 'Then you are not Mormon?'

'No. Not yet.'

There was hesitancy in her voice and he did not pursue his question, but he was intrigued.

'What happened in Kirtland?'

'We were not left in peace there, so we moved to Nauvoo.'

'And were not left in peace there either?'

'No. My father was not a religious man, but he said that intolerance was one of the worst sins he knew of. Intolerance and hypocrisy.'

His mouth crooked in a mirthless smile. 'He was right on that score,' he said, and Polly was shaken from her own reverie of the past by the depth of feeling in his voice.

'Have you, too, suffered from intolerance?' she asked curiously.

'I have and I no longer speak of it.' His voice was curt.

She wondered if she should return to her wagon. He showed no sign of speaking any further with her. His face was hard and uncompromising, his thoughts obviously far from her and the problems of the little wagon train.

At last, uncomfortably, she rose to her feet and he said: 'Do your companions realise that you are on the borders of Indian country?'

'Er . . . yes.' Polly did not know if they knew or not. 'We have had friendly dealings with Indians in the past,' she added, a trifle defiant.

He laughed. 'The Indians ahead of you are not Shawnees or Delawares. They are Pawnees and I doubt you will have any friendly dealings with Pawnees.'

'Do you know much about them, Major?'

'More than any man alive,' he said, and there was a strange note in his voice that she could not identify.

She wanted to ask more, but knew that if she stayed any longer it would be unseemly.

'I hope I have been able to help you with what you wanted to know, Major.'

'That the women are as stubborn as the men, no matter what their age? That death ahead is preferable to death in towns you have already been driven from? Yes, you have helped me.'

He did not wish her goodnight. She turned on her heel to leave him. So quickly that her foot caught in the hem of her cloak and she went sprawling face-down in the snow.

Before she could struggle to her feet strong hands had circled her waist. They lifted her and set her down, but did not release their grip. It was a pleasingly small waist. Dart Richards' fingertips met as he circled it.

The fall had rendered her breathless and for some unaccountable reason her heart was throbbing painfully.

His hold on her tightened as he drew her close to him and before she could utter a protest, his lips came down on hers in swift, unfumbled contact. She raised clenched hands to his shoulders to push him away, but she was helpless. As his lips parted hers, she was aware that though she fought and struggled, her one desire was to surrender. To circle his neck with her arms and to kiss him as passionately and as deeply as he was kissing her.

All too soon it was over. He thrust her from him, still keeping tight hold of her arms, a smile of delighted amusement on his face.

'Who would have thought it? The Mormons have a little passion-flower in their camp. I wonder if they are aware of it?'

Polly's pleasure turned immediately to fury. 'How *dare* you treat me like a . . . a whore of Babylon!'

He let go of her, shouting with laughter.

Polly's skirts whipped around her ankles as she raced for the sanctuary of her wagon. Hateful, detestable man. How dare he treat her so?

She pulled the blankets angrily over her shoulders. He would not have done so if Jared or Nephi had been present. He had taken unfair advantage of her. Major Richards was *definitely* not a gentleman. Her cheeks still burned scarlet. And she was not a lady. She remembered the tingling response that had seared her body as his mouth had closed over hers. She had never dreamed that a man's kiss could arouse such response. Certainly Jared's had not. Jared's kisses had been warm and comforting and safe. Major Richards' kiss had stirred her in a way that suffused her with shame, arousing in her longings she had never previously known existed. Worst of all, she would have to face him in the morning and behave as if nothing had happened.

His laughter still rang in her ears. She put her hands over them as if to shut out the sound. Lucy Marriot was right. Men outside the church were sensual and sought only their own gratification. The only happiness for a woman lay in marriage to a good upstanding member of the faith: to a man like Jared.

Her last, angry thought as she tossed and turned and tried to sleep, was that if Jared would kiss her as Major Richards had done, she would marry him tomorrow. But Jared would not do that for he had too much respect for her and she should be grateful for the fact. Her thoughts were low and impure and unfitting.

'God's teeth!' she said beneath her breath, and having given vent to her anger and shame, closed her eyes determinedly against all thoughts of Major Richards and his laughing dark eyes.

When morning came, Tom Marriot's fever had still not broken and Jared was harnessing the teams, his usual smiling face surly. Polly guessed that it would remain so until their unwelcome visitor left. She had no time to speak to him for there was breakfast to cook and the animals to feed.

As she hurried round the rear corner of their wagon she nearly fell headlong into a tin bowl of water balanced precariously on a drum of wheat. If the Mormons weren't hardy enough to strip to the waist and wash in conditions that froze water within minutes, Major Richards had no such inhibitions. He was in the process of reaching for his shirt as she staggered to regain her balance. She saw a broad chest of the same olive flesh tones as his face and a pelt of dark, curling hair. Whipcord muscles rippled as he said lazily:

'Good morning, Miss Kirkham. I hope you spent an uneventful night?'

'An unmemorable one, certainly!' Polly retorted and marched off, her skirts swishing.

Seeing his face and becoming fascinated with its strange handsomeness was bad enough. Being faced with the sight of the lean, tanned contours of his body was too much. She had seen Jared naked to the waist a hundred times, but had never taken any notice or thought it in any way remarkable. She knew she would remember the sight of the half-naked Major for a long time to come. Perhaps his sun-bronzed skin came from soldiering in California and Mexico, though that would not account for his raven-black hair and eyes. Sun would bleach, not darken, hair. She tossed her head and her ringlets danced around her face. She didn't care anything at all for the ungentlemanly, arrogant and rude Major Dart Richards.

'The Major tells us there's a wagon travelling many miles behind the main party and not far ahead of us. From his description it sounds like Charity and Fletcher Merrill,' Nephi Spencer said to Polly over breakfast.

The Merrills were close friends of both the Marriots and the Spencers. Emily Merrill was her own age, and they had shared an eighteenth birthday party only a month before.

'Then why did he not tell us so last evening?' she demanded indignantly.

'Because if he had, young Jared would have insisted on tearing off into the night and probably broken both his neck and that of his horse,' Nephi said equably.

'Why should the Merrills have fallen so far behind?'

'Sickness. They were afraid it was the cholera and did not want to spread it.'

'Is Jared going to them now?' Polly asked as she saw Jared saddling one of the horses and ramming a rifle down the side of a full saddlebag.

'Aye. Tis best if they wait for us rather than put more miles between us and remain constantly alone and unprotected.'

Polly put down her dish and crossed the frozen ground to Jared. The snow crunched crisply beneath her feet and her cheeks were rosy with colour from the sharp air.

'Brother Spencer has just told me of the Merrills.'

'I must go to them immediately, Polly. Brother

Merrill is no marksman and they are in Indian country now.'

'Can you not persuade them to return and join up with us? It would be better than waiting days or even weeks till we catch up with them.'

'That is what I intend.' He swirled his thick cape around his body and pulled his hat low over his ears. 'Look after Pa, Polly. You were right about mother. Her strength is failing, but I must go to the Merrills. You understand that, don't you?'

'Of course, and there's no one else who could ride so hard or so fast.'

She remembered Emily Merrill laughing gaily as they had danced at their birthday party.

'Pray God they are safe.'

'Aye, and that you remain safe while I am absent.'

He drew her into his arms and kissed her goodbye and she made no protest, but responded in a way that would have shocked Tom and Lucy Marriot if they had been witness to the scene. Fortunately they were not and Nephi's back was turned towards them. Only the Major could see and his face was completely expressionless.

She could feel Jared's heart thump wildly against hers and was unhappily aware that she was not reacting in a similar manner.

'Goodbye, Jared. Take care.'

She stood and waved and watched till he had ridden into the flat, barren wastes of the distance. He was a good man. Good men did not arouse lewd emotions. The knowledge brought her little comfort as she returned to her tasks.

The conversation between Major Richards and Nephi Spencer had developed into an argument on the Major's side. Tom Marriot was leaning weakly out of his wagon and doing his best to make his voice heard. Sister Lyman was making hers heard only too well.

'We go on, young man. How many more times do you have to be told?'

'White men killed two Pawnee squaws only days ago. What sort of reception do you think they will give you?'

'A friendly one as we shall give them. The red-men are our brothers, as are all men.'

'Commendable words,' the Major said drily, 'but hardly efficacious if uttered at the wrong end of a Pawnee arrow.'

'We go on.' This time it was Brother Cowley's voice. 'The Lord wishes us to establish a Promised Land in the Far West and that is exactly what we are going to do.'

The children were playing around them throwing snowballs and shouting with laughter, as they faced each other angrily. Sister Schulster descended falteringly from her wagon, a shawl covering her white hair, gnarled hands clutching it beneath her chin as she said bad-temperedly to the Major:

'How much longer before we start off? Are we to wait till the Day of Judgment, or are we to get there before it?'

The Major groaned and raised his eyes heavenwards, though not in the sort of prayer that the Saints would have found commendable.

'Come on, Pa. I want to see some Indians,' little Jamie was saying pleadingly.

Serena Spencer was fingering the gold braid on the Major's sleeve and gazing up at him with eight-year-old adoration.

Sister Lyman had returned to her wagon and her harnessed team and sat with the reins in her gloved hands. Brother Cowley, too, sat at the front of his wagon and showed every intention of driving his team, single-handed. Polly followed suit and vaulted into the teamster seat of the Marriot wagon.

Major Richards stood, his feet apart, his hands on his hips, every line of his body denoting his fury at the obdurate Nephi.

'Will nothing on God's earth make you change your mind?' he demanded seethingly.

'Nothing.'

The Major let out such a string of oaths that even Polly blanched. Then he swung on his heel and mounted his horse, the lines around his mouth white, his eyes as hard as frozen granite. Digging in his spurs he wheeled his horse not east, but westwards, galloping to the head of the convoy and saying to a delighted Nephi through clenched teeth, as he signalled the wagons forwards:

'Just don't sing! For the love of God, don't sing!'

CHAPTER FOUR

NEPHI didn't sing, but he whistled. The Major was just the man they needed, with Tom Marriot sick, and Josiah Cowley with one arm in a splint. The frozen wastes ahead of them no longer looked so forbidding. The Major was a man of the plains. They would reach Richardson Point in record time with his help.

Polly flicked her horses into movement with a surge of anger. So they were to have more of the Major's insolent company, were they? Well, *she* would have nothing further to do with him. All the same, she was aware of an undercurrent of elation that was caused by more than just the exhilaration of once more setting out on the trail.

Major Richards rode hard. If the fools behind thought they were going to have an easy time of it they had another think coming. By the time they pitched camp that evening they would be pleading with him to turn around and escort them back to Illinois. A blizzard began to blow with freezing ferocity and he grinned grimly. The worse the weather, the better, as far as he was concerned.

Richardson Point was several days' trek away and he knew that Nephi Spencer, no matter how determined, would never reach it. They had been only one day on the trail. They knew nothing of the realities of the hardships facing them. Today's trek would show them the impossibility of their task.

The snow blinded them, coating moustaches and seeping down the necks of capes and coats. After two hours' ride the Major cantered back alongside the four wagons, exhorting them to hurry their teams. They were making good time, considering that a man could not see further than two yards ahead of him for the swirling snow, but he had no intention of informing them of that fact.

Nephi Spencer beamed broadly at him, icicles forming on the corners of his drooping moustache.

'If you say so, Major,' he said cheerfully, and whipped his team encouragingly.

Lydia Lyman, hardly distinguishable as a female beneath her father's cast-off greatcoat and slouch hat, merely shrugged and showed not the least sign of flagging.

As he reined in beside Josiah Cowley he was sorely tempted to dismount and hitch his horse alongside the Cowley wagon and take the reins himself. Only his determination to break their spirit prevented him from doing so. The man was in obvious pain, but gritted his teeth and made no complaint at Dart's request that he speeded up his oxen. The Major shouted through the billowing canvas to Sister Schulster, asking how she fared.

'If I'd known this wagon would jolt so, I could have brought my butter churn and furnished us with fresh butter,' a tart voice replied.

Polly brought up the rear. Her cape was not as heavy as the one Brother Lyman had so thoughtfully passed on to his daughter and Dart could see at a glance that she was frozen to the bone. He crushed any feeling of pity.

'Get a move on,' he ordered curtly. 'You're lagging behind.'

'If I drove any faster I'd be sitting in the back of the Cowley wagon with Sister Schulster,' Polly replied through chattering teeth.

Despite himself he grinned and returned to the head of the column. Damn them to hell, but they were a stubborn lot. Another few hours of cold and damp would mellow them considerably.

It didn't. By midday the snow had stopped but the cold had intensified. He wanted nothing more than to call a halt and take some drink and dry biscuits for sustenance. For hour after hour he waited for one of the occupants to call out requesting the same luxury. None did. He cursed their hardiness and kept going. A Major was not going to capitulate before women and a band of inexperienced travellers did so.

Polly felt as if she would faint. Without the horse that Jared had taken the team was uneven and a constant strain on her arm muscles to control. Snow had seeped into her boots and melted. She could no longer feel her toes. She presumed blood still flowed in her fingers, for at least they still held the reins. It was the only proof she had that they were not frost-bitten. Serena had tucked herself up, in both Polly's bedding and her own, and was warm and a great deal more cheerful than she had been the previous day. Lucy Marriot sat at the side of her half-delirious husband and when the heat from the morning's refill of hot water had cooled, warmed him by holding him close against her own body.

Throughout the day Lucy passed Polly mugs of barley water that were virtually undrinkable because of their temperature, and several large slices of wheaten bread that had hardened before their time in the sub-zero weather.

Once or twice Sister Schulster peeped her wrinkled

face from beneath the heavy canvas of the Cowley wagon and winked an eye encouragingly. Polly had managed an answering smile and continued doggedly on.

On their left-hand side the ice cracked and broke into floats on the river. After the Fox they would follow the banks of the river Platte. Nephi had told her that the traditional trail West lay on the Platte's south bank, but that Brother Brigham was none too happy at the prospect of encountering hostile travellers and so was forging his own passage west. Polly hoped that Brother Brigham knew what he was doing. It seemed to her that no one could possibly have travelled this way before them, so desolate were their surroundings. She remembered the camp Major Richards had told her had been formed at Richardson Point and regained her optimism. Brother Brigham was a natural leader who had held the Saints together through the dark days after Joseph Smith's death. If he said this was the way, then it was. Even Major Richards had sounded grudgingly respectful when he told them of how Brigham Young was making plans for the establishment of a semi-permanent camp on the banks of the Missouri at Council Bluffs.

The intended camp had already been given the name of 'Winter Quarters'. All along the length of the Missouri wild-pea vines grew throughout the winter and so would provide an ample supply of food for the livestock of following church members.

The Major had wondered if the burly Mormon leader had ever been an army man. Certainly the way he had outlined his plans for the construction of a semi-permanent camp for the following winter showed that he was a man of vision. Log houses were to be built and a stockade. A meeting-house for worship and a school for the children. Workshops were to be erected and a water-powered gristmill for grinding the corn harvested the previous summer. All along the trail, come the spring, Brother Brigham intended sowing crops for those behind to reap. It was a plan of survival that not even Major Richards could argue with.

Those that followed would find the way prepared. Dart had been puzzled by Polly's declaration that there were only a few to follow from Nauvoo in the spring. So puzzled that he had overcome his irritability with Nephi and travelled alongside him apace.

'The preparations Brigham Young intends making at Council Bluffs are those of a man expecting thousands to follow this way. Yet Miss Kirkham tells me that Nauvoo is virtually a ghost town.'

Nephi had chipped the icicles off his moustache and blown hard on his mittened hands. 'Those that follow us to the Promised Land will come from Indiana and Ohio, Pennsylvania and New York State. Some from even further afield. Brother Pratt has preached the Gospel in England and found much success. Hundreds will travel across the sea and then across our great continent to our final resting place.'

Major Richards had shaken his head in disbelief and ridden away. It was as he thought. They were all completely mad.

He knew from talking to Brigham Young that the Mormon leader still had no idea of their final destination. That he believed thousands should follow him blindly into an uncharted wilderness was either megalomania or idiocy. Major Richards was accustomed to sizing up men. Neither megalomania nor idiocy were the right epithets for the man he had met at Richardson Point. Stern-faced when necessary, he could roar with laughter at the slightest provocation, and, for a religious leader, took great delight in music and singing and dancing. Dart shook his head in bewilderment. Lydia Lyman had spoken the truth when she had said they were a peculiar people.

Eliza Cowley had nervously replaced her husband at the reins. Josiah lay weakly against the canvas of the jolting wagon, his face haggard and drawn. There would be no opposition from *that* quarter when he ordered a return the next day.

In the Spencer wagon the youngest children, Thomas and Adam and baby Ruth, clustered around the shoulders of their parents, their earlier grins and waves turning to whines and complaints that stretched even Susannah Spencer's almost inexhaustible patience.

Several times Dart was tempted to reconnoitre to the last wagon, but did not do so. She was still keeping up and was only yards behind the Cowleys. He knew that her arm muscles must be hurting excrutiatingly by now, but he determined to offer no help. If they were to realise the foolishness of their venture and return to Illinois, they must suffer, and that included the women and children as well.

Religious fervour was the spur that drove the others on. Polly Kirkham lacked their faith. What drove her on in such deprivation and hardship? Fear of loneliness in Nauvoo? She had not said as much but he had guessed. He knew all about loneliness.

He had never intended to kiss her, but in the sharp clarity of day was glad he had enjoyed the experience. It had been a sweet kiss. He could never remember one sweeter. What had been more remarkable was the spontaneous passion he had felt beneath the surface as she had struggled so correctly in his embrace. Miss Polly

Kirkham was a young woman who only needed the right man in order to gain both unimaginable pleasure, and to give it. But the man would have to be experienced in the handling of women: gentle and sensitive in the early stages to overcome her innocence. Later, passion could be given and returned without restraint.

He bowed his head against the bitter north wind. He doubted young Jared Marriot was the man to accomplish such a pleasant task. Not only did the Mormons believe in keeping their women chaste, but their men also. Dart had roared with laughter at being told this principle by a church elder and then, realising that the man was speaking the truth, had leaned against the trees and watched them as they prepared to camp in conditions that would have deterred even his own, hardened soldiers. They were men all right, tough and hardy, yet with principles he had never encountered before. Principles he could not even begin to understand.

There was an ominous creak and a female shout of exasperation. Dart looked back to see the last wagon listing heavily at one corner and Polly urging the horses with little success. Her back right wheel had rolled into a hidden pit in the ground and the strength of the horses alone was not enough to haul it clear.

Nephi heard the cry too, and as Dart galloped towards her, reined in and ran back through the deep snow towards the Marriots' wagon.

'She's stuck fast,' Polly said unnecessarily.

Blue circles darkened her eyes and in the long hours since they had broken camp the rosy bloom of her cheeks had been replaced by a ghastly white pallor.

Dart cursed himself for not having come to her aid before, and cursed her for having put him in such a position. If only they would return. Two, three days driving and they would be back in civilisation. Every mile they took was a mile that would eventually have to be retraced.

He jumped from his horse and together with Nephi pushed hard at the offending corner as Polly whipped the horses and vocally urged them to move on. There was an imperceptible movement and then another. Then, with a suddenness that sent both men to their hands and knees, the wagon rolled free.

Nephi grinned. Dusk was approaching. Dart had not allowed them to stop once. Brother Spencer was supposed to be now on the point of capitulation.

'Not a bad little hitch for one day,' he said cheerfully and waded off back to his own horses.

Dart dusted the snow from his knees and gloves and swore.

When he remounted he walked his horse alongside the Marriot wagon. Polly's profile faced determinedly ahead. He noted the pert, straight nose and stubborn chin. She was no nearer capitulation than the defiant Nephi.

He said sourly, 'It's time we made camp, or dark will be upon us.'

'So it will, Major,' rejoined Polly, not trusting herself to look at him. 'I had noted that fact myself some while ago and wondered when it would occur to you. Lighting a camp fire in the dark is a difficult business.'

A corner of his mouth twitched. 'One I am sure you could accomplish, Miss Kirkham.'

'I can accomplish most things, Major Richards,' Polly agreed, aware that her nerves had begun to throb at his continued nearness. She was almost grateful for the fact. She had thought she would never feel sensation of any kind again, she was so cold.

'Even persuade your fellow travellers that to continue is an impossibility and they must return and wait until the spring?'

She turned and faced him defiant. 'We go on,' she said, using the words that had become a litany.

The amusement she aroused in him vanished and his temper snapped.

'What would have happened if I had not been here? Who would have helped Nephi push your wagon free?'

'I would,' Polly retorted. 'And Susannah Spencer and Lydia Lyman!'

They glared furiously at each other. Polly refused to be the first to avert her eyes. It cost her every last amount of strength she had not to turn her head away. His brows had flown together until they met. Sister Kimball used to say that one of the Anson boys was as handsome as Satan. Her husband had chided her for using such an expression and Polly had never been able to see the truth of it. She could understand it now, where Major Richards was concerned.

'You're a damned nuisance,' he said through clenched teeth. 'I should be in St Louis now, enjoying the comforts of a tavern and a soft bed, not shepherding a flock of women, children, horses, goats, oxen and hens through snow and ice!'

'Then leave us, Major,' Polly retorted hotly. 'I assure you that we are not dependent upon you for our safety!'

'Oh yes you are,' he said, and in the half light she saw that his face was taut with anger, his eyes blazing. 'If I wasn't certain of that I would never have given up my pleasures to act as nursemaid today!'

'Then act nursemaid in St Louis, Major, for you are not wanted here!' She blinked hard, determined not to let him see the weary tears that were so near to the surface.

'I will, never fear!' Furiously he dug his heels in and galloped away to the Spencer wagon. Her rage vanished, to be replaced by sweeping desolation. What pleasures awaited him in St Louis. A lady? Ladies? Major Richards was not the kind of man to live without feminine company. He was worldly and bad-mannered and ill-tempered, but he could be nice when he tried.

He had spent long hours alongside the Spencer wagon, telling the Spencer children hair-raising tales of Sioux and Navajo. Not many men would have given up their time to entertain children and take their minds off their discomfort. As the stories were relayed to her by young Jamie, who hopped from one wagon to another with monkey-like ease, she noticed the absence of any stories of Pawnees. It was a strange omission for a man who declared he was an expert on that particular tribe of red-men. If he could be nice to the Spencer children, why then could he not be nice to her? In a gentleman-like way. Not in the insolent, free and easy way of the previous evening. Then he had treated her as though she were a woman of easy virtue. Her cheeks stung with shame and anger. She wished Jared would return with the Merrills; that Tom Marriot would regain his strength. The prospect of another day's unceasing driving was daunting.

Nephi had halted. The Cowleys and Lydia Lyman's wagon were pulling around. Numbly she followed suit. Now, from somewhere, she would have to find the strength to make camp and cook a meal.

'Is Tom any better?' she asked Lucy as the horses came to a grateful halt.

Lucy shook her head, her eyes frightened. 'He's

shaking something terrible, Polly. Go ask Brother Nephi to give him a blessing.'

Hampered by knee-deep snow, Polly trudged to the centre wagon and passed on the message. The Major was still seated on his horse looking as fresh and alert as he had done when they started out. Polly shot him a look of pure hatred and then went for a shovel and began to help Lydia Lyman clear a patch of ground so that a fire could be kindled within the tiny encampment of the four wagons. Both Sister Fielding and Sister Schülster insisted on sitting with them by the camp fire.

Instead of the despair that Dart had depended upon, within the hour the Mormons were laughing and chattering as if they were on a Sunday afternoon picnic. Polly and Lydia had made a nourishing meal of bacon and beans and when the tin plates were cleared away, more brushwood from the back of Josiah Cowley's wagon was tossed on to the roaring blaze.

Nephi tucked his fiddle beneath his chin and Susannah sang Irish ballads taught her by her mother while her children indulged in snowball fights on the periphery of the camp. With child-like glee, Sister Fielding withdrew a bag of chestnuts from beneath her cloak and they began to roast them, shrieking and giggling as they tried to retrieve them with sticks from the burning embers. After Susannah had exhausted her repertoire Polly sang 'Greensleeves' in a perfectly-pitched voice that Dart found immensely appealing. He was amazed at the intensity of his disappointment when she refused to sing again. He juggled chestnuts and laughed with Josiah and didn't even mind when Sister Schulster's quavering voice broke out into 'Praise to the Lord'. Even Sister Cowley had regained her good spirits and though she could not sing, heated barley water and kept refilling their mugs and ensuring that the children did not stray out of earshot.

'How about a bit of dancing, wife?' Nephi asked.

Susannah cuffed him affectionately. 'You are the only one who can play the fiddle, Nephi. How can we dance with no music?'

'Why, the others will sing for us, of course,' replied Nephi, and seizing her in his arms, he began to polka around the circle of the fire while the others, Dart included, whistled, sang and clapped.

'Nothing gets the blood going like dancing,' Nephi said breathlessly when he returned to the drum of wheat that served as his seat. 'Now for the rest of you,' and he picked up his fiddle and played 'Susie, Little Susie' to his wife's secret delight.

Brother Cowley, hampered by his splints, executed a rather less energetic polka with his wife, and Sister Schulster, to Dart's horror, tottered to her feet and said 'Right, young man. Let's see your paces.'

Dart thanked his maker that none of his men could see him cavorting around with an eighty-year-old woman in his arms when he should have been holding the most beautiful belle of St Louis.

Polly suppressed an unkind smile at his discomfiture and returned to her wagon to check on Tom Marriot.

He was sleeping peacefully and Lucy explained that she thought the fever had broken, but that she would prefer to stay by his side and not exchange places with Polly, even for a little while.

When Polly returned to the camp fire Nephi's fiddle was well into 'The Minstrel Boy' and Lydia Lyman was dancing as well as she was able with the disability of her greatcoat. Her partner was Susannah Spencer and their cheeks were as flushed as those of young girls.

Polly's eyes were fixed firmly on the chestnuts roasting at her feet. She sensed the Major rise and begin to approach her. Her pulse began to race. She would not dance with him. She would *not*. He didn't ask her. He simply drew her to her feet and despite the encumbrance of her cloak, his hand seemed to burn as he placed it on her waist, his eyes holding hers, an unreadable expression in their dark depths. For a long second he held her, not moving, and then, with practised steps, he whirled her away from the light of the fire and into the shadows beyond.

'Do you always behave in such a cavalier manner, Major?' she asked, holding herself as stiffly as possible.

'Always,' he said, and there was amusement in his voice as he looked down at her.

She averted her head, but he did not take his disturbing gaze from her.

'I find you insolent, Major Richards,' she said, aware only too well of the appraisal in his near black eyes and the unfortunate effect it was having on her. Her cheeks were beginning to flush. She told herself it was from the heat of the fire and the exertion of the dance. Nephi showed no sign of stopping. 'The Ash Grove' merged, without pause, into 'Yankee Doodle'. Brother Cowley was on his feet again and the look of constant strain that had been on his wife's face since they had left Nauvoo, was replaced by one of carefree happiness.

'I find you infuriating, amusing and intensely desirable,' the Major said and Polly gasped. 'What's more . . .' His hold around her had tightened, '. . . I think the feeling is reciprocated.'

'Then you think wrong!' She would have delivered a stinging blow to his cheek but could not, for he was holding her hand in a grip like steel.

He continued as if she hadn't spoken. 'When I kissed you last night I found it a great temptation to continue.'

'Brother Spencer would take his whip to you if he knew how you had treated me or how you were speaking to me,' Polly hissed.

His black eyes gleamed. 'So you will not come and sit by me tonight when the others have gone to bed?'

Polly tried to kick him, but he moved adroitly and swung her round with panache.

'Not if,' she said, sparks flaring in her eyes, 'not if you were the last man on earth!'

'Where we are going, I probably will be,' he said, and as the music ended and he returned her to her place by the fire, he was laughing.

Lydia Lyman looked across at Polly's furious face and raised her steel-grey eyebrows quizzically. When Nephi began again to play, she gracefully accepted the Major's offer of a dance. Brother Cowley twirled a reluctant Polly round and round, and for the first time in her life Polly could not wait for a dance to end. Why, oh why, wasn't Jared here? Why had the Merrills fallen sick and needed his help? If he had been here she would never had been subjected to the Major's impudence or ridicule.

When the dance ended she excused herself with dignity. Shortly afterwards she heard Sister Spencer calling in her children and the sound of Major Richards' deep, resonant voice as he escorted Sister Fielding and Sister Schulster back to their wagons.

'Do you have a sweetheart waiting in St Louis?' Sister Schulster was asking with her usual forthrightness.

'One or two,' the Major replied carelessly. Polly fumed. She had been right. One woman alone would not be enough for a man of such carnal appetites!

There was the sound of more wood being thrown on the fire, of goodnights, of the low murmur of family prayers and then silence. Polly lay in her bed and seethed. Any other man would have apologised for his earlier behaviour—not exacerbated it by making fun of her.

She smiled grimly to herself in the darkness. His day-long trek had done him little good. No one was returning. In the morning Major Richards would set out for St Louis alone and she hoped the waiting sweethearts had grown tired and bestowed their affections elsewhere.

With the Saints in their wagons, Dart Richards' thoughts were moving along very much the same lines as Polly's. Alone, he hunched around the camp fire. They would not turn back. Only an angel from heaven could persuade them to do so, and whatever else he was, he was certainly not that. Richardson Point was fifty-five miles from Nauvoo, and when he had left it some five days ago, several hundred Saints had been camped there. Once at Richardson Point the Spencers, Cowleys and their friends would be safe. There they could wait with others of their faith for the snow to melt and the rains to cease, and continue West in a stronger and safer convoy.

At the speed they were now making it would take them three or four days to reach it. By that time, he thought ironically, his leave in St Louis would be curtailed by more than a week. He stared broodingly into the flames, and wondered if it mattered. If he had really wanted to, he could have been in St Louis now, enjoying the comforts of Bella Carling's notorious house with its pretty girls and excellent bourbon. And when he returned he might very well have passed the arrow-filled bodies of those he had so recently eaten and drunk and danced with.

If he decided against his weeks in St Louis and rode instead after Brigham Young, he could form the Mormon battalion even before his fellow officer, Captain James Allen, reached them. Captain Allen's orders were to reach the thousand-strong company of Mormons sometime in June. If he continued with Nephi and Josiah he would beat him to it and Captain Allen would be furious, which would please Dart as he had an old score to settle with James Allen.

The naive evening entertainment on the camp site had appealed to him. The Mormons, with their strange religion and stubborn obstinacy, accepted a man as he was. The antagonism between himself and Nephi had developed into firm friendship. Josiah Cowley was as pleasant a companion as he had ever met. The women suffered and did not complain. The children made him laugh. And Polly . . . He frowned. Polly Kirkham was a complication he could do without. When he was with her his firm intentions of ignoring her went with the wind. She was parentless, and he was. She did not fit in with the people she lived with. They knew it and she knew it. Nothing was ever said, but he could sense it. He was well attuned to such vibrations. He, too, had never fitted in. Not even in the army. He knew the way the men in the barracks spoke behind his back. The rumours that circulated about his birth and upbringing. The epithet 'half-breed' that was never uttered to his face, but was spoken often in his absence. It had been a long time since any man had said it within earshot and none who remembered the occasion was likely to do so again. For the first time in years he thought of Caroline Manningham.

He had been a Captain then, handsome and sought

after by the daughters and sisters of fellow officers. But not when it came to marriage. When it came to marriage he was a half-breed: the result of a Pawnee raid on an isolated homestead. Whether it had been his mother or her husband who had wrapped him in blankets and left him, hours old, on the outskirts of a Pawnee encampment, Dart never knew. Nor did he care. The Pawnees had shown more charity than the whites. Recognising the result of one of their forays, they had taken him in and reared him for the first eight years of his life. His Richards surname came from a fur trapper who had bartered guns and whisky for him. The trapper had been a kind man. His sister even kinder. During the next few years he had led a completely different lifestyle. He no longer ran barefoot with his Indian friends, but learned to read and write: at first with great objection and then with reluctant interest. As a young man he had entered the army and risen rapidly to the rank of Captain. He had fallen in love with Caroline Manningham who had made no secret of her feelings for him. Dutifully, he had asked her father for her hand in marriage. Her father had been outraged. So, to his complete stupefaction, had Caroline. He was a half-breed. How could she possibly marry him? From then on those who knew him were aware of a definite change in Captain Dart Richards' manner.

He was a courageous soldier and was soon a Major, but he did not mix. He kept himself to himself. He was a man, feared not only by the enemy, but by his own men as well. Nephi Spencer would not have cared if he had been a full-blooded Sioux. Nor, from her remarks, would Lydia Lyman, and he believed her. Without friends and family, he had enjoyed the carefree friendliness of the Mormon camp fire more than he would admit. No friends were waiting for him in St Louis. Only painted, perfumed and mercenary women. He threw another branch on to the fire.

Damn it to hell. He had nothing to lose. He would continue with the Mormons to Richardson Point and he would have his Mormon Battalion formed long before Captain James Allen put in his appearance.

Polly stealthily lifted the corner of the canvas sides of the wagon. He was still sitting there, staring moodily into the flames. The silver flask was not in evidence. She wondered when he slept. Perhaps he was waiting for her. He had the arrogance and utter assurance to believe that she would join him. She folded her arms tightly across her chest, and tried to shut out the deep, caressing voice with its undertone of laughter. He had told her he found her infuriating, amusing and intensely desirable. Polly tossed and turned. He had not meant it. He had been making fun of her. Or, worse still, attempting to seduce her. Treating her as he would treat the compliant ladies of St Louis. She closed her eyes tightly. He could wait till the Second Coming, but she would not join him at the flames of the camp fire. She would not be as easily flattered as the rest. Only utter weariness eventually brought on sleep and Lucy, hearing her cry out something unintelligible, wondered fearfully if she had caught Tom's chill.

CHAPTER FIVE

NEPHI and Josiah were delighted at the Major's change of plan. Their wive's relief at having an experienced soldier at their side was unconcealed. Sister Fielding was indifferent. They would reach the Promised Land, Major or no Major.

Sister Schulster poked her shawl-covered head out of the back of the Spencers' wagon and called, 'What about the ladies in St Louis, Major?' and received a chastening jab in the ribs from Susannah Spencer.

It was impossible to call a woman of eighty-four immodest, but sometimes Sister Spencer could think of no other way to describe her elderly companion.

Dart grinned at the wrinkled face and its wicked twinkling eyes. 'The ladies will have to learn patience,' he called back good-humouredly.

'Rogue!' Sister Schulster retorted, and was pulled back into the interior of the wagon with undignified haste by Sister Spencer, before she could commit any more indiscretions.

Polly pretended not to hear and kept her eyes firmly averted from the broad, straight back of the Major as he rode to the head of the small column and began to lead the way to Richardson Point.

Why had he changed his mind? Why was he retracing his steps? Surely not out of human kindness. That hard, strong face was not the face of a man given to such self-sacrificing gestures. He turned in the saddle and looked directly at her. She tilted her chin and kept her eyes straight forward, flicking the reins with unnecessary vigour, uncomfortably aware that the two high spots of colour on her cheeks were occasioned by his impudence and not by the cold.

Nephi's wagon headed the column, followed by Sister Lyman's and then the Cowley's. Polly, as in the day previous, brought up the rear. The snow fell steadily, but the sky had lightened and Nephi announced confidently that by afternoon they would be free of the blinding flurries that flew in their faces and made discerning their way so difficult.

At the Major's insistence, they stopped at midday and built a fire.

'Surely we should press on?' Nephi asked worriedly as the flames took hold and Lucy and Susannah hurried forward with pans and provisions.

'The women and children need warm food inside them if they are to survive the trek. An hour for food and rest is worth two on the trail.'

Nephi nodded. The man was right. He was the kind of man who would always be right.

'How is Brother Marriot?' he asked Lucy, as the stone jars were refilled.

'Better,' Lucy said, the strain of the last few days showing on her face. 'The fever has broken, but he's still weak.'

Polly poured hot barley-water into a mug and together with a plate of steaming ham and beans, turned to carry the food to the sick man. The snow was deep and with both hands occupied she could not lift her trailing skirts.

He did not speak. He simply took the plate from her hand and proceeded to walk along by her side.

Her pulse quickened. Throughout the morning she had been aware of his eyes returning to her and resting on her with disquieting frequency. She had not responded to his gaze. She dare not. She was unused to hiding her feelings and at the moment they were in tumult. He had treated her disrespectfully and she was justifiably indignant about it. He had laughed at her and her fury at his laughter had still not abated. He was not a gentleman and she had firmly decided to having nothing further to do with him. Yet she was continually aware of his presence. Whether he was at the head of the column, taking over the reins from Brother Cowley, reconnoitering; however near or far he was, however determinedly she did not look in his direction, she was painfully aware of where he was and what he was doing.

There was no way to shut out the remembrance of his lips upon hers, and the feeling his kiss had evoked in her. She had wanted to circle his neck with her arms and press herself closer and closer to him and it was useless to try to believe otherwise. Now, as he strode at her side, she was finding it harder and harder to hold on to her feelings of anger and indignation.

'I'll drive the team for you this afternoon. You must be exhausted.'

They were at the foot of the wagon steps. For the first time she allowed herself to look up into his face. She saw concern in his eyes and noted that his mouth was even more attractive when it was not set in a tight line of anger. His hand brushed hers as he handed her the plate. She felt herself tremble. Where was her anger? Her indignation? She remembered the ladies in St Louis and his careless reference to them. No doubt the Major believed she could be cuckolded just as easily. That an hour at the reins would arouse in her such gratitude that she would permit liberties to be taken with her person. Sparks glared in her eyes.

'I am *not* exhausted, Major, and I require no help. Least of all from you.'

The smile that had been curving his mouth vanished. The concern was replaced by studied indifference. He merely shrugged dismissively and returned to the fire. She found she was near to tears as she climbed into the wagon. He would not ask again, and even though it was of her own doing, she felt an overwhelming disappointment. It would have been pleasant to have sat beside him and allowed him to take the reins. To have talked as they had that first night, to have felt again the strange rapport that had existed so briefly between them.

'St Louis,' she said aloud to Tom Marriot's mystification, as she handed him his plate and mug. Instead of feeling better at the utterance she felt worse. She wondered what the unknown ladies in St Louis looked like. No doubt they were powdered and painted; sure of themselves and experienced in love.

She had no desire for powder and paint, but she envied the unseen city girls their confidence and knowledge of a world that she was so far ignorant of. Pride would not allow her to return to the warmth of the fire. She stayed with Tom Marriot and when Lucy arrived with the hot jars, helped wrap them in flannel and place them strategically around his weakened body.

'The Lord knew of our need when he sent the Major to us,' Tom said, finishing his meal and sinking back thankfully into the warmth of his blankets.

'Indeed He did,' Lucy agreed fervently.

Polly wondered what they would say if she told them of the Major's true nature. Of the kiss he had forced upon her. Of the ladies in St Louis.

Nephi's wagon began to creak as it pulled away from their resting place and back on to the trail. Polly clambered back into the teamster's seat and wondered why it was that none of them seemed offended by the Major's occasional blasphemies. Was it because he was a soldier and such things were accepted from soldiers? Or was it because he had charmed all of them as he had so nearly charmed her?

She had never known any other man take the Lord's name in vain and not suffer Nephi Spencer's wrath, and yet Nephi spent hours talking to Major Richards and had never once remonstrated with him. Only Jared had been impervious to the commanding attitude and strange charm of the Major. Jared . . . She must think of Jared. Perhaps they would meet up with him and the Merrills later that day, or early the next. Jared loved her and respected her. Jared would never seek diversions in a city as sinful as St Louis.

Nephi had been right. The snow dwindled and soon only an occasional flake settled on Polly's cape. The Saints began to sing hymns, and ahead of her the Major rode, straight-backed, talking to Lydia Lyman. After a few minutes he swung down from the saddle and vaulted up into the teamster's seat beside Lydia, his horse continuing to keep pace alongside.

Polly felt slightly sick. The Major could not possibly be contemplating seducing the grey-haired, tart-voiced Lydia, yet he was giving her a respite from the reins just the same. The thought that she had made a bad misjudgment entered Polly's head and was immediately quashed. It was a too-painful one. Whatever the Major's intentions towards Lydia Lyman, they were not the same where she was concerned and she had acted quite rightly and properly in refusing his offer of help. All the same, her arms ached and the cold pierced her cape and dress as if they were non-existent. If the Major had been beside her she could have warmed her mittened hands on one of the hot jars. She blinked away a threatening rush of tears. Let Lydia Lyman enjoy a rest. She did not care. Soon Jared would be back and they could be married any time she desired.

There was the sound of female laughter from the wagon ahead. Polly's mouth tightened. What sort of a man was he, that he flirted with a spinster of Lydia Lyman's years?

In mid-afternoon he returned once more to his horse, and galloped off up the track. When he returned it was to do the same courtesy to the Cowleys. Gratefully the injured Josiah allowed the powerfully-built Major to take the reins. Polly squared her weary shoulders defiantly. The Major could have no ulterior motive for relieving Josiah of the reins. Perhaps she had been wrong. She remembered the graceless, curt way she had refused his offer of help and the way his rare smile had immediately vanished.

She felt unaccountably miserable. Increasingly so as they made camp for the night and his eyes no longer flickered in her direction. When the work was done and the plates were washed and stacked away, she sat on her drum of wheat, as near to the flames as it was possible to get without setting her dress alight.

Nephi played his fiddle, the children danced, Josiah and his wife danced despite the encumbrance of the splints and sling. The Major and Lydia Lyman danced. Susannah and Josiah danced. Sister Schulster commandeered the Major yet again and this time he polka-ed her around the camp fire unselfconsciously, roaring with laughter at one or two of Sister Schulster's risqué asides.

His taciturn, intimidating presence had changed to one that Polly found even more unsettling. Only with her was he coolly indifferent. He spoke to Lydia Lyman of the merits of the United States President, James K. Polk, and of the merits of the Democrats as opposed to the Whigs. Polly felt ignorant and uninformed and was only too glad that the conversation remained between the two of them. Lydia Lyman's blue-stocking mind had never served to her advantage in Nauvoo. Polly could not think of any other man who would have sat and talked with her with such genuine interest and respect for her replies. It seemed even more surprising considering the Major's undeniable handsomeness and the fact that, never in his life, would he have had to work for the attentions of a lady.

With Josiah Cowley he spoke of the wars raging among the different Indian tribes. She overheard him saying that the Dakota and Sioux had threatened to wipe out their old enemies, the Pawnees. She heard mention of the Comanches, Kiowas and Cheyenne in Nebraska. Of how the place Brigham Young had destined for a semi-permanent camp was deep in Indian territory. He listened to Sister Schulster's memories of her youth patiently and with genuine interest. He half carried Sister Fielding back to her wagon when weariness overcame her. He listened quietly and non-committally as Nephi described Joseph Smith's vision to him. He retrieved Serena Spencer one-handed from a snowdrift and he spent a good half hour keeping the recovering Tom Marriot company. Only Polly did he ignore.

Her cheeks smarted and she stared steadfastly into the flames. She had never been very good at lying, either to herself or to other people. Now she was faced with a harsh truth. She found the Major far more attractive than Jared. Determinedly thinking of Jared, making plans to marry him, had failed to erase the Major from the forefront of her mind. Jared's kiss could never arouse in her the emotions that the Major's had. Jared's presence could never heighten her senses as the Major's did. Even now, when he so blatantly ignored her, her spine tingled when she heard his deep, rich voice. The lazy laughter, the careless self-assuredness that drew her like a magnet. She had been yearning for a man to love deeply and passionately and now she had found him. Only she did not know what to do. She had rebuffed him and he was no local boy that she could murmur an apology to and wind around her little finger. He was a man of twenty-seven or twenty-eight—possibly even thirty. A virile, handsome, experienced man and she had no idea how to approach him: how to say she was sorry for her rudeness earlier in the day. She knew now why she had reacted so vehemently to the mention of the ladies in St Louis. She had been jealous.

He emerged from the Marriots' wagon and strode back to the little circle around the fire.

'How many days until we reach Richardson Point, Major?' she asked, her heart hammering wildly, hoping that by her simple question she could renew contact between them.

He looked across at her uninterestedly. 'Three. Four.'

Her mouth felt dry, her throat tight.

'How many miles have we still to cover, Major?'

'In the region of thirty,' he said curtly, rising to his feet, and with a slight nod in Nephi's direction he strode away from them and into the darkness.

Very faintly Polly could hear the sound of the silver flask being unscrewed.

'From Sugar Creek to Richardson Point is fifty-five

miles,' Josiah Cowley said to a no-longer-interested Polly. 'We made ten miles yesterday and today, despite the heavy snow. If we keep up this speed we will be there in three days.'

Three days and then he would no longer be with them. Would he ride hard for St Louis or did he have other plans? Polly did not know, but wished that she did. She wished she had the confidence to walk away from the camp fire and into the darkness after Major Richards, and say that she was sorry and that she would have liked it if he had driven a little way for her. She could not. Not only because of the comment it would cause amongst her companions, but because she was certain that if she did so Major Richards would simply shrug and she would be left to feel foolish and childish and utterly mortified.

Her black-buttoned boots were nearly in the embers of the fire, but still she shivered. If her mother had been alive she would have been able to talk to her and her mother would have understood. As she had so often before, she felt utterly alone.

Dart fought down his anger. She was no different from all the rest and he had been a fool to have fallen, even momentarily, for her beguiling, wide-eyed, innocence. He was well used to the curtness with which she had rebuffed his offer to drive for her. Ladies, as he had learned the hard way, did not welcome close physical contact with a gentleman whose parentage was as mixed as his. Only under cover of darkness did they seek him out. He smiled grimly. She had been trying to appease him just now. Two days hard travelling had weakened her strong moral stand and no doubt she would have been only too pleased to have joined him secretly and in the darkness when the others had gone to bed.

He unscrewed his flask and took a deep swig of good

quality bourbon. She was in for a disappointment. No woman ashamed to be seen with him by day would enjoy his company by night.

He should never have kissed her. Until then he had thought her nothing but a pretty child. The kiss had made him revise his opinion drastically. He was well acquainted with desire, but her soft, sensual mouth had aroused in him something far deeper than that. Something he had thought dead and buried for ever. Was it because she was parentless and alone that he had felt so unaccountably drawn to her? He screwed the top back on his flask and replaced it in his hip pocket. He had felt her loneliness and had responded to it. He had also responded to pale golden hair, blue eyes, and the trimmest waist his hands had held for many a day. He laughed at himself without humour. Through the long night he had lain sleepless, disturbed beyond all reason by the encounter. And for what? For a jumped-up little miss who looked at him in the light of day as if he were no more than a fly to be brushed contemptuously away.

He waited alone in the freezing night until he heard the last of the goodnights. Then, and only then, did he return.

Lying beside Lucy in the Marriot wagon, Polly heard the quiet tread of his footsteps. She did not lift the canvas to look out in case he saw the movement. Besides, she had no need to look to know what she would see. He would be sitting on his drum of wheat, high-booted legs slightly astride, his military cape around his shoulders, his arms resting on his knees. He would be gazing into the flames as she had earlier, but his thoughts would be his own and she could not even begin to imagine them.

She knew one thing only. Even if Major Richards

never deigned to speak to her again, she would not marry Jared. She would not marry until she met a man who affected her as deeply as the man sitting only yards away from her. There was the sound of another branch being flung on to the flames. She wondered when he slept; if his long nightly vigils were for their protection. The exhaustion of the heavy day's driving overcame her. With her mind still full of him, still trying to fathom out his true character, she closed her eyes and slept.

The next morning was sharp and crisp, the sky a pale blue with no sign of further snow. Polly made breakfast and fed the animals. From the rear of the wagon she could hear water being poured and the sounds of vigorous splashing. Major Richards was having his morning wash. Polly tried hard not to think of the lean, muscled body oblivious of the sub-zero temperatures. She hurried to the Cowley wagon and checked on Josiah's arm.

'The Major says you did a fine job on it,' he said to her complacently. The bright fine day had lifted his spirits considerably.

'The Major?' Polly's voice was unusually sharp.

'Why yes. He asked to look at it and said whoever had tended it was an expert.' Josiah laughed. 'He thought the praise should be accorded to Sister Lyman, but I soon disabused him. "Polly Kirkham can tend anything from a sick, day-old chick to an amputation," I said to him. I told him about that time in Nauvoo when old Abe Wisley lost his leg . . .'

'Ready to roll?' Nephi shouted.

Hurriedly Polly clambered out of the Cowley wagon and, holding her skirts clear of her flying feet, ran back to her own. The Major, as immaculate as if he was on parade, was once more dressed and in the saddle.

He noted that she was in the teamster's seat with expressionless eyes, and then signalled them forward. It was quite clear that where he was concerned, she might as well not exist.

After an hour's steady travelling, little Jamie Spencer hopped down from the back of his wagon and clambered up beside Polly.

'There's a small town a little way ahead. About three miles east of our track. The Major suggests we stop and get fresh provisions there. He says we'll have very little opportunity for doing so afterwards.'

The prospect of a change from the ceaseless travelling cheered Polly. Ever since the morning that Dart Richards' eyes had flicked over her so carelessly, she had been plunged into a despondency that was unnatural to her. A three-mile walk on the hard-packed snow would give her the opportunity of putting her thoughts in order. The little wagon train had become increasingly claustrophobic. She wanted to be on her own for a little while. She wanted to be able to think.

'Josiah and I will go into Corrington for supplies,' Nephi said, marching down past Sister Lyman's wagon to her own. 'One wagon in the town will be enough. We don't want to make ourselves conspicuous.'

He had no need to say more. The Saints had suffered enough persecution in the past to know it could be found in the unlikeliest of places. Nephi was taking no chances with his little band.

With crushing disappointment Polly watched as Nephi and Josiah departed in the Spencer wagon.

Major Richards had dispensed with his cloak, and was carrying out repairs to one of Sister Lyman's wheels. The dark blue cloth of his jacket was stretched tight across his back as he worked, and Polly could see the strong muscles rippling as he braced himself, lifting the wagon in order to free the wheel. She turned away and busied herself with clearing a patch of ground clear of snow so that they could light a fire. By the time she had done so and was on her way to the Cowley wagon for an armful of dry timber, the Major had divested himself of his jacket and his white shirt was open, sweat gleaming on his skin despite the temperature. She averted her eyes quickly, burning with shame at the unfamiliar emotions of desire that leapt within her whenever she saw, or was near, him.

How long before Nephi and Josiah returned and they were back on the trail again? Until then there was no way she could avoid his presence. It was only natural that everyone would eventually gravitate to the fire. It was hard enough avoiding his eyes at night-time. In the daytime it would be impossible.

She marched purposefully across to her own wagon and said to Lucy, 'I'm going to walk into Corrington.'

'But there's no need, child,' Lucy protested. 'You will be able to carry very little back, and Nephi and Josiah have taken the wagon.'

'Nevertheless, I'm going.'

Lucy sighed. It wasn't often that note of obstinacy crept into Polly's voice, but when it did, it was not to be argued with.

'Then take one of the horses.'

Polly shook her head. 'No, I want to walk and three miles isn't far.'

Lucy was too tired to protest further. There was Tom to look after and Polly was eminently capable of looking after herself. She turned her attention to her husband.

Polly knew better than to inform anyone else of her decision. The Major was still engaged with Lydia

Lyman's wagon. The Spencer children were still playing, Susannah and Eliza were enjoying the rest, and the warmth of the fire.

She pulled her cloak closer around her shoulders and set off at a brisk pace, following the track left in the snow by Nephi and Josiah.

Polly had always found walking helped her think clearly. It did so now and as the first outcrop of houses appeared in the distance, the last of her doubts and confusion fled. She was in love with a man she knew nothing about and had spoken only a dozen words to. She was in love with Major Dart Richards.

Corrington proved to be so small that it scarcely deserved to be described as a township. It boasted one wide main street, a saloon bar, a dry goods store and a scattering of mean-looking wooden houses. Polly frowned. There was no sign of the Spencer wagon. The snow outside the dry goods store was churned and the indentation of footsteps indicated that a small crowd had recently gathered.

Polly felt a slight tightening of her stomach muscles. There was no one to be seen, the street was deserted, the air too cold for men to be loitering on the steps of the saloon with mugs of beer in their hands. She had taken it for granted that Nephi and Josiah would return the same way they had come, and that there was no way she could miss them and so hold up the party when they were once more ready to travel West. If Nephi and Josiah had left Corrington by a different route and were even now well on their way back to camp, by the time she returned on foot she would have aroused everyone's wrath, not least the Major's.

Apprehensively she stepped up and into the dry goods store. A grizzled-haired man sat on a chair, its two back legs tipped against the wall, a cheroot in his mouth. He made no move to rise to his feet when Polly entered, but his eyes sharpened as he looked her up and down, as if trying to discern her figure beneath the covering of her cloak.

'Have you just served two strangers?' Polly asked nervously. 'One of them a man with his arm in a sling?'

Something like amusement flickered in the unpleasant, blood-shot eyes. Without moving or removing the cheroot from his mouth he called out, 'Clay! Come out front and see what I have here.'

'Have you, or have you not, just served the two men I have described?' Polly asked again, trying not to let her unease show in her voice.

A heavily built, bald-headed man emerged from the inner door behind the counter. On seeing Polly he grinned, but it was not a friendly grin. On one side of his temple was the beginning of a large bruise. Dry flecks of blood were on his hand. Suddenly Polly was sure that Nephi and Josiah had been at the store and that their arrival had not been welcome. She backed away.

'Thank you, and good day,' she said and was angrily aware of the underlying tremble in her voice.

'Not so fast.' The front legs of the chair tipped creakily to the ground. 'A man with a sling, did you say?'

'Yes.' Her momentary halt while she answered was enough. The heavily-built, bald-headed man moved with surprising speed. The door was locked behind her, the shade pulled down.

Polly spun around and gasped in fear. He lounged against the bolted door and this time his grin was wolfish.

'Seems to me like the lady's referring to those two Mormons who stepped in here a while back, Clay.'

'Seems to me we've got ourselves another little

Mormon,' Clay replied, and Polly could see the ugly fat hanging over the broad leather of his belt. 'Reckon she's wife to one of 'em?'

'Mebbe she's wife to both of 'em. I've heard those Mormons have fancy habits. They're not content with just one wife. Why, my brother Frank in Illinois tells me they like to have a good round dozen to keep 'em warm on winter nights.'

'That so?' Clay's eyes ran lasciviously over Polly. 'Betcha those Mormon women are just as bad. Betcha one man ain't enough for them either.'

Polly had never known sheer, unadulterated fear before. Her heart pounded. She could feel the sweat trickling down the back of her neck and her knees felt so weak that she could barely stand, let alone walk. Yet walk she must. She held her head high and said again, as if the conversation had been about nothing but the weather.

'Good day to you,' and walked terrified towards the door. He must give way. He *must*. There were only three yards between them. She took another step and another. Still the man lounged indolently in front of her. She was so near to him now that one more step would bring them into bodily contact. She could smell the odour of his breath and the staleness of his unwashed body.

'Let me pass, sir,' she said calmly, fighting to keep her fear from showing.

The yellow teeth were bared in a grin. 'Seems to me like we'd be letting this little lady down if we didn't show her some appreciation.'

She dared not turn her head for a second away from the monster in front of her, but from behind she could hear the creak of the chair as its occupant rose to his feet.

'Let me pass.' A sob strangled in her throat. Two

dirt-ingrained hands reached from behind her and caught at the strings of her cloak. Before she could raise her hands to prevent him, he had wrenched her cloak open and tugged it from her shoulders so that it fell in deep folds at her feet.

Clay whistled appreciatively through his teeth. 'Those Mormons sure know how to pick women, Ed.' In the dim light of the store her pale gold hair shone silkily. Because of her fear, her breasts rose and fell beneath the cambric of her gown, up-thrusting and sharply defined.

'No . . . Please . . .'

She was caught around the waist from behind and as she struggled wildly, the obscenity in front of her moved forward. He wound a hand in her hair, wrenching her head back painfully. And then, as she kicked and sobbed, he brought thick, wet lips down on hers.

She couldn't breathe, couldn't move. Her wrists were caught in a vice-like grip and as a foul tongue probed the depths of her mouth, a hand covered her right breast, kneading and squeezing. She was going to be sick. She was going to faint. She struggled wildly and at last freed her head enough to bite savagely at the loathsome face. She was rewarded by a blow that would have sent her reeling across the room if it had not been for the cruel hands holding her fast.

There was blood on her tongue and she could no longer see clearly. Her small, booted feet kicked out in vain and then, as Ed's hands reached the neck of her gown and tore the material apart, she screamed and kept on screaming.

Another blow sent her head sharply sideways and she was barely conscious, aware only that defiling hands were no longer on the cambric of her gown but on her bare flesh.

At first Polly thought it was a gunshot, the door was kicked in so violently. She was sent sprawling to the ground as the men leaped forward to meet their adversary. Dart sprang through the door like an eagle in flight. The lumbering, ox-like Ed was circled by the neck as he charged at the spoiler of his fun, and his head was rammed into the wall so hard that the wood splintered.

Clay, jubilant reaction at the prospect of a fight with the returning Mormons changing instantly at the sight of a uniform, was scrambling for the gun and holster hung on the far wall.

'No . . .' Polly hurled herself bodily after him, catching hold of his legs, sending him sprawling against the counter, a boot kicking cruelly into her face as he rid himself of her restraining grasp.

He struggled to his feet, his hands reaching out for the gun a second too late. Another hand, darker and well-shaped, wrenched it away and a clenched fist connected with Clay's jaw, sending him reeling across the counter top. As Clay slipped over the far side of the counter, Dart dived after him. There was the sound of bone against bone and again and again Clay went sprawling, his face a bloodied mask.

At last, panting harshly, Dart kicked the unresisting body contemptuously with his foot. Clay groaned, rolled on to his belly and retched. At the other side of the room Ed sprawled senseless, the connection of the wall and his head too much for even his thick skull. Polly felt giddy and nauseous as she stumbled to her feet and half sank. Immediately his arms were around her, and she clung to him, shaking convulsively.

'It's all over. You're safe now.' His voice was gentle and the hands that had just laid two men unconscious stroked her hair tenderly.

The most curious longing swept through him. He wanted her to remain in his arms and he wanted to tilt her heart-shaped face to his. He wanted to kiss her long and lingeringly and he wanted her to respond to him. He wanted what he could not have. Miss Polly Kirkham was only clinging to him now out of shock and relief at being saved from a fate she could barely comprehend.

He smiled grimly to himself. He doubted if she yet realised it, but she was naked down to the waist and her bare breasts were even now pressed tantalisingly against his chest. If he had known the situation in advance, he would have removed his jacket in order to enjoy the experience more. He stifled his desire with the iron will that had become second nature to him.

'It's time for us to go, before any of their friends arrive and delay us further.'

'Yes. Of course.'

She released her hold on him. She had imagined the tenderness, for his near-black eyes were as coolly indifferent as his voice. She stood dazedly while he lifted her cloak and placed it around her shoulders. As he fastened it at her throat, she was aware for the first time of the torn material of her gown and her exposed breasts. Her face flamed, but the Major had already covered her nakedness. How long had she been exposed to his gaze? She remembered that his enigmatic eyes had never left her face. Her cheeks burned with fresh shame. She had told herself that he was not a gentleman. Now she knew that she was wrong, as she had been about so many other things. The black stallion pawed the trampled snow outside the saloon. Silent spectators stood in small, isolated groups. The Major ignored them and swung Polly up easily in his arms, placing her on his horse. Then he mounted behind her and she had no option but to lean against his chest as they cantered down Corrington's lone street and towards the waiting wagons beside the Fox River.

When she could trust herself to speak, she said:

'Brother Spencer and Brother Cowley. What happened to them?'

'They returned without provisions and Brother Spencer had a few cuts and bruises to show for their venture. Fortunately he entered the store alone and for a God-fearing man is useful with his fists. If Brother Cowley had entered with him it might have been a quite different tale. No man can fight one-handed.'

'When did you . . . How did you . . .' She did not know how to phrase the question.

'Nephi and Josiah returned speedily and not by the same route they had taken. We were all ready to break camp when Sister Marriot told us that you had left for Corrington on foot.'

'I see.'

'It was a very foolish thing to have done.' He was once more master of his feelings and his voice cut like ice.

'Yes.'

'You've wasted a good three hours' travelling time.' She remained silent. For good measure he added, 'And you've blooded my uniform.'

'I'm sorry.' Her stiff little voice did not sound sorry. That he was more concerned about his uniform than her was mortifying.

She tried to move so that she was not resting against his chest, and as she did so the piece of cloak she had been holding against her cut cheek shifted and brushed his hand. He reined the horse in sharply.

'You're bleeding!'

'It will stop in a little while,' she said, trying not to give in to the faintness that threatened to overwhelm her.

He turned her face to his and gazed horrified at the gash on her cheek where the vicious boot had gouged the skin. He had been so busy stifling his desire for her, so conscious of the rose-tipped breasts, that he had not realised the extent of the wound. If she had not acted as quick-wittedly as she had done, he might very well be a dead man and he was complaining of the damage done to his uniform!

'Here, let me,' he said, and a soft linen handkerchief was pressed gently against her cheek. The horse remained still; dusk had fallen. In a wood of trees nearby the wind soughed softly through the branches. Her mouth was only a fraction away from his. Slowly he bent his head, his lips barely touching hers. She did not move away. The pressure of his lips increased and she did what she had yearned to do for so long. She lifted her arms and circled his neck, parting her lips softly and willingly beneath his.

She could feel the breath catch in his throat and then he was kissing her long and deeply and her whole body responded. She clung to him, pressing her body nearer and nearer to his in a need that was primeval.

In the distance came the faint sound of a hymn being sung, not joyfully, but fearfully. The Saints were anxiously awaiting their safe return. The sound penetrated Dart's consciousness and was the only thing that restrained him from swinging her to the ground and imprisoning her body beneath the weight of his. She would not have protested. The passion he had sensed the first time he had held her had been fully awakened.

He shut his eyes tight, steeling himself to regain control. She had just endured a traumatic experience and he was taking advantage of her innocence and vulnerability. He opened his eyes and firmly disengaged his lips from hers. Then, just as firmly, he removed her arms from around his neck. In the growing darkness she looked up at him in bewilderment.

'Our friends will be waiting for us,' he said. His voice betrayed nothing and it was now too dark to see the expression in his eyes. Uncomprehending she turned away from him as he flicked the reins and the horse began again to canter forward.

Her cheeks burned. His kiss had been nothing but the reaction of a man after a dangerous fight. She had shown herself to be shameless, eager for the kisses of a man who was indifferent to her. She remained stiff-backed, her lips burning and bruised, fighting back tears of humiliation.

The faint singing grew louder and Polly struggled to compose herself. Hating Dart Richards. Hating herself. Hating everybody.

'They're back! They're back!' Little Jamie Spencer was running across the snow towards them. Relieved, welcoming faces greeted and surrounded them. With her eyes firmly averted from Major Richards' face she allowed herself to be lifted to the ground, immediately stepping backwards, away from his blue-uniformed figure.

Lucy's arm was around her shoulders and she went willingly with the older woman to their wagon. She had no desire for the rest of the Saints to see her torn gown or the extent of her bruises. As she climbed the step she could hear Nephi asking anxiously.

'You caught up with her before she reached Corrington? There was no harm done?'

'None' Dart lied and then, changing the subject, 'That

broth smells good, Sister Lyman. I am more than ready for it.'

Polly felt weak with relief. For all his faults he was not going to tell what had happened in the hateful little dry goods store in Corrington. Nor would he tell what had happened on the journey back. Why should he? To him it had meant nothing. His kisses were freely and easily given. With trembling hands she bathed her face and bundled the torn gown away until it could be stitched. Then, in the darkness, she began to cry, his linen handkerchief clutched tightly in her hand.

CHAPTER SIX

In the morning the first thing she did was to tend anxiously to her face. She gave a cry of horror when she saw the damage that the flailing boot had inflicted. Her right cheekbone was bruised and to Polly's eyes the cut was so deep it would surely leave a scar. She bathed it, put salve on it and when an anxious Lucy asked how it had been inflicted she said only that it was of no moment and would soon heal. Lucy knew better than to press her. Tom was rapidly recovering his strength and insisted that he take the reins for the day's drive. She turned her attention to him, beseeching him not to be so rash. Polly had lived with them for five years and Lucy loved her dearly, but she was still a stranger to her in many ways. It was obvious from her attitude that she had no intention of divulging what had happened to her in the hours that she had been absent from the camp. That something *had* happened was patently obvious.

Polly stared aghast at herself in her treasured hand mirror. It had been dark last night when he had kissed her. He could not have seen how swollen her cheek was, how damaged. If he had he would not have done so. Would his contempt of her shamelessness be touched with distaste when he saw her? Would he flinch or turn his head away?

She lingered in the wagon and allowed the other women to prepare breakfast.

'See what eggs we have this morning,' Lucy called from outside.

The hen coop was so placed that it was virtually impossible to reach it from inside the wagon. Polly tried and failed. She could hear the Major's lazy deep voice in conversation with Nephi. He sounded remarkably good-humoured.

'The eggs, Polly,' Lucy called.

Polly gritted her teeth. She would have to emerge sooner or later. With as much carelessness as she could affect, she jumped down on to the snow and walked briskly to the rear of the wagon and the hen coop. She was aware of Susannah's quick intake of breath. No one, the previous night, had been aware of her injury. Out of the corner of her eye she saw Nephi's horrified expression and his quick movement in her direction. She also saw a blue-uniformed arm restraining him. Despite her warring emotions she felt grateful to him. He had known, without being told, that she did not want what had happened in Corrington to become public knowledge.

Her hands trembled as she lifted the eggs. He was still with Nephi, only yards behind her. She would have to turn eventually.

'How many eggs?' Lucy called impatiently.

'Five,' Polly answered, with forced light-heartedness. She could delay no longer. She lifted her chin and turned, a falsely bright smile on her face. His eyes were on her, but she would not meet them.

She crossed to the fire and, at a warning glance from Nephi, Susannah and Eliza averted their eyes from her face and continued their conversation without questioning her or making any remarks.

Wherever she went she was aware of him. A brilliant

winter sun was beginning to melt the packed snow and the Saints' spirits were high as they breakfasted. He was sitting directly opposite her on the other side of the fire. Her lowered head could see black hessian boots and dark blue breeches. When he put his plate to the ground, her heart seemed to turn in her breast at the sight of the olive-skinned, strong hands. Hands that had held her and fought for her. Hands that had coldly removed hers from around his neck.

'The weather's on the turn,' Josiah said cheerfully. 'The going should be easier.'

'Nothing will be easy until the snow has thawed completely,' Nephi replied practically. 'The sooner we're on our way, the better.'

The women took the hint and rose to their feet, carrying the dishes towards a bowl of melted snow.

Polly rose hastily, anxious not to be left on her own. Dart watched as she hurried towards the Marriot wagon, his near-black eyes narrowing, his good humour gone. He had made a fatal error of judgment. Polly Kirkham was showing him that what had happened yesterday was meaningless in the light of day. Her eyes had never once met his. Her manner had been as frosty as the snow around them. With even more curtness than usual he ordered the men to prepare to break camp.

Miserably Polly sat beside Tom Marriot as the wagons rolled onwards. Susannah Spencer began to sing a rousing hymn, but Polly could not bring herself to join in. Her mind was full of darker thoughts, trying to understand the reactions of her heart and body to a man who showed passion one moment, and indifference the next. A man who could be crushingly cruel and yet exceptionally kind. Her head ached. She knew too little of men even to begin to understand him, yet she could sense his inner unhappiness. It did nothing to alleviate her own. He rode at the head of the wagons, his broad back firmly turned to her. Eliza Cowley began to sing an old English song taught her by her mother, and the early March sun continued to shine down and soften the hard-packed snow.

Dart eyed it, mentally estimating how long it would be before it melted and flooded the creeks and made their way impassable. He did not have long to wonder. Ahead of them a creek roared, bursting its banks with the rush of melted snow from higher up the valley. The Cowley wagon stopped abruptly and Polly had to rein in the horses and veer to the side to avoid a collision.

'What is it? What's the matter?' Lucy asked anxiously from the interior of the wagon.

'A flood,' Jamie Spencer ran down to tell them, an expression of immense satisfaction on his face.

'But the creeks are not until after Richardson Point,' Tom Marriot protested as he sat beside Polly.

They waited. When Dart rode up to them he was grim-faced. His eyes flicked over Polly as if she didn't exist. He said curtly to Tom,

'One of the creeks is bursting its banks with melted snow. Normally the water would be no more than two feet deep, now it's a raging torrent.'

'What do we do?' Tom Marriot's face was ashen. The floods would increase before they subsided. They could not survive in such a small party and endure a camp that could stretch into weeks. That could only be achieved with their friends at Richardson Point.

'We cross it,' Dart replied grimly, 'though the Lord alone knows how.'

'He's even beginning to talk like a Mormon,' Sister Schulster said with irritating complacency from the back of the Cowley wagon. The others paid her no attention.

They had known of the Chariton River and the Locust and Modkine Creeks that lay after Richardson Point. It had not occurred to them that they would be held up by a flooding creek before then.

Silently all four wagons drew slowly up to the banks of the offending and nameless creek. Polly's heart sank within her. A creek conjured up a stream. What faced them was a river, rushing and surging with tremendous force into the broad waters of the Fox.

'It isn't possible,' Susannah Spencer whispered. 'We'd be swept away.'

Eliza's face was white, her lips moved in silent prayer. It was their first big obstacle. She had known there would be difficulties and had prayed she would not let her companions down when faced with them. The fear that gripped her was almost paralysing. Tom and Lucy Marriot silently clasped hands. Sister Fielding poked her head out from between the flaps of canvas and said:

'Moses's faith parted the Red Sea. I can't see why twenty foot of water should disturb us!'

Dart and Nephi stood on the bank, Dart's brows pulled close together.

'What would you have done if you'd been alone?' Nephi asked quietly.

'Ride it. It's broad, but I doubt if it's more than four feet deep at the centre.'

'Then why can't we do the same?'

'Because of the current. Wagons are cumbersome and easily tipped over. Not even being able to swim would help the women and children in a torrent like that.' His eyes narrowed. 'The first thing to do is to make quite sure how deep that flood water is.'

'How will you do that?'

'The only way there is. By riding into it.'

There was a concerted intake of breath as the Major strode grim-faced back towards his horse and mounted it, edging it slowly towards and into the foaming water. Even the Spencer children remained quiet, eyes wide as saucers as they clutched their mother's skirts. Polly's nails dug deep in her palms as the stallion stepped carefully into the swirling water. Part of the bank began to crumble and give way and Eliza Cowley turned her head away. Polly's heart hammered and her eyes were riveted firmly on him as slowly, inch by inch, he moved his horse further out into the torrent.

The water covered the fetlocks and then rose higher. Dart reined in. The horse's hindquarters staggered under the weight of water. They were still not mid way. Then, as Susannah Spencer began to pray quietly and Nephi drew in a horrified gasp, Dart slid from the saddle and, keeping hold of the reins, lowered himself into the icy current. The water swirled around his waist, buffeting him, only his hold on the reins and the steadying body of the horse holding him upright. Carefully, step by step, he moved forward until both horse and man were in the centre of the stream. Another step and another. Then they were on their treacherous way back and Dart was calling to Nephi:

'I was right. It's just over four feet, but damnably strong!'

Polly felt sick with relief as he emerged soaking wet, his trousers clinging to him like a second skin.

'Will a wagon make it?' Josiah asked fearfully.

'No reason why it shouldn't, but not with any occupants save the teamster. If it overbalances there will be little chance of saving anyone.'

'Then how . . . ?' Nephi began.

'Rope,' Dart answered curtly. 'We secure one end round a tree this side and one end the other. Then you and I each take a child across separately, holding on to it. We help the women across in the same manner.'

Nephi blanched and for the first time in his life said unthinkingly, 'Good God, man. That would be eleven trips, and there's also Josiah to help!'

'And a man won't survive that water temperature for long, so we'd best set to,' Dart said tersely, his teeth chattering. He marched across to the Spencer wagon and rummaged for a coil of sturdy twine.

'Here, Nephi. Secure this as though your life depended on it, for it does. Susannah, Lucy, Eliza—move all the bedding and all else you can, above the water level.'

His commands shook them from their stupor of shock.

'I'll take the first wagon over,' Dart said, moving to the Spencer wagon.

Nephi stayed him with his hand, saying softly so that his wife could not hear, 'I'll drive it. If the wagon should be lost, it's you the rest of them will need.'

Dart didn't argue. The rope was tied with the other end around Nephi's waist. It would serve to pull him clear from the icy torrent, if necessary.

The sturdily-built, home-made wagon had never looked as clumsy and vulnerable as it did when Nephi urged the protesting horses into the icy flood. Within a few feet of the bank it was rocking perilously and Serena Spencer started to cry. Inch by inch Nephi continued, the horses whinnying in fright.

'He's halfway over,' Sister Schulster said as Susannah Spencer could no longer bear to look. 'The water line is receding. He's coming out of it! He's made it!'

'A triumphant cry went up as the horses clambered up

the far bank, the wagon resembling a giant sea creature, its canvas soaked and an assortment of Sister Spencer's possessions bobbing merrily downstream.

'Praise the Lord,' said Josiah fervently.

Nephi wiped the sweat from his brow and fastened the other end of the rope around the stoutest tree he could find.

'What now?' he shouted back to Dart.

Dart did not even look in Josiah Cowley's direction. The man could not possibly drive through such a strong current.

'You make your way back, using the rope, hand over hand, and we'll drive the other wagons across.'

Lydia Lyman whipped her horses and edged towards the bank. 'I can drive my own team, thank you, Major.'

Dart's eyes held hers for a long time.

'Very well,' he said at last. 'If the wagon should go, leap for the rope and hold on.'

She nodded. Slowly, ponderously, the Lyman wagon entered the flood waters. Every muscle of Dart's body was flexed and ready for action. Lydia Lyman's voice could be heart exorting her team. The expression on Nephi's face changed from one of horror to one of hope and finally to joy as the horses slithered up the far bank and wild shouts of triumph were emitted by the Spencers and Cowleys.

'Now me,' Polly said tentatively. He turned on her with a savagery that took her breath away.

'No!'

Her eyes flashed in uncomprehending fury, her voice shaking as she said, 'You allowed Lydia!'

'You're not Lydia Lyman,' he rasped, and turned his back to her.

'Hand over hand,' he called to Nephi.

Polly's face flamed. She was just as capable a teamster as Lydia Lyman. Was she to be treated like Eliza Cowley, who had been city-bred? Or the children or the two old ladies?

'Damn,' she said furiously as Nephi made his arduous way back to them. 'Damn, damn, *damn*!'

Little Jamie Spencer listened with interest. It was a word he had never heard before.

'Damn,' he said happily as he ran back to his mother. 'Damn, damn, damn.' Susannah's concern for her husband made her deaf to her son's profanities. His father emerged from what so easily could have been an icy grave and Jamie ran up to him, circling his father's soaked boots with chubby arms.

'Damn,' he said with a broad grin on his face as Nephi hugged him tightly.

'What next?' he said to Dart.

Dart had heard Jamie's new word and had a good idea where it had come from. Despite himself he felt a flicker of amusement.

'The children next. I'll go first with Jamie.'

Susannah stifled a cry as Dart hoisted Jamie on to his back.

'Hold tight, but don't choke me.'

'Damn,' Jamie said cheerfully, and had to be screamed at by his mother not to wave goodbye as Dart descended into the swirling waters.

For one terrifying moment, Dart lost his footing, staggered and grabbed the taut rope. This time, to Polly's eyes, the water was higher, submerging Jamie's booted feet as he clung, piggy-back fashion, to Dart. The hat with its gold tassel had been dispensed with, as had his jacket. Blue-black hair grew thickly away from his forehead, hanging glossily low in the nape of his neck. His saturated shirt might just as well have been invisible. The powerful arm and shoulder muscles flexed and strained.

'He doesn't look like an American, does he Pa?' Serena Spencer commented as they watched Dart traverse the twenty-foot width.

'Nonsense,' Susannah Spencer said briskly, her eyes never leaving her son's back and fat, water-soaked legs.

Polly's eyes were on Dart. He *didn't* look like an American. Not the Americans of Kirtland or Quincy or Nauvoo. Beside Dart, all the male inhabitants of the towns Polly had previously lived in paled into insignificance. They had none of the unleashed power that she was aware of when she was with him. None of his animal-like grace. None of the mystery caused by features so unlike those she met daily. Who else had slanting black eyes and high cheekbones, a strong nose and a jawline that would deter the hardiest fist fighter? Or skin that made her ache to touch it. Or a mouth so finely chiselled that her eyes never tired of studying it? She had never before met a man like Major Dart Richards and neither had anyone else in their little wagon train.

Jamie Spencer was deposited on the far side with Lydia Lyman. As Dart began to make the gruelling return crossing, Nephi hitched his youngest on his back and Susannah secured him tightly with her shawl. A nod from Dart indicated that it was all right for Nephi to take the plunge. They crossed mid-stream and when Dart finally emerged, saturated and shivering from the water, Susannah Spencer immediately hoisted Thomas on to his back and with Eliza Cowley's shawl, anchored her son more securely.

Polly watched aghast. There was Sister Fielding and

Sister Schulster to ferry across and they would not be as easy as the children. And Josiah, who had only one usable arm. Already she could see that both men were on the point of exhaustion, the icy water cutting into them like knives as Thomas joined his brothers in safety.

'You have a choice,' Sister Schulster said with unconcealed delight when he returned. 'I either walk holding on to that rope or you carry me like you did the children.'

Dart glanced at Sister Schulster's gnarled hands. 'You'd never hold on. The rope is drenched and freezing.'

'Then someone had better give me a leg up,' Sister Schulster said unwaveringly.

Susannah and Eliza exchanged appalled glances. 'She's right,' Dart said, 'it's the only way.'

Sister Schulster grinned and circled his neck. 'A leg up, if you please, Sister Spencer,' she said demurely.

'You'll have to lift your skirts high out of reach of the water,' Dart said as Sister Spencer reluctantly complied.

'No problem,' Sister Schulster said equably and, gathering her skirts, she lifted them high and tucked them down her waistband.

Susannah and Eliza could not bear to look at such immodesty in a lady of her years and both privately determined that no matter what the danger, they would not be subjected to a similar indignity. Sister Fielding watched with a jutting chin. Sister Schulster would live for years on the story of how she crossed the creek on Major Richards' back. She gritted her teeth. Sister Schulster was not going to outdo her.

'Nephi!' she commanded as Dart deposited a cackling Sister Schulster with Lydia and the children. 'A carry, if you please.'

'But Sister Fielding . . .'

'A carry,' Sister Fielding demanded, her skirts already hitched out of the way.

Neither Susannah nor Eliza showed any sign of helping with this new foolhardiness. Polly linked her fingers and made a step for Sister Fielding, hoisting her up on to Nephi's back.

'Away we go,' Sister Fielding cried defiantly, and closed her eyes.

'It's rising,' Nephi said to Dart when they were once more on the same bank. Dart nodded. Time was fast running out and their strength was rapidly waning. There was blood on Nephi's hands and his own felt like raw meat.

'Your wife next,' he said. 'If we do get separated into two parties she needs to be with the children.'

Susannah was crying, adamantly refusing her husband's offer to carry her. Instead, with Nephi only inches behind her, coaxing and encouraging, she began the long crossing, gripping the rope hard, stumbling on the uneven bed of the creek, breathless with the unbelievable cold.

'Surely we could risk a wagon?' Josiah asked. 'My wife will never manage it. She's of a nervous nature.'

'You can see how strong the current is. If the wagon overturned . . .'

'Please.' Eliza Cowley was clinging to her husband. 'Please let me drive across in a wagon. Please!'

Dart hesitated and then said with an authority that brooked no argument, 'No, into the water, Sister Cowley. I shall be with you.'

It was harder guiding Eliza Cowley to safety than it had been with all the others. Halfway across she became hysterical and everyone watched horrified as Dart first shook her viciously with his free hand and then slapped her sharply across her face. It was the first time Eliza Cowley had ever been struck. Weeping and half-senseless, she was finally pushed ashore to Lydia Lyman who was waiting with warm blankets.

'He'll answer for that,' Josiah was saying, white-faced.

'Don't be a fool, man. He's just saved her life,' Nephi retorted curtly.

Only Nephi, Josiah, Polly and the Marriots remained. Each crossing took longer, the fatigue becoming more apparent. Nephi had to literally haul Dart out of the water on his return to them.

'The Cowley wagon,' Dart gasped. 'Can you drive it across?'

'Yes.'

Neither man allowed their glance to fall to their own or each others' bloodied hands.

'If you ever want an army career,' Dart said as Nephi took the Cowley reins, 'come to me and I'll rate you a Captain on your first day!'

Nephi grinned and goaded the reluctant oxen into the water.

Polly's anger at not being able to drive her own team as Lydia had, had long since vanished. She watched fearfully as Nephi struggled with the reins, and then screamed as the oxen plunged wildly and the wagon teetered, crashing into the bed of the river. Dart leapt into the swirling torrent, ignoring the rope, ignoring everything but the fact that Nephi was trapped between wagon and oxen, and was not surfacing.

The children were crying. Pans, blankets, Bibles floated free of the wagon, but both men had now disappeared. Polly rushed down to the bank and into the water. She was just about to plunge in and begin swimming when first one head and then another appeared. Waist-deep in water she watched, sobbing with relief, as both men grabbed the rope, hanging over it as they fought for breath. Then she could see Dart order Nephi to the far bank.

Stumbling and falling, with Josiah reaching down to help her, she clambered back to the bank.

'What the devil did you think you were doing?' he asked, struggling ashore like a beached fish.

'I . . . I . . .' She had been going to save him. Her foolishness rendered her speechless. He shook the water from his eyes and glared at her.

'You stay exactly where you are until I tell you differently. Do you understand?'

There was no warmth or kindness in his voice.

She nodded, blinking back tears, watching as he plunged into the water yet again, this time behind Josiah. Josiah's courage and stamina saw to it that Dart's remaining strength was not overtaxed. Nephi was intent on returning for the Marriots and Polly and Dart exhaustedly denied him permission.

Tom and Lucy had withdrawn from the rest of the little group. Tom had only just recovered from a fever. It seemed impossible to Lucy that he could survive the icy waters and she knew instinctively that she could not. Years younger than Sister Fielding and Sister Schulster, she did not have their strength. Breathing painfully, saturated and freezing, Dart recrossed the creek and walked the twenty yards down the bank to where they stood, hand in hand.

'We cannot do it,' Tom Marriot said simply. 'My wife has a sickness and as for myself . . .'

'We'll go in the wagon,' Dart said. 'It's the only way.'

'But you would not allow the others, and look what

happened to the Cowley's wagon.'

'The others could survive by crossing in a different manner. I know that you cannot. The Cowley wagon overturned, but the other two didn't. I want you to sit very, very still. Is that understood?'

They nodded acquiescence. Alone, Polly watched as Dart helped them into the wagon. Both Tom and Lucy had aged in the last few days. No one spoke as the wagon began to teeter perilously into the depths. Polly knew that Dart's stamina was almost exhausted. Once he had struggled with the Marriot's team, she alone remained. She was young and strong. With the aid of the rope she could cross alone.

She hitched up her skirts, took a deep breath and plunged into the torturously cold water, gripping hold of the rope.

One step: another step. The cold was crucifying. It was hard to keep her balance. One step: another. Dear Lord, how had he managed to cross so many times? The cold was unbearable. It numbed the limbs until movement was almost impossible. One step: another. The water surged around her breasts. How tall was she? Surely she was five foot three. The water should never reach her chin. Another step.

He was coming towards her and then there was such a scream that Polly lost her footing and felt her skirts trailing out in the current, pulling her off her feet. She fought for balance. Susannah's mouth was a gaping hole as she screamed and continued screaming, her eyes on the far bank. Polly gasped, spluttered water, and turned her head. Serena Spencer had emerged from the tree she had been hiding behind and was howling pitifully.

Polly paused. Dart was near to collapse. It would be far easier for her to retrace her steps for the girl. She began to move back, hand over hand, towards the bank she had just left. She was aware of a shout of protest from Dart, and Nephi and Lydia plunging into the water and dragging him forcibly ashore. If Nephi judged him to be at the end of his strength, then her judgment had been correct.

Behind her pandemonium was breaking out, but she could not turn her head to see, nor break her concentration to hear. One step, another. The water slid down over her breasts, her waist, her dripping skirts.

'Come,' she said through chattering teeth to Serena. 'Hold the rope tightly and move one hand and then another.'

Serena's terror at the reality of being left behind was greater than her terror of the crossing. She did exactly as Polly told her. The water reached Polly's waist and Serena's chest.

'Let your feet and legs float,' Polly gasped to the girl. 'Keep hold of the rope. Keep moving one hand and then another.' She was aware that from the far bank help was coming. The child obeyed, but the rush of water was too strong. With a cry she let go and instinctively Polly struck out after her.

She was holding Serena's chin, but the child was struggling. Water closed over her head, she was sinking, dragged down by the weight of her skirts and the struggling child. Serena slid from her grasp and no matter how hard she tried she could not reach the surface. Then, as she clawed vainly, strong hands gripped hold of her, pulling her upwards.

'You bloody fool!'

'Serena,' she gasped, coughing up water, choking for air.

'Nephi has her.'

The flood water swirled around them, one arm released her, striking out for the rope, the other holding on to her. As his hand gripped hold of it she could see, blurred and unfocussed, the blood oozing from the cuts, dropping into the water, staining it an ugly red.

'I can manage,' she protested, seizing hold of the rope, knowing how intolerable his pain must be.

His arm did not release her. Together they hung exhausted on to their frail lifeline.

'You can't,' he said at last, shaking the water from his face. 'You damned well nearly drowned.' His eyes were black pits in a ghastly white face.

'Would it have mattered?' Her voice was bitter. She had nearly died and her emotions were naked. The roaring water tossed and buffetted them.

'Of course it would have God-damned mattered!'

Polly's feet made brief contact with the river bed and then slipped, her heavy skirt fanning out in the water. She clutched at the rope so tightly that she could feel it cutting into her frozen flesh. Struggling to regain her balance, she said savagely,

'Is your pride so intolerable that you would take even my death as a personal insult, Major?'

His eyes were frightening. The blazing anger was extinguished. Only cold fury remained.

'I would take no action of yours personally,' he spat, gasping for breath. 'You're not fit to wipe the shoes of those you travel with. You're shameless. A tease and a flirt of the worst kind—showing one face to your companions by day and another at night when none can see.'

With a cry of rage Polly let go of the rope to slap his face. The torrent seized her, swirling her away as if she were a leaf, the gushing waters closing over her head. Her ears pounded, her heart felt as if it would burst. She struggled vainly and then he had hold of her, dragging her above the surface, his face a barely recognisable mask of pain and anger.

'You little fool! Are you trying to drown us both?'

She tried to speak and could not. She could no longer breathe. Her hands clutched him, her eyes agonised.

'No . . . !' The words tease and flirt rang in her ears. She heard him shout her name and then the roaring blackness engulfed her and she lay limp in his arms.

'Here!' Nephi had plunged in, one hand on the rope, the other stretched out to Dart. 'Take hold, man!'

Twice Dart stumbled. Neither time did his grip on the inert body in his arms weaken. Step by painful step he struggled to the bank. Eager arms stretched out to take Polly from him, but he would not let her go. Swaying on his feet, he carried her to the nearest wagon and laid her on dry bedding. Rasping for breath, he rolled her over and began to press down on her back, releasing the pressure, pressing again.

'Please . . . Please . . .' His words were incoherent. It was the first time in his life that he had prayed. 'Please Lord. *Please*!'

Nephi and Josiah stood by, their eyes anguished as tears merged with the water streaming down the Major's lean, hard features.

There was a moan and then a gasp and then Polly was violently and convulsively sick. Dart's legs buckled and he sank to his knees as Josiah and Nephi gave thanks to their maker and Susannah Spencer said authoritatively:

'Out of here, all of you. If she isn't stripped of those wet clothes she'll die of pneumonia!'

Reeling with exhaustion, Dart allowed Nephi and Josiah to help him to his feet and to lead him away.

'If we don't get those breeches off you soon, they'll be

frozen so hard they'll have to be chipped away,' Nephi said gruffly.

Dart nodded and staggered. Together Nephi and Josiah helped him into the Lyman wagon and stripped him of his sodden shirt and breeches.

'Here,' Nephi said, as Josiah wrapped him in warm blankets, 'I reckon you'll be needing this.'

Dart grinned weakly and accepted the silver flask of bourbon from the non-drinking Mormon.

'I reckon I will,' he said, and fell into an exhausted sleep.

CHAPTER SEVEN

When he awoke the wagon he was in was moving. He swung his legs to the floor and looked around him with the immediate reflexes of a soldier. Five pairs of eyes gazed at him with interest.

'We're pretty bunched up,' Serena said, perched comfortably on the end of what served as his bed. 'Pa says to thank you for saving my life. I wish you'd woken earlier, though, as he was awful mad with me.' She rubbed her bottom reflectively. 'Brother and Sister Cowley are travelling with the Marriots. Ma said it wouldn't be proper for you to travel with them, though I don't know why. Anyhow, you're in here with us and Sister Lyman.'

Dart was relieved to find that Nephi had had the foresight to dry his breeches and reclothe him. He dragged on his shirt and jacket and shouted to Lydia Lyman as he pulled on his boots.

'How far have we travelled?'

'A good twenty miles. We had freezing weather and have ridden far. It's Tuesday today.'

'For the love of God!' He burst out of the wagon. 'Why didn't you wake me?'

'There was no need,' Lydia said complacently. 'Never wake a sleeping babe or a tuckered-out man.'

He grinned and jumped to the ground and found his horse reined alongside.

'How you managed to remain a spinster beats me. Someone should have snapped you up years ago.'

Lydia laughed. 'It was completely voluntary, Major. But don't tell anyone else. They might stop feeling sorry for me.'

He mounted his horse, wheeled it around and paused uncertainly. His memory of the last few minutes of the river crossing was hazy. He remembered quite clearly the sight of Polly struggling to save the Spencer child, and he could remember his own horrified reactions, the sensation that he was about to lose all that he had ever longed for. He remembered his plunge into the icy torrent and his relief when he had caught hold of her and they had clung together, choking and exhausted. His lips tightened. He remembered her contemptuous words: her loathing to have him anywhere near her when all could see. Her reaction had been very different when he had rescued her from the dry goods store in Corrington. Then, with no watching eyes and under cover of darkness, she had surrendered to him willingly and warmly. He remembered his feeling of savage bitterness, his desire to wound and hurt her. And then she had let go of the rope and been swept away, and he had thought she was drowned.

Time had spun out in an eternity as he had struggled to seize her, to drag her above the surface and back to the bank.

Miss Polly Kirkham owed him her life. He wondered if she would be grateful and doubted it. The knowledge of such a debt would only make her more hostile. The sensible course of action would be for him to ignore her. To carry on as if the incident had never taken place: as if the angry words had never been spoken. His knuckles clenched till they showed white. He could not do it. He had to speak to her. The need to see her again was insurmountable.

With every muscle in his body taut, he cantered towards the Marriot wagon. She was up front, perched precariously on the edge of the wooden seat as Tom drove and Josiah sat next to him.

Her face had flushed with colour the minute he had emerged from Lydia Lyman's wagon. Her eyes avoided his, her fingers twisting torturously in her lap as he asked in a voice feigning indifference,

'Are you all right?'

'Yes, thank you, Major.'

Tom and Josiah cleared their throats and began to take an uncommon interest in the countryside they were passing through. The silence stretched uncomfortably.

'I . . .' Polly swallowed and wished that he had not ridden so close. If she reached out her hand she could touch him. 'I believe I owe you my life, Major Richards. I . . . I . . . am most grateful for it.'

Beneath the broad brim of his hat, Dart's face remained impassive. It was not her stiffly spoken words of gratitude he wanted. He stared broodingly ahead of him. The sun was shining and they were making good progress. They would be at Richardson Point by dusk. Polly Kirkham would soon be nothing but a memory. The knowledge brought with it a pain that was like a knife wound. He cursed himself silently. He had made a fool of himself once over a woman and had vowed never to do so again. It was a vow he had kept. Until now. They had only a few hours left in each other's company. It would be easy to dig his spurs in and ride away. He need barely set eyes on her again. Instead, he found himself saying curtly,

'You look pretty cramped up there. How about riding with me for a while?'

Polly gasped, her heart beating wildly, her cheeks burning. 'I'm sorry . . . I don't think . . . It would not be proper . . .'

'T'will do no harm,' Tom Marriot said easily. 'And it will give Josiah room to breathe for a while.'

Polly gazed from Tom to the Major helplessly. A slight smile curved the harsh lines of Dart's mouth. She looked prettier when she was mortified than she did when she was angry.

Tom reined in and, still protesting, Polly allowed herself to be swung in front of Major Richards on his powerful black stallion. It evoked memories that were all too clear and recent. Memories of the ride from Corrington, of his mouth on hers, hard and sweet. Of the blissful strength of his arms as they had held her, protecting and shielding her. Of the cold reality when he had removed her arms from around his neck. In the icy torrent of the creek he had accused her of being shameless. With her face primly averted from his, she knew that what he said was true. With the heat of his body against hers, the rough feel of his uniformed arm around her, she was overcome with a longing that was unbearable.

They left the Marriot wagon behind them and cantered beside the Spencers. Nephi eyed them with affection and seemed to see nothing amiss in Polly sitting in such close proximity to a man she was not betrothed to.

'How come I slept and you didn't?' Dart asked Nephi, already regretting his unwise impulse. He could not be so near to her and not touch her. Her hair smelt of lavender. He longed to take her cumbersome cloak and cast it aside, taking her slim, supple body in his arms, feeling the softness of her lips once more beneath his.

Nephi grinned. 'I only woke four hours ago. Sister Lyman got things moving. Susannah drove our team, and at the rate of progress we've made, I reckon Brother Brigham should install Sister Lyman at the head of one of his convoys.'

'Will Brother Brigham still be at Richardson point?' Polly asked tentatively.

'That depends on the weather they've had. I know that he intends to leave as soon as possible with a pioneer party for Council Bluffs.'

'Is that in the Rocky Mountains?' she asked, acutely aware that however straight she sat she could not avoid contact with Major Richards' uniformed chest.

There was dry amusement in Major Richards' voice as he said,

'Council Bluffs is only the beginning of the trail Brigham Young intends to blaze. From there he can follow the Platte River and make for Fort Laramie. Then he intends crossing the south pass over the mountains into the desert beyond.'

'To the Promised Land,' Nephi said cheerfully.

Dart shook his head in exasperation. 'There's no Promised Land in the desert, Nephi. Mr Young talks of settling at the Great Salt Lake. You'll never build a city there. It's a waterless desert.'

'We'll make the desert bloom,' said Nephi confidently, and began to whistle his favourite tune.

Dart listened to him with half an ear. His thoughts were centred entirely on Polly. There was only one way to free himself from the unremitting desire he felt for her, and that was to satisfy it. In doing so he would lose the respect of Nephi and Josiah and Tom. That would be a pity, but could not be helped. She had teased and tormented him enough. His decision made, he bade goodbye to Nephi and tightened his hold of Polly. Then he dug in his spurs, and, as Polly gave a gasp of surprise and fear, he galloped furiously off up the snow-bound track until the three wagons were out of sight.

'We have some unfinished business to attend to,' he said grimly, reining in at a copse of beech trees.

Polly gazed at him like a rabbit at a stoat. Was he going to vent his anger on her here? Was that why he had asked her to ride with him? So that he could abduct her and vent his anger on her, out of earshot of any that might intervene? He had ordered her to remain on the far bank and she had disobeyed him. In doing so she had nearly lost both their lives. Major Richards was not a man who would take disobedience lightly. Her mouth felt dry. She wanted to cry, but knew that to indulge in tears would be the lowest form of weakness.

He swung lightly to the ground and when he seized hold of her waist and her frightened eyes met his, she knew that her fears were unfounded. It was not anger that Dart Richards wished to vent on her. Her heart began to beat wildly and irregularly.

She opened her mouth to make a cry of protest, but it was silenced by the heat of his lips. His arms were around her and with a sob of capitulation she made no effort to free herself.

'Polly . . .' The words were strangled in his throat. He had anticipated resistance, outrage. Now his anger and hurt were lost in a rush of passionate tenderness. He swung his military cape to the snow-covered ground and lowered her beneath him with infinite tenderness.

'Polly . . .' The words he wanted to say were never uttered. She was in his arms and his mouth was on hers, warm and demanding, sliding down to the hollow of her throat so that she gave a little cry of pleasure, and then returning to her mouth, kissing her with increasing urgency and hunger until her senses reeled.

The fever possessing her rose higher and hotter. His warm hand was on her breast, his fingers gentle and caressing. Her hands moved up the length of his back, burying themselves in the thick black hair as he lowered his head, kissing her throat, opening the buttons of her gown, kissing the soft flesh of her bared breasts. She was oblivious of the sharp, cold air, of the improprieties, of the liberties he was taking with her body—for he was taking none. She was giving to him freely, locking loving arms around his head as his mouth burned hers like a flame. With a small gasp she pressed herself closer and closer to him and then she felt him freeze, and heard the unmistakable sound of approaching wheels.

Slowly, carefully, he re-buttoned the bodice of her gown. She traced the harsh contours of his face with her forefinger, gazing up at him in wonder and love. This time there could be no mistake. The expression in his eyes reflected the expression in her own. She loved him and he loved her. He had not said so, yet there could be no other explanation for what had passed between them. As he lifted her to her feet she was trembling. What would happen to them? Where would they go? There could be no question of her continuing to the Rocky Mountains with the Latter-day Saints. Her place was with him.

Dazedly she rejoined the wagon train, unaware of the curious glances Susannah and Eliza were giving her. Even her voice had changed, imbued with an emotion that had previously been foreign to it.

* * *

'A wagon! A wagon!' little Jamie Spencer called out suddenly as they made camp at midday.

Lucy dropped the ladle with which she had been spooning beans and ran to Jamie's side. 'Praise the Lord!' she shouted exuberantly. 'It's Jared and the Merrills!' and despite her husband's protests she picked up her skirts and ran to greet them.

'Now there's a funny thing,' Josiah said, sitting on a water cask and continuing with his meal. 'Richardson Point is only a couple of miles away. What have those plum idiots been up to?'

'I don't know, but it hardly matters, seeing they're safe and with us again,' Tom said jubilantly.

The Merrill wagon came towards them at a rattling pace. Polly could see Jared at the reins, Emily beside him. With the others she ran forward, overjoyed at seeing him again, knowing he was safe. The horses slithered in the snow and Jared leapt to the ground, hugging his mother tight.

'Son, son, I've been so worried. You've been in my thoughts every minute of every day.'

Polly had the grace to feel ashamed. He was part of her adopted family, yet she had taken it for granted that he would be able to look after himself and her mind had been too full of Dart to have room for Jared.

Emily had already sprung to the ground after Jared, and Charity and Fletcher Merrill followed more slowly. Fletcher Merrill's face was emaciated and he looked a poor replica of the vigorous man who had departed from Nauvoo.

'Come near the fire. Where have you been? Why are you not at Richardson Point with the others?'

Question followed question. Jared disentangled himself from his mother, clapped his father stoutly on the back and then his eyes immediately searched for Polly.

She ran towards him, her arms wide, all the constraint of the last few months vanishing. They were brother and sister again, for now she knew that she had never been in love with him. Love was what she felt for Dart.

He swung her round in his arms and only when he kissed her on the lips did realisation flood Polly. Jared had left the camp in the belief that she was on the point of marrying him. She pushed her hands against his chest and he released her gently.

'It's good to be back, Polly. You should have your hood up. The cold is biting.'

Tenderly he lifted the hood of her cloak and tucked the golden ringlets out of sight.

Dart, leaning negligently against the Lyman wagon, watched the scene through narrowed eyes. He had not taken Jared into account. He was a mere boy who had left camp before his own feelings for Polly had manifested themselves. Now, with pristine clarity, he saw that not only did the boy love her, but that he fully expected a like response from Polly. How long had she lived with the Marriots? Four years? Five? It would be only natural that two young people, living together in close proximity, should fall in love; especially when the young man was as personable as Jared and the girl as breathtakingly beautiful as Polly. His eyes shifted to Emily Merrill. She was watching the reunion with agonised eyes, the lines around her mouth white and painful.

Jared loved Polly: Emily loved Jared. Who did Polly Kirkham love? He remembered the way she had kissed the Marriot boy on his departure and frowned, reflectively unscrewing the top from his flask and swallowing a mouthful of bourbon.

'Why did you not head on to the camp at Richardson Point if you were only a half day's travelling away?' Josiah was asking Jared.

'We had food enough and were relatively sheltered by a hill and a handful of trees. Brother Merrill was reluctant to travel until he was fully recovered. The slightest movement made him nauseous. I saw you from the top of the hill an hour ago, and as Brother Merrill was feeling more like his old self we thought we'd surprise you and join you. We can all enter Richardson Point together now.'

'That boy has been so good,' Charity Merrill was saying to Lucy. 'He shot enough birds to keep us in meat every day.'

'And how have you fared?' Fletcher Merrill asked as they gathered around the fire. Only Dart remained apart, standing in the shade of Lydia Lyman's wagon.

'Nearly lost our lives a while back,' Josiah said, giving a graphic account of the flooded creek.

'If it hadn't been for the Major we'd still be at the other side of it with our provisions dwindling.'

'If it hadn't been for the Major, my daughter would be drowned, as would Polly,' Susannah said quietly.

The Merrills turned and looked curiously at the blue-uniformed, gold-epauletted figure.

'He looks kind of intimidating,' Charity Merrill said with a whisper to Lucy Marriot.

'He certainly doesn't look the kind of man to be travelling with God-fearing Christians,' Fletcher agreed in a low voice.

Nephi leant across to him, a strange light in his usually-kind eyes. 'The Major is the friend of every man, woman and child on this train, Brother. He may not be a Mormon, but we Mormons don't have exclusive rights to courage and integrity. Brother Brigham has said that himself and I'd like you to remember it.'

The Merrills remained silent but unconvinced. Emily Merrill kept sliding her eyes in Dart's direction, as if he were the devil incarnate.

Dart noted the tight little mouth and unbecoming hairstyle. Emily Merrill's face was one full of character, but not seduction. For her, Jared Marriot would be the answer to a prayer. He noticed that though Polly had welcomed her warmly, Emily had quickly removed herself from Polly's touch and had seated herself as far as possible away from her. Two girls of the same age should have been talking ten to the dozen. Emily Merrill seemed reluctant even to look in Polly's direction.

Dart replaced his flask in his hip pocket and strolled across to them.

'We can either camp here and ride into Richardson Point tomorrow, or continue and arrive at Richardson at dusk.'

'Onwards!' Nephi cried, leaping to his feet. 'Are we in agreement?'

The women, hoping that those ahead of them had contrived comforts that they so far lacked, agreed, and the drum of flour and water casks that served as seats were hastily rolled back into the wagons.

Emily Merrill moved forward to speak to Jared, but he was already striding towards Polly and at the expression in his eyes Emily halted, her face a mask of misery.

'It will be good to ride together again, Polly,' Jared said, seizing her hand and leading her towards the Marriot wagon.

'Jared, I must talk to you . . .'

'And I to you, dear heart. But not now. Later, when we can speak without being overheard.'

He grinned at her and helped her into the teamster seat. Behind them Lucy and Tom Marriot sat within inches, Lucy's knees jolting occasionally into Polly's back.

Emily spun on her heel towards the wagon Jared had driven so jubilantly only a short while ago. If she had hoped he would ride it again, she had been mistaken. Blinking back tears she climbed up into her seat and took the reins while her parents made themselves comfortable behind her.

Dart mounted his horse and rode down the line. When he reached the Marriots' wagon he raised a quizzical eyebrow at Polly, but said nothing.

'I suppose,' Jared said with unaccustomed bitterness as Dart returned to the head of the convoy, 'that I should thank him for saving your life, but truth to tell, Polly, I can't help feel that it was he who endangered it.'

'What on earth do you mean?' Polly nearly fell off the seat with surprise.

Jared flicked the reins bad-temperedly. 'Ordering you to cross the creek as he did. He should have waited until the water subsided. It was foolhardy and why Brother Cowley and Brother Spencer can't see it, I can't imagine.'

'The water would not have subsided,' Tom said soothingly. 'The snow had only just begun to melt. If we hadn't crossed when we did, we could have been stranded there for months—and without food.'

'Nevertheless, I don't like the man,' Jared repeated stubbornly.

Polly's hands were screwed up tightly in her lap. She could not tell Jared of her change of feeling when his parents were within earshot. She could say nothing until they were alone.

'He's arrogant and overbearing,' Jared continued undeterred. 'Who does he think he is, assuming leadership as if it were his by right?'

No one answered him. The subject of the Major was not even one that Tom wanted to discuss further. He was tired and weak, but he had seen the way the Merrill girl had looked at his son. Now, if Jared would only turn his attention in that direction, they would have no more worries.

Jared showed no intention of doing so. His eyes were so often on Polly's pert little profile that it was a wonder the Marriot wagon remained in the convoy. He talked incessantly to her: about Brother Merrill's illness, about how calm and unflappable Emily Merrill had been, alone on the trail with two sick parents; of how he did not intend to stay at Richardson Point, but to forge ahead with Brother Brigham and his party of pioneers. Unspoken, but obvious, was the assumption that she would travel with him and that his parents would remain at Richardson Point with the main body of pioneers until the spring came and the journey West would be less hazardous.

If he intended her to accompany him West with Brother Brigham and the others, then he also intended that she should marry him before they set out. Marry him at Richardson Point.

Polly's fingers continued to twist in her lap. If only Tom Marriot would take the reins and allow her and Jared to walk awhile. Then she could tell him that she could never marry him. That she was in love with Major Richards.

Twice it was on the tip of her tongue to ask Tom to take over, but on his son's return Tom had sunk back into exhaustion and looked almost as ill as Brother Merrill.

Dart remained at the head of the party and Polly tried to listen to Jared's eager conversation and not to be constantly trying to catch a glimpse of Dart. If Jared and the Merrills had not returned, she would probably be riding with him, or at the very least sitting beside him as he drove the Marriot wagon, seeing strong brown hands on the reins instead of fair, blunt-fingered ones: a tailored, blue uniform instead of buckskins and cape. More importantly still, a dark laughing face instead of Jared's boyish countenance. She pursed her lips. It was a face that did not always laugh. Sometimes it looked distinctly forbidding and she could well understand Sister Merrill's reluctance to approach and be friendly with him. In repose, there was a savagery in Dart's features that intrigued and aroused her. It was a face she would never tire of looking at, not by sunlight nor by moonlight.

'We're there!' little Jamie Spencer cried. 'I can see the tents and wagons!'

Polly felt a tight knot of apprehension growing in her stomach. Very soon she would have to speak to Jared and she knew he would not take the news placidly.

Guided by the Merrill wagon, the little convoy drew up to the outskirts of the large camp and stopped. Close on five hundred wagons formed in an orderly manner, some with tents pitched alongside, some without. Friends that had not been seen since Nauvoo ran to meet them—Lees, Kimballs, Fieldings, Smiths.

Lucy was in tears of relief. Just being amongst so many friends and neighbours gave her the sense of security she so badly needed.

'I'm off to tell Brother Brigham we have joined him safely,' Jared said, springing to the ground and raising his arms to circle her waist.

Polly was quite capable of jumping to the ground with the same agility, but there was no refusing the outstretched arms without being hurtingly impolite.

Lydia Lyman pretended not to notice, but Dart made no such pretence. He felt a sudden blazing anger at the sight of another man touching that supple waist, holding her close.

'I must talk to you first, Jared. It's very important.'

He frowned. 'Is something wrong? I noticed that you were quiet on the wagon, but then I thought you were tired . . .'

Throngs of well-wishers were milling around them. She took hold of his hand. 'Let's move away, Jared. We can't talk in the middle of a crowd and what I have to say is very private.'

She led him away from the camp fire and the sound of reunions and greetings. As he watched them walk away into the darkness, there was a sudden flexing of muscles along Dart's jawline.

Whatever suspicions he had held were now confirmed. His first assessment of Polly Kirkham's character had been correct. He had been a diversion for her—nothing more. His blaze of anger turned cold and hard and he turned on his heel and went in search of the Mormon leader.

Emily Merrill stared unwaveringly at Jared and Polly's retreating backs. He hadn't looked at her once since they had joined up with the others. For three days he had laughed and talked to her, begun to teach her to shoot, promised to teach her to fish. He had not kissed her, nor said he loved her, but he had enjoyed being with her and once, when his arm had circled her shoulders as he taught her to hold a rifle, she had been sure that he had been as aware of her body as she had been of his. She would make him a far better wife than Polly Kirkham. Blonde ringlets and summer-blue eyes were not enough to compensate for being an unbeliever. After living for five years with a Mormon family and not embracing the faith, Emily doubted very much that Polly ever would. There was an undercurrent of wildness beneath Polly Kirkham's pretty exterior. The mother had been an unknown quantity and the daughter was as well. In Emily's opinion Polly would never fit in: would never become one of them. Why was the same instinct so lacking in Jared? Why could he not see how unsuitable Polly was to become the wife of a future church leader?

She blinked her tears away angrily. She would try praying. It was the only course left open to her.

'What's the matter?' Jared asked again, as they stumbled away from the clamour of the camp.

Polly stopped walking and turned to face him, her heart racing uncomfortably.

'I cannot marry you, Jared. Major Richards has made it impossible . . .'

Jared's face whitened. 'What did he do to you? In what way did he harm you? Did he . . .' He gagged on the words, his eyes glazing with such ferocity that Polly nearly fainted with fright.

'No! No! You don't understand Jared. He . . .'

Jared swung on his heel, his hand on the knife at his belt. She ran after him, pulling on his arm.

'Please stop and listen. It isn't as you think.'

'It's enough! I knew the man was carnal the minute I set eyes on him, but that he should take advantage of you the minute I rode away . . .'

He shook her off and began to run back towards the camp.

'Jared! Jared! *Wait*! *Listen*! Oh please! *Please*!'

He was yards away from her now, running and leaping, and she could not catch up with him. Her long skirts caught on unseen brambles and then she fell. Sobbing, she stumbled to her feet but could no longer see him.

She lifted her skirts and began to run, her heart hammering wildly. She was aware of people giving her strange looks, but she did not care.

'Have you seen Jared Marriot?' she asked breathlessly. 'Have you seen the Major?'

'The Army man went off to see Brother Brigham,' an unknown voice said. 'Down there's the way. At the far end of that row of wagons.'

'Thank you. Oh, thank you!'

She began to run again. Jared would not know where Dart had gone. He would look for him among their own tiny party.

'I think you've an infernal cheek,' Brigham Young thundered, his mane of white hair making him look like a patriarch from the Old Testament. 'You expect me to round up a battalion of men to fight for a government that has failed to protect us, that has forced us out into the wilderness?'

'Those are not my orders, but they soon will be. I'm only advising you of the facts and asking that you supply the men now and so save time later.'

'Rogue!' roared the Mormon leader with a gleam in his eye. 'You're out for promotion and to beat someone else to the job.'

Dart nodded. 'So I am. A Captain James Allen has orders to intercept you at Council Bluffs and form a battalion of your men to fight in the Mexican war.'

'And if you can do it, so much the quicker, there'll be more gold braid to fancify your shoulders?'

'Maybe, but I think you should listen to the proposal carefully. On the surface it *is* insufferable that after such persecution and lack of help from the government, they should call on your men to fight. But every man who volunteers will be paid full army wages. They'll go first to Fort Leavenworth and then to California.'

The Mormon Leader's eyes sharpened beneath his bushy eyebrows. 'California?'

'Exactly. You can have a whole army of men transported to the far side of the Rocky Mountains without expense to yourself. Your food supplies will last longer, for there will be fewer mouths to feed.'

Brigham Young rose to his feet and slapped Dart on the back. 'I like your gall, Major, and I like your way of thinking. But until we reach Council Bluffs I need every man that I have.'

Dart shrugged. What the Mormon leader was saying was true, and he would not want to argue a case that would leave women and children in hazardous conditions. It was a pity though. It would have done his career no harm to have arrived at Fort Leavenworth with a full battalion of Mormons ready and willing to fight in the war against Mexico.

'Good day to you, sir,' Brigham Young said, shaking him vigorously by the hand. 'I've heard good things of you from Nephi Spencer, and Brother Spencer is not a man to give praise easily. May I ask what your plans are now?'

'I shall return East,' Dart said uninterestedly.

'Then our ways diverge, for we go forward to establish a camp on the banks of the Chariton.'

Dart did not press him further. He knew the route the

formidable man in front of him intended taking and he had heard enough about the so-called Promised Land.

Cordially they parted and he strode away between the wagons and tents and camp fires, to his horse. He would not think of her. Let her marry her Mormon man and let her go into the wilderness with the rest of them.

At the sight of his grim profile, the Saints fell silent. There was something menacing about his striding figure. Charity Merrill saw him and shuddered. She could not share her friends' views of him. As they had been the last to arrive, the Spencers, Cowleys and other wagons were on the very perimeter of the camp and had not, as yet, made their own camp fire. Instead, with great relief, they had joined friends and relations and the wagons were deserted except for Charity's as she returned for provisions.

It was dark away from the fire and there was no moon. She could no longer see him, but she heard the rattle of bridle and reins. He was leaving them. 'Thank the Lord,' Charity whispered and descended from the safety of her wagon with a fresh supply of wheatcakes in her apron. Jared knocked them flying to the ground as he raced up to her, gripping her arm so hard that she cried out in pain.

'The Major! Where is he? Have you seen him?'

'Jared, my arm! You're hurting . . .'

'The Major!' Jared's face was that of a man half crazed.

'You wanted me?' The voice was insolently careless. The reins were dropped as he jumped lightly to the ground.

Jared's hesitation was momentary and then he lunged at the shadow in the darkness, hitting out viciously with his fist, and sending Dart reeling.

'That,' he yelled triumphantly, 'is for Polly. For defiling her. For . . .' He got no further.

Dart had hoped to avoid the indignity of a fight with a mere boy by talking to him and pacifying him. Now, with lightning speed, he retaliated. From being the victor, Jared found himself victim, sprawled flat on his back, the breath knocked out of him.

'She's not worth fighting over,' Dart said contemptuously, making no attempt to continue the fight.

Jared struggled to his feet. 'She's betrothed to me! You knew that, yet still you . . . You . . .'

'I did *not* know it and certainly the lady, if that is the correct terminology, did not advise me of the fact. Indeed, she seemed most forgetful of it.'

'*Liar!*' Jared's fist shot out again and Dart's lean hand circled it with panther-like speed.

'Have sense. I'm leaving. You'll only get hurt if you continue this idiocy.'

'Not me, Major! Not me!' With his free hand he reached for his belt.

Dart saw the flash of steel and sighed. The young man would have to be taught a lesson. He hit him once and then again. At what point the crowd began to appear, Dart had no idea. He only knew he was not going to be stabbed in the back by a stripling youth, demented with jealousy.

Jared bled from the nose and the mouth. Barely able to see, he staggered to his knees, fumbling for the elusive knife.

Dart hauled him to his feet, steadied him with one hand and struck him on the jaw with the other. When he released him, Jared fell senseless. In Dart's judgment he would remain like that for several hours.

The crowd that had gathered backed away, horrified.

They were accustomed to violence from outsiders, but not in their midst. Not in their hymn-singing camps on the trail.

Polly saw only a half-senseless, defenceless Jared being dragged upright, only to be hit with calculated viciousness. She pushed through the crowd, eyes wide, barely comprehending what she had seen. All fear for Dart's safety fled. Jared was the one who was hurt. Jared the one lying unconscious. She flew to his side, cradling his head in her lap. Above her Dart drew on his gauntlets, his face cold and hard, the face of a stranger.

'Savage!' she hissed as Jared moaned in pain. *'Savage!'*

Dart shrugged and mounted his horse. Silently the Saints made way for him as he cantered out into the night. The last sound he heard was Polly's uncontrolled weeping as she helped carry Jared into the family wagon.

For Polly the next few days were a haze of misery. Jared, despite swollen eyes and a cut lip, was cock-a-hoop that he had driven the 'damned' Major from their midst. The Spencers, Cowleys and even the Marriots turned away whenever she approached, blaming her for the hideousness of the fight, for setting one man against another. Jared's elation only died when Polly steadfastly refused to marry him. His perplexity was pathetic, but Polly could say nothing to enlighten him. She could not bear to speak Dart's name. It hurt too much.

As she had helped Lucy sponge Jared's face of blood, and heal his cuts, Jared had spoken wildly of his confrontation with Dart. Of how he had told him Polly was his betrothed. Of how he would let no man insult his future wife.

Mechanically doing her daily chores, Polly knew only

too well what Dart had believed and why he had left. She did not know how the fight had originated, but she could guess. If Dart had knocked Jared senseless, it had been for Jared's own good. Knowing did not ease the pain, because knowing did not bring him back. She could not set off on her own in search of him. He might have returned to St Louis or continued on to his camp at Fort Leavenworth: or he might have ridden West towards California. At night she cried herself to sleep and Jared's bewilderment turned to impatience. He gave vent to his feelings with Emily, who at least had the sense to see him as the hero who had rid their camp of an evil malignancy.

The story of the fight had spread, coloured by the telling. Polly found herself increasingly isolated, only Lydia Lyman behaving as if nothing had happened.

Brigham Young and a small party set off to forge the way ahead and only Jared's hope that Polly would change her mind and marry him, kept him from joining them. As the days passed, and it became apparent that no marriage ceremony would take place at Richardson Point, he spoke with increasing fervour to Nephi of the advantages of being amongst Brother Brigham's band. Their present camp site seemed overrun with chattering women and noisy children. Nephi, too, was regretting not having the courage to have been among Brother Brigham's company.

'We know they were going to make their first camp on the Chariton. We could catch them up easily,' Jared urged.

'Seems like we're always catching people up,' Nephi observed drily.

All the same, he was tempted. He spoke to Josiah, but Josiah was not of the same mind. Neither were the elder Marriots. Lydia Lyman, overhearing their conversation one evening, said casually that if they decided to set off on their own, she would join them. Neither man demurred. They knew by now that Sister Lyman was a help in a crisis, not a hindrance.

To Emily's anguish her own parents were steadfastly opposed to journeying further until the last of the snows had melted and the flooded rivers had subsided. Tom and Lucy did not argue when Jared said he was accompanying Sister Lyman and the Spencers and joining up with Brother Brigham. They had had enough of life on the trail for quite a while, and the settled camp at Richardson was relatively comfortable.

It was still dawn when the two wagons bravely set out, Susannah Spencer sitting beside her husband, the children in the back. Sister Schulster was remaining with friends at Richardson, as was Sister Fielding. Lydia Lyman followed them, Jared at the reins.

'Wait!' The voice was so faint it was a wonder Lydia heard it.

'Hold the horses, Jared. It's Polly,' she said, as a dark-caped figure ran breathlessly after them.

'I couldn't stay,' she gasped as Lydia helped her up into the wagon. 'Eliza Cowley has not spoken a word to me for days and neither have the rest of the women. Without you I would be completely friendless.'

Jared grinned, not understanding the reason for her ostracism.

'Let's hit the trail,' he called joyfully. Lydia's hand squeezed Polly's and Polly was deeply grateful. One person, at least, understood.

Instead of snow, their wagons were lashed by incessant rain and they made only three miles the first day. Time after time Polly and Jared had to jump to the saturated ground and in mud up to their ankles push the rear of the wagon as Lydia urged the horses onward and tried to free mud-bound wheels.

'My sense of adventure is rapidly dying,' Polly said wearily to Lydia as they heaved the wagon free once more of the quagmire.

'It's to our advantage,' Lydia replied composedly. 'With rains like this, Brother Brigham will still be encamped at the Chariton. We will be with them in a few days.'

The thought gave Polly no elation. She had no further desire to be with Brother Brigham or anybody else. She desired only to be with Dart and he believed her to be a flirt—a faithless-hearted girl who had toyed with his affections in the absence of the man she was to marry.

Suddenly Nephi's horrified voice shouted, '*Indians*!'

At first Lydia and Polly expected to see only the friendly Indians they had been used to in Illinois. One glance at the furiously galloping party racing towards them through sleeting hail, disabused them.

'It's a war party,' Lydia said, paling.

Nephi had already slithered his team to a halt. 'Have the children lie on the wagon floor,' he shouted to Susannah, 'And keep loading those rifles!'

Jared swerved alongside of him. There was no question of being able to outdistance the approaching redmen.

'Get down behind the seat and keep on firing!' he yelled as Lydia nearly fell over herself in her haste to reach the rifles and ammunition.

'Lord have mercy on us,' Lydia prayed fervently, as the blood-curdling cries drew nearer and they could see the hideous paint-daubed faces.

The two wagons were each surrounded by galloping

horsemen; one arrow and then another struck the Spencer wagon.

'Let them have it!' Nephi cried, and blasted at the nearest rider with his rifle.

Polly had no time to feel afraid. Lydia was loading the rifles as fast as she knew how and lying beside Jared behind the teamster's seat, Polly fired and fired again.

Her rifle was knocked sharply upwards as an arrow hit Jared and he rose with a cry of pain, trying to pull it free. As he did so he toppled sideways and down on to the ground, an easy target for the shrieking attackers.

'Oh God!' Polly heard herself call and then, disregarding Lydia's clawing hand on her cloak, she was stumbling over the seat and leaping to the ground.

'They're toying with us!' Nephi cried to his wife. 'They could have killed every last one of us by now if they'd wanted to.'

Jared stumbled against Polly and Lydia's hands reached down to them, hardly aware that the hail of arrows had halted. The Indians rode nearer and nearer, circling them only yards away, grotesque painted faces grinning gloatingly. Polly shrank back against the wagon as Jared was hauled inside by Lydia.

As Jared fell finally on to the floor of the wagon, and as Nephi was beginning to feel a growing confidence that their lives were not seriously at risk, a wheeling horse almost trampled Polly underfoot. Lydia's hand was within inches of hers, stretching out to help her.

With a cry of terror Polly felt herself lifted off her feet. Vainly she reached for Lydia's hands, but they were no longer within reach. There was a grip on her waist like steel as she was pinioned against the throbbing flank of the horse. She could see Jared struggling for his rifle and heard Nephi fire vainly, and then the horse wheeled around and she could see nothing but a blurring landscape and the ground speeding dizzily beneath her kicking feet.

With whoops and cries the raiding party headed off in the direction they had come from. No one in the two wagons, apart from Jared, had been injured. Within minutes the plain was as empty and as silent as before.

CHAPTER EIGHT

'SWEET Jesus,' Lydia Lyman whispered, sinking to her knees, her smoking rifle still in her hands. She had remained firing after the retreating figures long after it was possible even to see them clearly.

Susannah sat huddled on the floor of her wagon, white-faced and trembling, her crying children gathered around her, shielded by her protecting arms.

Nephi stood, a dazed expression on his face, staring into the empty distance. Jared was the first to come out of shock. There was no boyish charm on his countenance now, only rank fear. In two minutes he had aged twenty years.

'We must go after them, give chase!' His voice was trembling, his hands shaking as he fumbled while trying to release one of the horses from the team.

Nephi stopped him, breathing deeply, struggling for control and command of the situation.

'T'would be useless. One man in search of a war party, no doubt already amongst a larger encampment? And where? How? The plains and the hills have been the Indians' home for centuries. It would take an army to find them.'

'But we can't just leave her!' Jared's voice broke on a sob that indicated how near he was to losing complete self-possession.

'Of course not. We must return. Seek help.'

'From *who*?' The full horror of the situation had permeated Jared's numbed brain. 'The men at Richardson know no more about this country than we do. They cannot leave their womenfolk to fend for themselves in this weather. We would get no help there!'

'Then at the Chariton. Brother Brigham has plenty of men with him.'

Jared leaned against the horse. The Chariton. How long would it take them to reach it? How long to make the Saints understand and form a search party? How long to rescue Polly? And in the meantime? What would her fate be in the hands of the vermillion-painted redmen? He was violently, convulsively sick. Lydia Lyman threw his cloak around his shoulders.

'It may not be too bad,' she said, reading his thoughts all too clearly. 'I believe the red-men take women for extra work. To cook and fetch water.'

Even her strong voice lacked conviction. Jared looked at her with agonised eyes.

'Not Polly. They will . . .' He leaned over the side of the wagon and vomited once more.

'To the Chariton!' Nephi called. 'We have no time to lose.' Lydia didn't need to be told twice. While Jared clambered beside her, his face the colour of a dead man, she whipped her horses to the utmost.

Women taken by the Indians did not return to their family and friends alive. Nor, in Lydia's opinion, would they have wanted to. The sooner an arrow was put through Polly's heart, the better. Every hour alive would only be an hour of unspeakable suffering and humiliation. She kept her thoughts to herself, her lips tight and her eyes on the galloping horses before her. The Chariton. Pray God they made it soon.

'We can go no further,' Nephi called out at last. 'The

horses will drop without rest and water.'

Dusk had fallen. In the distance came the lone cry of a wolf.

'One horse, just one, to let me ride ahead,' Jared pleaded.

Nephi shook his head. 'The horse would drop dead beneath you. Give them rest and then ride on ahead.'

Susannah and Lydia exchanged quick glances and lowered their eyes, remaining silent. Two women, five children and one man alone on the plains. If the Indians had attacked once they might very well do so again. Yet how could they delay Jared in his fevered, desperate ride for help?

Lydia slept as best she could, but it was precious little. If only Polly had been killed at their feet. If only her fate wasn't so unknown . . . so unthinkable.

At three in the morning Jared saddled the best of the horses.

'May the Lord go with you,' Nephi said, clapping him on the shoulder.

Jared did not reply. He was already digging in his heels, riding westwards into the all-encompassing darkness.

Lydia called softly, 'Nephi?'

He walked across to her wagon. She clutched her cloak tightly beneath her chin.

'I calculated it to be a three-day journey from Richardson Point to the Chariton when we set out. Riding alone Jared will make Chariton tomorrow.'

'To what good?' Lydia asked bleakly. 'There can be no saving Polly now.'

'No.'

Lydia could not see, but knew that tears were coursing down Nephi's cheeks.

'But we cannot deny the boy his hope, Sister Lyman. Try and sleep. We must be off at first light.'

Jared rode as if all the hounds of hell were at his heels. It was his fault. Everything was his fault. He had been the one to suggest they set out in an undefended party of two wagons, to catch up with Brigham Young. It was because of him that Polly had insisted on joining them. And then the attack. The grotesque figures galloping down on them through the sleeting rain, naked except for breech cloths and beads and ochre and scarlet painted faces and bodies. *He* had been the one foolish enough to have been hit. He could barely feel the pain in his arm. Sister Lyman had removed the arrow, cleansed the wound and bound it tight. The pain was nothing. It was infinitesimal compared with the agony he felt at Polly's fate.

If he hadn't been fool enough to have leapt to his feet when he had been hit, and thus toppled to the ground, Polly would still be safe. Nephi had already called out that the Indians were playing with them. There had been twenty or thirty braves. If they had wanted to kill them, they could have done so easily. To both Nephi and Jareds' chagrin, no dead Indians had been left behind. Their rifle shots had been futile.

He took no food, no water, no rest. When, late the next afternoon, he rode into Chariton camp and slid from his sweating horse, he was immediately surrounded by helping hands and questions.

'Brigham Young,' he gasped, as his horse was led away to be rubbed down. 'Brigham Young.'

'I'm here, boy. What brings you in such distress. Is Richardson safe?'

The gathering crowd around Jared parted to allow

their white-maned leader through.

'Aye,' Jared said, lights dancing before his eyes, blackness pressing in on him. He must not faint now. He must not delay Polly's rescue by so much as a second. He was conscious of many hands holding and supporting him. Of the sweat rolling into his eyes, of his painfully cracked lips. Magnetic blue eyes bored into his.

'One of our women has been taken by Indians,' he managed at last, and was aware of uproar around him.

'From Richardson?'

'No, sir.' The noise subsided.

'We set out two days ago to catch you up. Sister Lyman and Brother and Sister Spencer.'

'Sister Spencer has been taken by Indians.' The word went quickly from mouth to mouth. Brigham Young remained silent, waiting, listening.

'A day's ride from Richardson a war party surrounded us and began to attack.' His strength left him, his knees sagged and he sank to the ground.

'Sister Kirkham, Polly Kirkham, has been taken.'

'The orphan child the Marriots took in,' someone said to Brigham Young.

'She's no child,' another voice said. 'She's a woman, full-grown. Eighteen last month.

'We must form a party at once.' Jared's words were barely coherent. 'We must find her, rescue her.'

The Mormon leader's face was grim. 'The boy is exhausted. Help him to my tent.'

The way was ankle-deep in mud. Brushwood and limbs of trees had been thrown on the ground in the tent in order to keep the bedding and provisions free of the mire. A water cask served as the Mormon leader's desk. He stared at the map that rested on it.

'How long had you been travelling from Richardson

when the Indians attacked?'

'A day.' Jared could scarcely keep his patience. Why did they not do something? Why were their horses not being saddled? Men being called?

A formidable finger made a circling motion on the map in front of him, a jutting jaw even more pronounced as he thought deeply.

'We must go!' Jared cried despairingly. 'Now! Immediately!'

Slowly the Mormon leader shook his great head. 'No, brother. We would be riding off without directions, and even if, guided by the Lord, we found the Indian camp, we would stand no chance of rescuing Sister Kirkham.'

'You're going to *leave* her?' Jared asked incredulously. 'You're going to stay here, safe and secure, while one of our sisters is . . . Is . . .'

A strong arm circled his shoulders. 'No, brother. I am not going to leave any sister in the hands of Indians without moving heaven and earth to free her. Neither am I going to act incautiously and to no avail. Sit, drink the water Brother Kimball is offering you, and listen.'

'But . . .' Jared glanced around him wildly. They could not sit talking, while Polly, smiling-faced Polly with her merry blue eyes and bobbing ringlets, was helpless in the hands of savages.

At the pressure on his shoulder, he sat. Brother Brigham drew up a box of provisions and sat opposite him.

'The Indians you spoke of must have been Pawnees.'

'Does it matter?' Jared felt that he was losing control of his senses. 'They were Indians . . .'

'Listen.'

At the authority in the deep-sounding voice, Jared did as he was bid.

'I had the pleasure of meeting with a Major of the United States Army a week or so back. He warned me specifically of raiding parties of Pawnees. Two of their women were taken by trappers and treated shamefully before being left to die, their throats slit from ear to ear. The Major warned me that because of this infamous incident, which reflects great shame on our race, the Pawnees were striking with unusual frequency and ferocity.'

Jared felt the blood in his veins turn to water, colder by far than that which ran in the Chariton River.

'Brother Spencer was right. He said the Indians were toying with us . . . That they had no intention of killing us. They wanted revenge. Two white women for the squaws that were killed.'

'Yet they took only one of your party?'

'Sister Lyman does not look like a woman in her father's greatcoat and Sister Spencer was in the Spencer wagon, loading rifles for Nephi and pacifying the children. So they took Polly.'

The nightmare was real and tangible. Polly being treated as the trappers had treated the squaws. Polly left to die, her throat bleeding from the knife of a brave. He groaned and buried his head in his knees.

The strong, calm voice continued. 'The only person who can help us is the man who will know where the Pawnees are camped. The man who can gain entry and plead for the release of our sister.'

'Where is such a man to be found,' Jared asked brokenly. 'Any man approaching the Indians would be killed by an arrow before he even had the chance to state that he came in peace.'

The Mormon leader rose to his feet. 'The man we need is on the trail East to St Louis.'

Jared staggered to his feet. 'Then give me his name. Let me be on my way.'

'His name is Major Richards, the army man I told you I had spoken with when we first reached Richardson Point.'

Jared staggered and was caught in the steadying arms of Brother Kimball. 'You are mistaken, sir. The Major is of a carnal nature. He is not a man who could give us help.'

'The Major is the only man who *can* give us help,' Brigham Young said in a voice that brooked no argument. 'He is half Pawnee himself and if any man can gain entrance to their camp, he can. As for his being carnal minded, I am a shrewd judge of men, brother. The Major may be a man whose private life may not be fitting for a member of the Church of Jesus Christ of Latter-day Saints, but to be carnal is to be evil and the man I met and spoke with is not evil, nor ever could be.'

Jared's head reeled, unable to accept that the only man capable of saving Polly should be the man he had so totally alienated back at Richardson Point. That he was half Pawnee he did not question. If Brigham Young had told him Major Richards was a full-fledged Indian chief, he would have accepted the fact. But Major Richards was the man who had made free with Polly, distressed her. Why, he had fought the man for Polly's honour. How could he now go to him for help?

He stared blindly ahead, seeing nothing—not Brigham Young nor Brother Kimball. Only Polly. Laughing, pretty, Polly.

'Oh Lord, my God,' he groaned, sinking to his knees on the brushwood. 'Help me and guide me.'

The two older men left him to his prayers.

'Send the Adams boys back to Richardson,' Brigham

Young ordered. 'They can change horses there and tell them to ride hard for St Louis and the Major.'

When Jared emerged, hollow-eyed and grey-faced, the boys were already on the trail.

'A horse,' he said weakly to Brigham Young. 'A fresh horse and I'll be on my way.'

'The Adams boys have already left. All that can be done is being done.'

'No . . .' Jared shook his fair hair, his grey eyes hard—those of a man and not a boy. 'Polly Kirkham was to be my wife. A horse, Brother Brigham, if you please.'

The boy was exhausted and swaying on his feet. Nevertheless the Mormon leader nodded at Brother Kimball and a saddled horse with packets of biscuits and water cannisters was led towards them.

'It is my place to ask the Major for help,' Jared said bleakly as they helped him into the saddle. 'Good day, to you, brothers.'

Silently Brigham Young and Brother Kimball and the rest of the party watched as Jared rode away in the direction of Richardson, quickly disappearing in the darkness.

'Was it wise to let him go without his resting first?' Brother Kimball asked tentatively.

The Mormon leader frowned at him so fiercely that Brother Kimball quaked.

'What else would you expect the boy to do?' he roared. 'Of course it wasn't wise, but it was human. Now let's pray to the good Lord to give him strength to accomplish his mission,' and he strode away and offered up a prayer in a resounding voice and as he did so, Jared felt new strength flow into his exhausted limbs.

The Adams boys had already passed Lydia Lyman and the Spencers on the trail. The weary travellers showed no surprise at seeing Jared riding hard towards them in the early dawn. He barely reined in, and then only for long enough to ask how far ahead of him the Adams brothers were.

Time began to blur. When he reached Richardson he had been without any sleep, apart from that taken in the saddle, for countless hours. The Adams boys had changed horses and were already riding hard for St Louis. Lucy Marriot thrust a plate of hot food into his hands as he waited for a fresh horse and provisions.

Josiah Cowley came across to him and said thoughtfully, 'If I were you I would not follow the Adams boys to St Louis.'

'I shall not rest here like a milk sop and allow others to do my work for me,' Jared replied angrily.

'Nay, brother. I do not say that you should. Only that three men in one direction is bad policy when that direction is not known for sure.'

Jared put down his fork. Josiah continued.

'It *was* the Major's intention, when we first met up with him, to ride on to St Louis, but I know that after he left, Sister Kirkham felt it possible he had returned to Fort Leavenworth. Or even to California.'

Jared was beyond asking why Polly should have spent time talking to Brother Cowley on the subject of the hated Major's whereabouts.

'And do you propose I set off to search the whole of the United States between here and California?' he asked bitterly.

'No,' Josiah said. 'I'll ride along with you to Fort Leavenworth. If he has gone to St Louis, the Adams boys will find him. But he may not have. He might very well be returning to his quarters at the Fort.'

There was a quiet conviction in Josiah's voice that

could not be argued with.

'We ride across country for Independence and then on to the Fort. It is a trail I know well, for our home was in Independence before we were driven from it and turned to Nauvoo.'

Jared sat silently for so long that Josiah thought he had fallen into an exhausted sleep. When he spoke he said quietly, 'You are right, brother. Let us ride towards Leavenworth and pray God we catch him on the trail.'

Josiah nodded. 'I see no reason for him to be riding hard.'

Jared hoped fervently that the Major's horse had broken its leg, but did not express this uncharitable view to Josiah, who was busy soothing Eliza, convincing her that he would be safe, and that she would be well looked after by friends in his absence.

Together, Josiah's arm still in a sling, they left Richardson Point and turned South-westwards in the hope of seeing before them a lone, blue uniformed figure. At Josiah's insistence they stopped at regular intervals, feeding and watering the horses and themselves, and resting.

'Did *you* know the Major is half Indian?' Jared asked Josiah on one of the rare occasions they lapsed into conversation.

'No, but it don't surprise me. Not on reflection.'

'No.'

There was nothing else to be said about the Major. He was the last man on earth Jared wished to have to ask for help, and Josiah knew it. Silently they continued on the trail that Josiah could only pray was the one Dart Richards had taken before them.

For a while the weather held and they made good speed, but there was no blue-uniformed figure in the distance and with every day that passed Jared, as well as Josiah, was forced to recognise that their mission was likely to be in vain. Polly could not possibly still be alive.

'Independence,' Josiah said grimly, and pulled his slouch hat low over his brow as they rode into the town. Independence had not been kind to him and his fellow Mormons. He had no desire to be recognised, not with one arm in a sling. The rain began again, coming down in blinding sheets, sending those on the street scurrying to the shelter of their homes. The two tired men turned up the collars of their cloaks and wearily cantered down the main street. By now, not even Josiah expected to see a black stallion or an unmistakable broad-backed figure.

The horse was tethered outside the saloon—a saloon that Josiah, in all his years of living in Independence, had never entered. Saloons were not built by Mormons: nor were they frequented by them.

'It's his horse all right,' Josiah said as Jared hesitated. 'I'd prefer it if you could conduct your business in there without me. I'm no coward, but my face is known in these parts and yours is not.'

Jared nodded, a strange reluctance settling over him. His legs felt like lead. To voluntarily face the Major again, the scornful, insolent eyes: to have to plead for a favour from a man he despised. And to what avail? Polly would no longer be alive to save. She would have been raped. Tortured and murdered by savages, blood kin to the man he was going to for help.

The rain poured down, running in between his cloak and his neck in rivulets. He slammed one fist on top of another. He couldn't. He could *not*. His mind ranged back over the years. Polly, pale faced and quiet in the days after they had taken her in. Polly, racing him to the forge. Polly singing in the kitchen as she baked oatcakes and wheatcakes. Polly, her lips parting softly between his in the autumn darkness as she had shyly accepted his first kiss. Polly helping his mother. Always cheerful, always smiling. Polly, with hair so beautiful Brother Carson had declared it was sinful. Polly, sweet-mouthed and sparkling-eyed. Polly, who had leapt without hesitation to his aid when he had fallen from the wagon. Polly, who would not have been taken if it had not been for his stupidity.

He slid from his horse and walked with a pounding heart towards the wooden doors of the saloon. The moment of entry, when he expected every eye to swivel in his direction, was relatively easy. He had forgotten how near Independence was to the Army Fort. There was more than one man in a blue uniform. There were girls in plenty. Girls dressed as Jared had never seen before: low blouses showing creamy-skinned shoulders and breasts. One black-haired girl stood, a dainty foot on a chair, her skirts over her knee, showing a slim, naked leg. Quickly Jared averted his eyes.

Lazily the girls looked him over. By his appearance and the quality of his clothes, his pockets would be empty. They returned their attention to the soldiers.

There was a haze of blue smoke and as his eyes adjusted themselves to it, Jared saw him. He was leaning negligently against the bar, ignoring the efforts of the girls trying to win his attention. His face was set in the brooding, forbidding lines Jared knew so well. Across the room their eyes met. Only a man completely in control of himself could have refrained from showing surprise at Jared's entry. None showed in the Major's.

A girl with cheap bracelets on her wrist caressed the back of his neck. He brushed her away and the girl pouted. This time, as Jared made directly for the figure at the bar, every eye turned.

'Can I help you?' Dart asked uninterestedly. 'An introduction perhaps?' He carelessly removed the girl's hand from his sleeve and planted it in Jared's to squeals of feminine laughter.

The blood boiled behind Jared's eyes. Cheap perfume clung to him. The girl's laughter was anathema. He wanted to hit the man in front of him as he'd never wanted to hit anyone else before, ever in his life.

'Polly,' he said tightly, exerting all the self-control he was capable of. 'The Pawnees took her.'

Dart's movement was so sudden and unexpected that the girl literally fell. He turned so that his back was to the room, his face to the bar. His hands circled his glass of bourbon.

'How long?' he asked abruptly. 'How long have they had her?'

Jared's exhausted mind refused to work. 'Five days . . . A week . . .'

'Sweet Christ!' Dart said with such savagery that Jared involuntarily stepped backwards.

'What of the others? Susannah and Eliza and Lydia?'

'Susannah and Lydia are safe. Eliza was still at camp.'

The Major seemed to freeze. 'What do you mean? Still at camp. Where were the rest of you?'

'On the trail.' Jared could not seem to raise his voice above a whisper.

'Who was on the trail?' The question was like a whiplash.

'Sister Lyman, the Spencers, Polly and myself.'

Jared had to turn away from the contempt in the older man's eyes.

'Help us,' he mumbled. 'Help *her*.'

Dart didn't drink the bourbon. He pulled on his jacket

and seized his cloak and hat. Outside in the rain Josiah waited with dogged patience. Dart strode across to him.

'Where?' he asked tersely. Josiah told him in as few words as possible.

'Keep him away from me,' Dart said through clenched teeth, indicating Jared. Then he mounted his horse and without another look in their direction galloped off down the mud-bound street.

'Shouldn't we go with him?' Jared asked nervously.

'Not if you value your life,' Josiah replied drily. 'We'll continue on to the Fort and seek further help. We'll be able to rest up there awhile as well. I'm plum tuckered out.'

Jared resisted the impulse to follow in the Major's wake. Josiah had ridden one-armed and the strain had begun to show. Reluctantly he wheeled his horse in the opposite direction to that which Major Richards had taken and, immersed in their own thoughts, they rode towards Fort Leavenworth and help from the army.

Dart had known anger many times, but not the cold, all-pervading fury he felt now. Why the devil had he ever stopped the little wagon train in the first place? Why hadn't he let it rumble on to its own destruction? He could have continued to St Louis and remained oblivious of Polly Kirkham's existence and that of her damnable companions.

He swore volubly and dug his spurs in harder. He had told them they were fools to continue. He had warned them. He had told Nephi explicitly about the scattered bands of marauding Pawnees and *still* they had travelled on. By the time he had left them at Richardson Point he had formed a grudging admiration for Nephi Spencer and a strong liking for the man, yet, despite all Dart had told him, he had been fool enough to set off across country with a handful of women and children and a hot-headed youth.

Damn them to hell, but it was a miracle the lot of them hadn't been killed. Unbidden was the thought that it would have been better if they had been. Better for Polly. Red-Cloud was no lover of the white men or their women. She would get little mercy there.

A watery sun broke through the clouds and the rain drizzled and finally stopped. Red-Cloud, chief of the Pawnees and the man who had been his closest childhood friend. The man who was his half-brother.

He left the track and set off across wild country. As a child the land he was now traversing had been thick with buffalo and elk. Wild herds of antelope and deer had roamed in droves. Now, apart from a few stray herds, they had been driven further West, away from the trappers and encroaching settlers.

He knew where Red-Cloud would camp and he found Indian tracks just before dusk. Tomorrow he would enter the camp, though not as Major Dart Richards of the United States Army. He would enter as the son of a Chief. He would enter as Fire-Dart, the name he had borne for the first eight years of his life.

Despite the biting cold, his jacket and hat were discarded when he remounted his horse in the early hours of dawn. The cloak would go the minute he saw the tepees and the braid had already been ripped from his breeches. A kerchief circled his head, Indian-fashion, his coarse black hair falling straight like that of his half-brother.

They had settled in Happy Valley as he had known they would. He smiled bitterly. Happy when he was a child, and the herds ran thick and wild. Not so happy now when braves became beguiled by rough whiskey and weaker chiefs exchanged their lands for worthless bits of paper. He dismounted, unbuckled his saddle, and left it with his cloak beneath a tangle of brushwood. Then, looking so much like a red-man that Charity Merrill would have fainted in a fit, he rode towards the tepees, his black hair flying in the wind, and the whoop he made was one that could not possibly have come from a white throat as he galloped into the camp.

His manner and bearing, his shouted commands in their own language, deterred the braves who rushed furiously towards him, knives drawn.

'I am Fire-Dart, brother of Chief Red-Cloud,' he cried, his eyes flashing dangerously.

The braves hesitated. He wasn't Pawnee, yet he looked Pawnee. He spoke Pawnee. Beneath his ice-cool exterior Dart's heart was beating with unfamiliar speed. If he had misjudged the situation and the Chief was not Red-Cloud, then he was a dead man, and he knew better than any the painful ways of death that the Pawnees devised.

Squaws in beaded and quilted moccasins gathered around, babies on their hips, eyeing him curiously and admiringly.

'Take me to my brother, Chief Red-Cloud,' he demanded arrogantly, and then, seeing the tepee with the wolf's ears on its apex, he scattered them as if they were dogs and moved towards it.

There was no sign of Polly and if the man who emerged from the Chief's tepee was not Red-Cloud, then it would not matter if she was here or not. He would be unable to save either her or himself.

As he dismounted the braves and squaws waited and watched. Red-Cloud strode to the opening of his tepee and stared at the insolent intruder. Dart Richards returned the stare.

A wry smile curved the corner of his mouth as he faced the man before him. The likeness was indisputable.

'So . . . you have returned.'

'I have returned as I have before.'

'The last time was seven years ago. Seven years is a long time, brother.'

'Not in the life of a man.'

Red-Cloud knew of his life as a man. That he rode and fought with the enemy, but the bonds of childhood had held fast and when they were together they were Red-Cloud and Fire-Dart, friends of equal status and not Indian Chief and Army Major.

A slow smile touched the olive-dark face with its frame of magnificent feathers. 'Come,' he said and held out his hand.

His wives flitted round, silver earrings tinkling, bracelets flashing. Together the two men sat on a sofa of furs and skins and Dart knew that not until after the ritual smoking of the calumet could he ask after Polly. To do so would be insulting. Polly. The tightness in his chest was a physical pain. Merely thinking of her was a torment. To imagine her fear made his flesh run cold. He did not, like Jared, have to wonder what the Pawnee brave who had taken her would do with her. He knew. But would he have killed her after he had raped her, or kept her? Squaws did not like white women. Perhaps her body was even now rotting by the side of a creek or wood. Beads of sweat broke out on his forehead.

'My new wife,' Red-Cloud said as a ravishing dark-haired girl of Polly's age entered with a dish of sweetmeats.

A wide-sleeved scarlet shift, richly embroidered,

reached to her knees and her leggings were fringed and tasselled, her moccasins gleaming with gold. There was gold too, at her ears and throat and dozens of bracelets circled her smooth brown arms. Red-Cloud was obviously pleased with his new wife.

'I, too, have a new wife,' Dart said. To admit to having no wife would be beyond Red-Cloud's comprehension. He kept his voice deliberately careless. 'One of your braves took her from the wagon train she was travelling in five days ago.'

With a click of the fingers the new wife was dismissed. Red-Cloud frowned. 'Was she an important wife to you?'

'Very.'

Their eyes locked.

'Was her hair gold like the sun and her eyes blue like the sky.'

'Yes.'

How Dart found the strength to speak, he did not know. He was experiencing a terror he had never experienced even on the battlefield. In the next few seconds he would know if she was alive or dead.

Red-Cloud's face was grim. 'It is true. Such a one was taken and brought here.' Dart could tell by the intonation in Red-Cloud's voice that she was still alive. The prize of some brave. Captive in a tepee perhaps only yards away. He had lived among Indians long enough to know how they thought—how Red-Cloud was thinking now. A wife was only one of many and a despoiled wife was of little use to a man. Red-Cloud would offer him one of the prettiest of the squaws in recompense for Polly.

He said, still sitting Indian-fashion on the pile of skins as the fire in front of them burned and the smoke wound upwards and out of the hole in the apex of the tepee,

'Even if she has been spoiled, I want her back.'

'She has not been spoiled.' Red-Cloud's face looked like a carving in wood. It was impossible, even for Dart, to know what was going on in his mind. Still only thirty, he was as inscrutable as a practised statesman of eighty. 'Black-Feather brought her here. He wanted to keep her.' He shrugged. 'You know my feelings towards the white man, Fire-Dart. They bring trouble. As do the women. I told him he must enjoy her and kill her.'

How Dart remained immobile he never knew. 'And . . .' he asked, knowing that if he showed any emotion now he would lose all standing in his half-brother's eyes.

'The woman had her flow. Black-Feather has had to wait for his pleasure.'

Dart gave silent thanks to nature and to Indian superstition.

'He will not like to let her go. He has argued with his wives over her. They, too, do not want her in the camp.'

'They will not have her in the camp,' Dart said, feeling his hands tremble with relief as they rested on his knees. 'I shall take her with me.'

Red-Cloud nodded assent, but his eyes were dark. 'Children by the white woman will not be Pawnee, Fire-Dart. They will be our enemies. My new wife has a sister—younger, nearly as beautiful. Come back to us and help us keep our lands from the whites.'

They had met five times since the fur trapper had taken him away. Once, when Dart was twelve, again when he was seventeen and then three more times when he had been in his twenties. At every meeting the distance between them had become greater. Blood brothers; their lives destined them, eventually, to become enemies.

Dart knew that this time was the last that Red-Cloud would ever offer him the old way of life. He knew, too, that he could never come back. The Indian life was the life of his childhood, not his manhood.

He shook his head. 'My life is elsewhere.'

'Then we will not meet again,' Red-Cloud said, and there was sadness in the impassive voice.

He nodded at the brave who waited at the open flap of the tepee and the vermillion-tipped feathers on his head-dress swayed. 'Bring the white woman. Tell Black-Feather she is my brother's squaw. He must look elsewhere for his pleasure.'

Instinctively Dart's hands clenched. When Polly stepped into the tepee she would have to react to him as a rescued wife and there was no way he could speak to her and explain. He had only his eyes. Pray God she read the message in his eyes and had sufficient wit to grasp the situation. He saw himself as she would see him; sitting cross-legged on the furs and skins, his shirt discarded and no sign of a reassuring blue uniform. The bandanna around his head turned him instantly from an arresting-looking man into an unmistakable Indian—a savage. That was the last word she had shouted after him. Would she behave any differently now? He stifled a groan. All his mental senses strained towards her. If he could not reach her by speech he must reach her some other way.

The tepee flap was flung back. 'She is here,' the brave said, and flung a dishevelled and terrified Polly before them.

CHAPTER NINE

POLLY had kicked and struggled, but there had been no mercy in the arms that had captured her.

Lydia Lyman's terrified face receded, thudding hooves covered the icy plain at breakneck speed. If the iron arm released her now she would be crushed instantly by the horses behind. The air was squeezed from her lungs and with a sob she capitulated, hanging as weakly as a rag doll. The Indian heaved her unceremoniously up and across his horse so that she hung like the sacks of wheat Jared brought home from the mill, her fingertips only inches from the snow that flashed beneath her semi-conscious eyes.

She could hardly breathe for the pain in her chest. If she did not raise her head she would pass out completely, yet she could not. Movement was impossible. She could do nothing but grit her teeth and pray for survival.

The horse sweated beneath her and against her body she could feel the rough leggings of the Indian and his heat and his smell. Dear Lord. What sort of survival? She had heard rumours of what happened to white women if they fell prey to marauding Indians. She remembered the men in the dry goods store in Corrington. She had thought that nothing could have been worse than that. From her undignified position she caught fleeting glimpses of the other riders. Near to the painted faces were even more terrifying. She became dimly aware of a shouted conflict between her captor and the others and hope rose within her breast. Perhaps, after all, they would let her go. A hand came down hard on her calico skirts as the Indian emphasised a word that was an unmistakable no. Polly closed her eyes and fought hysteria. She had not been taken by the raiding party as a whole: she had been taken by one warrior and the hand that came down, slapping her where no one, not even her father had slapped her, was one of ownership.

Fear drowned all thought. Her mind was paralysed with it. The incessant movement of the horse beneath her chest was too much to be borne. She could breathe no longer. The snow swam, merging into blood red and then darkness and her last conscious image was not of Lydia Lyman's outstretched hands, or of Jared's agonised face, but of Dart Richards. If he had been with them she would not have been taken. Yet it was she herself who had driven him away, calling him a savage. She had not truly known what the word meant, but she did now. She whispered his name helplessly and sank into merciful oblivion.

She was returned to consciousness by being thrown brutally to the ground. The Indian slipped lightly from his horse and again she was aware of angry voices and of conflict. She struggled to her knees, her hands clenched tightly in her lap, her legs too weak to support her.

The ground of the campsite had been cleared of snow, churned into mud by many feet. The raiding party had dismounted, hurrying squaws led the steaming horses away. Children stared at her curiously. She strained her eyes beyond the tepees and into the distance, hoping vainly to recognise some landmark. All was strange and devoid of any other habitation. They were in a valley bounded by ice-covered rocks. A stream ran nearby, rushing swiftly with melting snow. Stark, leafless willows clustered on its banks.

The children were joined by dogs and from the nearest tepee squaws in shifts of rough linen and beads eyed her hostilely. She rose unsteadily to her feet. The tepees were clustered in threes and fours, and then, from one far bigger than all the others, she saw the brave who had taken her emerge. He had been to his Chief. She saw the rich bison skins that covered the tepee, the wolf's ears that crowned the apex, the ornamentation of crosses, circles and arabesques that surrounded the entrance. Perhaps the Indian Chief would have pity on her, would allow her to return to Richardson Point or the Chariton.

Her captor's headband was black and beaded, his feathers a blue-black plume. The expression in his eyes as he caught hold of her was no different to the expression in the eyes of the men at Corrington.

'No . . . Please . . .'

There was no way she could escape him and throw herself on the Chief's mercy. He began to drag her in his wake and she called imploringly to the squaws who watched.

'Please! Help me! Oh please!'

No help was forthcoming. The women turned their backs. The children watched and the dogs nosed at their heels. She was flung inside a tepee full of strange smells, dark and overpowering. A girl not much older than herself spat angrily at her captor and was rewarded by a stinging blow to her cheek. As Polly was flung on to a pile of skins the girl was ejected forcibly.

He stood above her and in the darkness white teeth flashed in a smile of anticipation.

'No . . .' She tried to scramble to her feet, but with

animal speed he pinioned her to the ground. She screamed and screamed, but this time there was no Dart to hear her and to save her.

Her legs were cruelly parted and then, as suddenly as he had seized her, he let her go with an oath, kicking at her violently. She shrank back, panting. The triumphant expression on his face had turned to one of cheated fury. With a shower of abuse he kicked at her again and then turned on his heels, the tepee flap opening and falling closed behind him.

Polly began to tremble and then to shake. She wrapped her arms around herself, hugging herself tightly, fighting for control. For some reason she had been given a respite. She had to make use of it. She had to overcome the paralysing effect of her fear and think. Slowly the shaking eased. Her teeth no longer chattered. She took deep, steadying breaths. Think. She must think. Instinctively her arms lowered to press against the ache in her stomach and then halted. The inconvenience that she had to endure each month had saved her. She had more than minutes in which to think of a way of escape: she had days. He would not touch her again until her time of the month had passed.

The squaw came back into the tepee and sulkily handed Polly a plate that contained meat and beans. Unwillingly she ate; whatever happened to her she would need her strength and she would need allies. The squaw might prove to be one, for she obviously resented Polly's presence in what appeared to be her home. Was the Indian who had taken her the squaw's husband? If so, it would account for her bitter anger. The food warmed her. The ache in her stomach comforted her. She was, for the moment, safe. She had only to gain the squaw's compliance, and escape would be easy. Even without help she would achieve freedom. She was filled with determination and confidence. It received its first dent when the squaw adamantly refused to enter into any sort of communication with her. No matter how much she wanted to be rid of Polly, she feared Black-Feather's wrath too much to be active in aiding her.

That night Polly was ejected from the tepee and left with a covering of skins on the frozen ground, staked by the wrists to a stout wooden pole. The squaw's eyes had been gloating as she retreated into the warmth of the tepee with her brave. Polly wished her well of him and concentrated on freeing her wrists from the thongs that bound her.

The dogs prowled around, growling and then falling silent and sleeping. She chafed the leather against the poles. She chewed it with her teeth and she cried in exasperation as nothing weakened it. In the morning she was still bound as ignominiously as a beast of burden.

For the next few days that was how she was treated. The hard work she had endured on the trail was nothing to the work Black-Feather's squaw demanded of her. At her first proud refusal the squaw called her husband and the Indian had whipped her back until it had bled. She had not refused again. Her determination and optimism was gradually eroded as the third day slipped into the fourth and she was still no nearer escape. The braves were constantly armed, small tomahawks at their belts. On the fifth day she washed in the bitterly cold stream and knew there was no longer any reason for Black-Feather to refrain from taking her inside his tepee.

The squaw knew too, and her eyes were malevolent as Polly ground kernels of wheat for bread and carried back-breaking buckets of water from the stream to the camp.

The weather was changing. The stream gushed with the melted snow from the hills in the distance. Spring was coming, but it was a spring Polly doubted she would see. That night, and perhaps for several nights after, Black-Feather would take her in his tepee and then he would kill her. The escape she had thought so easy had proved impossible. Dusk was approaching. Across the campfire she saw Black-Feather nearing her, and she realised that he knew she was no longer untouchable.

She brushed her hair away from her eyes in a helpless gesture. It would have been better if he had taken her days ago. Better if she had died that first or second night and not lived for days with vain hopes of escape or rescue.

She turned her head sharply as she heard the sound of a galloping horse. The hunting parties had returned long ago, and a wild, unreasoning emotion surged briefly through her. It was extinguished almost immediately. Why should she think that he would come and save her? He did not even know of her capture. He would be in St Louis now, or at his fort. Yet she felt so near to him. She began to cry. Not for the fate that awaited her, but for Major Dart Richards, who would never know that she loved him. Jared, foolish and headstrong, had seen to it that they had parted in anger. She wiped her tears away. It was possible that Dart Richards had already forgotten her. Possible that he had never wanted her love in the first place.

The stranger was entering the bison-covered tepee with the wolf's ears on its crown and Black-Feather was approaching.

She began to run, making one last attempt to throw herself at the mercy of the Indian chief, but Black-feather had seized her shoulders. Time had, at last, run out.

The squaw had gone, but a meal was prepared: a meal that Black-Feather ate alone, the whip on the ground beside him, within hand's reach if Polly dared to move from the pile of skins that served as bedding.

From outside Polly smelt the now-familiar aroma of wood smoke mingled with buffalo chips. Black-Feather sat cross-legged, eyeing her lasciviously whilst he ate. There seemed to Polly only one decision left to make: to be killed making a hopeless attempt to escape, or to be killed after being subjected to the violation of her body. The first choice seemed preferable. She saw the whip and the tomahawk in his belt. She knew she would never succeed, but she was beyond caring. She would not go to her death passively and after satisfying Black-Feather's lust. He rose and threw the bones of his dinner to the dogs outside. Polly sprang to her feet and hurtled towards the open flaps. He caught her so violently that she screamed with the pain, and then she was on the floor, thrashing in the straw and dirt, fighting to free herself of his weight and the unspeakable, brutal, searching hands.

The voices were loud and sharp and authoritative and the nightmare paused. He was on his feet and she was being dragged to hers. Dragged by braves who had never shown interest in her before. Dragged outside, away from the tepee—away from Black-Feather whose fury showed in every line of his face and in the virulent words he hurled after her.

Polly felt fleeting relief and then increasing panic. She had been saved from Black-Feather's attentions, but for what? What further horror awaited her? It was dusk now. The Indians were quiet and watchful as they crowded around the camp fires. Half falling in the wake of the two braves who held her, Polly saw the tepee with the wolf's ears loom large.

The Chief. She was being brought before the Indian Chief. Her eyes had grown accustomed to the darkness of the tepees and this one was large, a fire burning in the centre, smoke escaping through the apex above.

Behind the flames was a large bank of rich furs and skins and two men, one with a vermillion-tipped headdress of hundreds of white feathers, the other an unadorned replica.

A squaw she had seen before only at a distance, with gold at her ears and throat, glided past her and for the first time Polly was almost sure the glance she was given had been friendly.

The braves who had brought her had now released her. She stood upright and free. She tilted her chin defiantly. Whatever the reason for her summons she would not plead nor cry.

The Chief was speaking and asking a question, but not of her. The voice that answered was unmistakable. Polly swayed on her feet, her eyes searching the firelit gloom. Where was he? How had he found her?

'Dart . . .' She stepped forward and then halted.

The flames from the fire crackled and burned brightly. The Chief's face, framed by its headdress, was impassive. As impassive as the face of the man next to him. The Indian next to him. Familiar eyes burned in the still, expressionless face. They held hers, forbidding her to cry out, halting her where she stood.

'My woman,' Dart said in a voice of near-indifference, 'has not been well looked after.'

Her hair had not seen a brush for a week. There was dirt on her face from her struggle with Black-Feather. Her gown was rent and filthy with mud.

She opened her mouth to speak, but his black eyes gleamed with a desperate urgency that did not accord with his indifferent manner.

She remained silent and uncomprehending. The Indian Chief nodded, and with a clap of his hands the gold-ornamented squaw reappeared. He spoke to her in Pawnee and the girl took hold of Polly's arm, intent on leading her away.

Polly protested, her eyes seeking Dart's. He gave an imperceptible nod of his dark head and her fear died. No harm would come to her now. No harm could possibly come to her when Dart was near.

The adjoining tepee was full of giggling, mischievous squaws. All hostility had vanished. Water steamed in a large bowl. Her clothes were removed; her hair fingered and commented upon.

How on earth had Dart managed it, Polly thought wonderingly as she was bathed and the pretty squaw, who she rightly assumed was the Chief's favourite wife, stroked perfumed oil on her temples and wrists.

He had spoken to her in English, but English was not the language he was speaking to the Indian Chief at his side. Did the Pawnees believe him Indian, or did they know he was in the army? Was his Indian mode of dress a sign of friendship or had he deceived them into thinking he was one of them?

The Chief's young wife gave her a pair of leggings like her own, lavishly fringed and tasselled, and an overdress with a beadwork sash and moccasins for her feet. Her hair was rubbed with oil and brushed sleekly, the squaws giggling as it sprang stubbornly back into curling ringlets. At last it was to their satisfaction, firmly smoothed and hanging glossily to her shoulders and down her back.

When she was returned to the Chief's tepee the air was sweet with the smoke of the calumet. The Chief's wife sat, cross-legged, and Polly sat likewise, watching and wondering and waiting.

Red-Cloud's eyes held more than a flicker of interest as they rested briefly on her. Black-Feather had not been as foolish as he had thought, and his brother had been quite right in insisting on the return of such a wife.

Long into the night the two brothers talked, knowing it would be for the last time. Polly could feel, but could not understand, the intense emotion that pervaded the tepee. By the time Dart rose and walked towards her, her back ached and her eyes smarted from the smoke of the fire.

'Come, wife,' he said and as Polly gasped, his glittering eyes silenced her protests.

He wore only breeches and his powerful shoulder and chest muscles gleamed in the firelight. Outside was snow and ice. Where was his jacket? His cape? He had already passed her. Instinctively, as she had seen the Indian women do, she fell into step behind him. The Chief's squaw smiled, her eyes dancing. What was amusing her? Where were they going without cloaks and in the middle of the night? By the light of the remaining campfires she could see the familiar outline of his horse, but Dart did not walk towards him. Instead, he entered a nearby tepee and held the flap back for her to follow. A fire had been lit for them. The skins and furs were more opulent than those in Black-Feather's tepee. Clean straw covered the ground. They were alone.

In the firelight he looked strangely forbidding, the coarse black hair hanging Indian-style, the high cheekbones so like those of the Indian chief.

'Why have we not left?' she asked, and was ashamed of the tremor in her voice.

'We will leave in the morning.' His voice was curt. 'To leave now would be discourteous when Red-Cloud has offered us his hospitality.'

'But how . . . ? Why . . . ? I don't understand.'

His manner was so unexpected that she felt like crying. In her relief at seeing him, at being saved, she had forgotten the hideous scene at their last parting.

'It is not for you to understand. It is for you to do as you are told.'

Polly's eyes widened. 'Like a *squaw*?' she asked indignantly.

His eyes were mirthless. 'Yes, Miss Kirkham. Like a squaw. *My* squaw.'

'Never. I'd rather die first. I'd . . .'

Lazily he opened the flap of the tepee so that the cold night air blew frostily into the dark warmth.

'Then die, Miss Kirkham. Or return to Black-Feather. Whichever suits you best.'

'You're a fiend!' she hissed, misery and fury fighting for mastery.

'I'm a fool,' he agreed carelessly. 'Risking life and limb to save an empty-headed chit for an even emptier-headed young man who would stab me in the back given half a chance.'

He was gazing at her with unconcealed contempt. There was not a trace of the love that had shone so briefly in his eyes in the copse of beech trees. It had been there. She knew it as surely as she knew the light that had kindled her own. And she, herself, had killed that love. She had allowed Jared's hot-headedness to destroy her happiness, and she knew no way of rectifying it. The man in front of her was a cold, menacing stranger who would listen to no excuses or explanations. She had only her pride left and it found its outlet in anger.

'Am I to understand that I owe my safety entirely to the fact that you told the Indian Chief I am your wife?' she asked, trying to keep her voice steady.

'I imagined that was clearly obvious to you when we were in Red-Cloud's presence. I did not see you object then.'

Her eyes flashed. 'To have done so would have been to have lost my life!'

'I'm glad your grasp of the situation is so acute,' he said dryly. 'As it is, no doubt you realise that unless you lower your voice and behave more in the manner of a rescued and loving wife, Red-Cloud may well become suspicious.'

Her cheeks flushed as he gave her a cool look of appraisal.

'Indian dress suits you.' His smile mocked her. '. . . wife.'

She drew back her hand to deliver a stinging blow to his cheek, but he caught her wrist in a steel-like grip. 'One word of protest from you, Miss Kirkham, and you go back to Black-Feather's arms and not your Mormon's.'

His face was only inches away from hers. She could feel his breath on her cheek and she was helpless, her whole body responding to him. He felt her tremble, saw the heat at the back of her eyes and, unable to stop himself, he seized hold of her, kissing her with barely suppressed violence. She resisted furiously, and then, as his mouth crushed hers, gave a sob of capitulation and yielded willingly as he lowered her beneath him to the soft richness of the skins.

She was helpless, murmuring his name, clinging to him in desperate need. Her breasts in their thin covering were pressed flat beneath his naked chest. The warmth of his touch spread through her like a fire. Her body strained against the weight of his and as his hands gripped the waistband of her leggings, pulling them down till the slim, white outline of her hips showed, she moaned in eagerness to be free of her clothes, to feel his flesh against hers. Suddenly he became perfectly still, staring down at her, the abrasively masculine lines of his face accentuated by the firelight.

'Whore,' he said softly, imprisoning her wrists above her head, kneeling astride her.

'No . . .' she whispered dazedly, 'it's not true.'

'It is true.' His voice was cruel. 'I saw with my own eyes. The moment Jared Marriot entered camp I was forgotten, wasn't I? And in case I was foolish enough to betray you, you lied to young Marriot and said I had forced my attentions upon you. I've met women before like you, Polly Kirkham. Women who like to see men fighting over them. Women who make love in dark corners and ignore the objects of their desire in the light of day.'

'No!' her voice was anguished.

A bitter smile twisted his mouth. 'I understand perfectly,' he said. 'When you lay in my arms in the beech wood you were betrothed to Jared Marriot, as you still are.'

'No! You *don't* understand.'

He laughed softly and the sound sent chills of fear down her spine. 'There's no one to see now, Polly Kirkham. No Latter-day Saints; no Jared Marriot. Only I will know the unfaithfulness of your heart.' His hands tightened their hold so that she cried out in pain.

'Whore,' he repeated, as his mouth came down hard on hers.

She tried to push him away, but he was too strong for her. His lips seared hers and even as she struggled she could feel desire surging through her. She fought it as she fought him—desperately and vainly. Her shift had been ripped from her back. In the firelight his hands were olive-dark on the rose-tipped whiteness of her breasts. She moaned, begging to be free, knowing that resistance was no longer possible. His tongue inflamed and tormented her. She was his to do with as he pleased and the knowledge brought shameful tears. She was everything he said she was. All the ugly words he had called her were true.

Abruptly he raised his head, gazing down at her anguished face, at the tears that flowed unrestrainedly. Then, with a groan and an oath, he rolled his weight away from her and lay silently, staring up to where the first pale light of dawn filtered into the tepee. She turned her face into the furs, her hands pressed close to her mouth so that he should not hear the sobs that wracked her body.

They left an hour later, their only well-wisher Chief Red-Cloud himself. The two men embraced and in the cold of dawn the Chief undid his cloak of mink skins and fastened it around Dart's shoulders. Numbly Polly accepted Dart's hand and allowed herself to be seated behind him on his stallion. As they left the last of the tepees, he turned. Red-Cloud stood alone in the early light, a soft breeze ruffling the feathers on his magnificent head-dress. The brothers raised their arms in a last gesture of farewell and then the horse broke into a gallop. Polly had no alternative but to circle Dart's waist with her arms. As she did so she felt his body stiffen in tense hostility and the knife in her heart went deeper, inflicting even more anguish. He thought her a whore and she had no way of proving otherwise.

At the point where he had hidden his saddle and clothing, he reined in and dismounted. Polly stood and shivered as he saddled his horse and then removed his cloak and headband and replaced his jacket and cape. With his fingers he brushed back his hair and put back on the blue, wide-brimmed hat with its gold tassels. The transformation was nearly complete. Only the ripped braid from his breeches prevented him from looking as immaculate and commanding as ever. Silently he put the cloak around her shoulders and silently she accepted it. For a second he paused, as if about to speak, and then the moment was gone. It was too late.

They rode until the sun was high in the sky and Polly tried hard not to feel hungry and harder still not to feel thirsty.

'Where are we going?' she ventured at last.

'To the Chariton and your Mormon friends,' he replied curtly.

At last, just when she was beginning to think she could hold on no longer, he reined in beside a stream.

'The water is clean,' he said, bending down on the bank and scooping up handfuls to drink. She did likewise, though the cold nearly numbed her fingers.

He walked back towards his horse, but she remained standing, biting her bottom lip, summoning courage.

'I'm waiting,' he said tersely.

She swung around, looking strangely royal in the ankle-length fur, her gold hair shining like a crown in the sunlight. Her voice trembled as she said bravely,

'I was never betrothed to Jared Marriot. I never told him that you forced your attentions on me. I tried to tell him that I was in love with you and he would not let me finish.'

She walked back towards the horse and he made no move to help her mount.

'And I,' he said slowly, 'did not pick the fight with Marriot. I would never have knocked him unconscious except that he had a knife in his belt and intended to use it.'

They stared at each other and the water rushed by, filling the silence.

'I am not a whore,' she said after a few minutes, and there was defiance in her voice.

'I am not a savage,' he said, and there was the merest hint of amusement in his.

She gave a tremulous smile and asked tentatively: 'Then may I ride with you as I did before, and may we be friends?'

His hands reached down and she was drawn into his arms and lifted in front of him.

'We may not be friends,' he said, and she felt a plunging sensation near her heart.

'But why? I have explained . . .'

'Because I do not wish to marry my friends,' he said huskily, and then he was kissing her, his mouth hot and demanding. Beneath them the horse moved impatiently. Dart raised his head, his eyes full of unsatisfied desire.

'Why does making love to you always have to be so damned difficult? We're either in a snowdrift with a wagon train of hymn-singing Mormons rumbling towards us, or astride a horse, or . . .'

'. . . in a bed of furs and skins and calling each other names,' Polly finished, her cheeks flushed, her eyes glowing.

'I've changed my mind about heading for the Chariton,' he said, his hands tightening on her waist. 'We'll ride straight for the Fort instead.'

'Why?' She laid her head against his broad chest as the stallion once more began to canter steadily forward.

'Because there is a preacher at the Fort,' he said.

Polly smiled, thinking of the Latter-day Saints. 'There are hundreds at the Chariton.'

'A marrying preacher,' Dart said, his voice deep and tender and loving.

'If you were a Mormon then Nephi or Josiah or any of the elders could marry us.'

'If you were an Indian, then Red-Cloud could have married us.'

She sighed contentedly. 'Then as you are not a Mormon and I am not an Indian, a preacher at the Fort it will have to be.'

He smiled his devastating smile. Wrapped from head to foot in skins of wild mink, held securely in the arms of the man she loved, Polly put away for ever all memories of Black-Feather and Corrington. The past was past. Only the future mattered. The future and Dart.

The blast of the bugle startled her from sleep.

'What is it? What's the matter?'

'Nothing,' Dart said with barely concealed annoyance. 'Only my brother officers and half the United States army.'

Polly was acutely aware of her fringed leggings and exotic cloak.

'God's teeth!' he uttered furiously. 'There's half a division of Mormons with them!'

Polly looked and her heart sank. Jared's fair hair was unmistakable.

'I think they've come to rescue us,' she said unhappily.

Dart's face was grim. 'Then the sooner we tell them they're not needed, the better,' he said and dug his spurs in, riding hard to meet them.

CHAPTER TEN

'POLLY! Polly!' Disobeying the strict orders of the Captain, Jared broke ranks and rode at breakneck speed towards them.

'You're safe!' His face was so boyishly joyful that Polly had not the heart to do anything but smile and say,

'Yes, Jared. I'm safe.'

'Your clothes!' His grey eyes registered her bizarre clothing and were instantly concerned.

'Petticoats and cambric gowns are not very suitable in an Indian encampment,' Polly answered lightly, showing no intention of removing herself from the blue-jacketed arms that surrounded her.

It was obvious from her demeanour that she had suffered no harm. Jared steeled himself to face the silent Major and said uncertainly,

'I thank you from the bottom of my heart, sir.'

Dart merely nodded. The boy's very presence annoyed him. He turned his attention instead to the approaching Captain.

The Captain had halted his perfectly-drilled men some little way distant. Instinct told him that Major Richards might not want details of his chivalrous rescue of the Mormon girl made public. His riding into the Pawnee camp would only renew gossip as to his background—and his loyalties. It was a delicate subject and one the Captain intended handling tactfully.

He saluted respectfully. 'I was informed by this young

man and others that one of their party had been taken prisoner by marauding Indians. I had heard that the Pawnees were at present at their old camping ground and was on my way there.'

Dart's face showed none of the relief he felt. A contingent the size the Captain was leading could never have entered Red-Cloud's presence peacefully. There would have been deaths on both sides and a further rift between the Indians and the army.

'Very commendable of you, Captain. But you would have done better to have approached with a smaller party. The girl was unharmed and treated respectfully.'

Polly grimaced. She was sure Dart knew what he was doing, but being manacled to a pole, like a dog, was not her idea of being treated with respect. Neither was the rape Black-Feather had so obviously intended.

'Yes, sir.'

'Order your men back to the Fort.'

'Yes, sir,' and then hesitantly, 'The Mormons, sir. Some of them are pretty distraught.'

'Leave the Mormons to me, Captain. I'll rejoin you later.'

'Yes, sir.'

The Captain saluted again, stole a curious look at the fur-clad, blonde-haired girl sitting so complacently against his Major's chest, and did as he was bid.

Nephi and Josiah and Tom Marriot rode up to them, their faces wreathed in smiles.

'I thought you were dead, child,' Tom Marriot said as he dismounted and held out his arms.

Polly slid from the horse's back and hugged him tightly.

'I am quite safe, as you can see.'

'But the Indians . . .'

Behind her, Dart cleared his throat. She smiled wryly.

'The Indians were perfectly respectful to me, as the Major has just informed the Captain.'

She could almost feel Dart exude a sigh of relief.

Jared wanted to hug her too, but she no longer looked like the Polly he knew. Her hair still gleamed with aromatic oils and hung sleekly down her back. If some of the Latter-day Saints had thought her ringlets sinful, they would surely have thought the sight of her long flying hair pagan. The rich skins, clasped at her throat by an amulet depicting a wolf, clothed her as though she were a fairytale princess—or an Indian princess. He felt strangely ill at ease with her.

'We rode on to the Fort,' Josiah was saying to Dart. 'By the time we had persuaded the Captain to act, Tom and some of the others from Richardson and Chariton had joined us. The Adams brothers had spread the news of Polly's capture and everyone that could be spared rode with us.'

'So I can see,' Dart said drily, surveying the motley array that clustered on horseback around them.

'Come, child.' Tom Marriot turned his attention to Polly. 'Let's have you out of those heathen clothes and looking like a decent Christian again.' He was already making room for her on his horse.

Polly hesitated, aware of the score of eyes upon her. She had no desire to ride with Tom. Her place was with Dart. Their eyes met and he nodded his head fractionally. Understanding, she gave him a reluctant grin and mounted Tom Marriot's horse.

'Tell the rest of your company to ride back to their camps, whether it be Richardson or Chariton,' Dart said to Nephi authoritatively. 'I want Miss Kirkham to be brought to the Fort.'

Nephi nodded. No doubt there were many questions for Polly to answer. Josiah waved a cheery goodbye, but Jared rode steadfastly behind them, accompanied by Nephi. Where Polly went, he went. He owed heartfelt thanks to the Major, and felt them, but still he did not like the man—or trust him.

The sun shone, the snow was rapidly melting. Young grass sprang bravely upwards, replacing the blanket of white with tender green shoots.

Dart rode ahead of them and Polly savoured the sight of him. At Leavenworth they would be married. There would be no more bitter-sweet moments curtailed all too soon by misunderstandings on both sides. They would have all the time in the world to love: the rest of their lives. And not in snowdrifts or tepees or on horseback. She smiled happily at her thoughts and Tom looked at her curiously.

'Your adventure does not seem to have harmed you, child.'

'No, Tom, it hasn't. And Tom . . .'

'Yes?' He looked at her fondly, this girl who was like a daughter to him.

'I'm not a child. I'm a woman.'

'Aye.' Tom's assent was wry. Jared knew that well enough; as did the Major. He had a feeling that his difficulties were still not over. His son had spoken as if his marriage to Polly was imminent, yet Tom was astute enough to have seen the protective way Major Richards' arms had enfolded Polly as they had approached. He also knew that Jared, as was his nature, was being over-optimistic. Polly had never agreed to marry him. He had tried to warn him, prepare him for disappointment, but all to no avail. When Polly was rescued from the Indians, Jared insisted he was marrying her. His father had tried to warn him that Polly might be no more eager for marriage than she had been previously, but Jared had turned a deaf ear. It seemed to him that Jared would have to learn the hard way that it was unwise to assume anything. Especially if that assumption concerned women.

Polly's heart was exultant as they rode between the sun-dried brick towers flanking the gates of Fort Leavenworth and into the spacious quadrangle. Soldiers, going about their daily business, stopped and stared. Then, seeing the Major at the head of the strange party, they hurried on their way. Major Richards was not a man to appreciate open curiosity as to his doings.

As they slid from their horses Dart strode across to her, saying briefly, 'I must report at once to my commanding officer. Say nothing at all about what happened at the camp—for my sake.'

'All right.'

Why did it matter so much? She had no time to ask him. He was already striding towards a long, low building, removing his gauntlets, while a young soldier led his horse away for a well-deserved rub-down and rest.

The Captain who had greeted them earlier crossed quickly towards them.

'My wife has arranged a suitable change of clothing for Miss Kirkham, and also a hot meal.'

Polly followed him gratefully: a hot meal. When last had she eaten one? Or at least one that was appetising.

The Captain's wife was young and pretty and chattered incessantly. Nothing of what she said penetrated Polly's tired brain. So much had happened and now she was overcome with weariness and she wanted to sleep. But not until after she had seen Dart again.

Polly ate gratefully and then discarded the Indian shift

with its delicate embroidery and the leggings which had been so suitable for riding, and allowed herself the pleasure of a soak in a hot tub of soapy water. The gown that had been laid out for her was a little less modest than the ones she was used to. A lace fichu at the neck plunged quite daringly before it reached the tiny buttons of the bodice.

'Your young man wishes to speak to you,' the Captain's wife said and disappeared discreetly before Polly could stop her.

As she left the room Jared entered. The dress Polly wore exposed the crevice between her breasts. Jared averted his eyes manfully. Immodest or not, at least it was better than the heathenish clothes she had escaped from the Indians in.

'I hope you don't think less of me for not riding to the camp with the Major, Polly, but he would not let me. I pleaded with him to let me join him, but he forbade it utterly.'

'He was quite right to do so,' Polly said gently. 'You played your part, Jared, and without your ride to the Major I would not be alive now.'

He took her hands in his and she grasped them tightly. 'Thank you, Jared. I know what I owe you and will never forget it.'

His grey eyes were tortured. 'I know the Major says you were treated with respect, but though the others may believe him, I do not. I saw the way you were taken . . . the warrior . . .'

Polly looked away quickly, afraid her eyes would betray her.

'Polly, dearest. I *know*. I know what you have suffered at the hands of those unspeakable savages.' His throat tightened. 'I have come to tell you that it makes no difference to me.'

'No difference?' A small frown creased her forehead as she returned her gaze to his, not understanding.

He licked his lips and said awkwardly, 'I still want you for my wife, Polly. No matter what happened to you at the Indian camp. I swear I shall never mention it between us. I shall treat you just as if, just as if . . .'

'Oh, Jared!' Polly did not know whether to feel despair, impatience or amusement. 'Nothing happened to me at the Indian camp. Nothing that could prevent me becoming the honourable wife of any man.'

The relief in his eyes was pathetic.

'But I will *not* marry you, Jared. I've told you so many times and I have not changed my mind.'

'You must.' His voice was urgent. '*I* believe that you are telling the truth, Polly, but others will not. For ever you will be pointed out as the girl who was captured by the Indians. No decent man will marry you now.'

'He would, if he loved me,' Polly replied tartly.

Jared shook his shock of fair hair. 'If you don't marry me, Polly, you will have no husband.'

Sparks flashed in her eyes. 'That is where you are wrong, Jared. I am to marry the only man I want to marry. I am to marry Major Richards.'

If she had slapped him across the face she could not have shocked him more.

She said, trying to soften the blow, 'I am the last person in the world you should marry, Jared. You would for ever be apologising for my behaviour, chastising me, forgiving me. It would be awful tedious for both of us. The girl you *should* marry is Emily Merrill. She would make a fine wife and she loves you. I also think that you love her, but are not yet aware of it.'

'Polly!'

She was at the door. She turned, her happiness seeming to give her an inner luminosity. His next four words destroyed it utterly.

'The Major has gone. He left the Fort almost immediately.'

The smile froze on her face. 'No! He can't have! It's not true!'

She opened the door and began to run. He could not leave her. He would not. She half fell up the wooden steps leading to the building Dart had entered. The grey-haired man at the massive desk paused in his conversation with the Captain. Both stared at her. She was clutching her chest, gasping for breath.

'The Major! Where is he?'

'My dear young lady, I . . .'

'When will he be back? He must be coming back. He hasn't left for good: he couldn't have!'

The men exchanged glances and the Captain saluted and retreated. As the door closed behind him, the General emerged from behind his desk and took her arm, leading her protestingly towards a chair.

'Major Richards had duties to perform elsewhere.'

She shook her head, trying to clear it. Trying to think.

'No,' she said repeatedly, clasping and unclasping her hands in agitation. 'He would not go without speaking to me. When will he be back? By nightfall? By morning?'

'I'm afraid you do not understand. The Major is riding for Fort Kearney. He will not be returning to Leavenworth.'

The blood thudded in her ears and her heart drummed painfully in her chest.

'But he must! There has been some mistake.'

'There has been no mistake. I gave the Major his orders myself.'

'Is there no message for me?' she asked wildly. 'No letter?'

'The Major wished to leave a letter, but I advised against it.'

'*You* advised against it!' Polly's anguish was replaced with blinding anger. 'What right have you, sir? What right to send him away without even allowing him to speak with me!'

The Captain, stationed outside the door, flinched. No one spoke to the General like that. Least of all a slip of a girl young enough to be his grandchild.

The General's eyes were grave. 'I see that you will not be satisfied with my explanation, Miss Kirkham, and must be given a fuller one. Major Richards told me that he had made a proposal of marriage to you. Indeed, after giving me a most unsatisfactory account of your rescue from the Pawnees, he requested not food or drink, but a preacher.'

Polly trembled with relief. For a moment she thought she would faint and then the mist cleared and she said, 'Why then did you order him away?'

'My dear child, you were in a vulnerable situation. Naturally you felt an overwhelming gratitude to Major Richards and . . .'

'I felt love for Major Richards,' Polly said defiantly, refusing to let his eyes slide away from hers. 'I did so *before* I was captured and I do so now.'

'I'm sure that you did,' the General said indulgently, in a voice that indicated he felt nothing of the kind. He was used to infatuations and the havoc they could cause. He had reared five daughters of his own. 'Unfortunately, Major Richards has been less than truthful with you.'

Her heart began to thump irregularly. What did the General mean? Was Dart already married? Had he proposed and regretted it and asked for a preacher out of honour and obligation?

'He has not told you of his background or why it is impossible for a girl of your upbringing to marry him.'

Polly's confusion deepened. His background? He was a Major. As for her upbringing, she was nothing but an orphan, travelling homeless across the plains with a party she knew the General would classify as religious fanatics.

'Mr Spencer has informed me that your mother was Mary Ellen Jameson, the daughter of Charles Jameson of Wilmington.'

Polly nodded.

'I knew your grandfather very well. I'm a Wilmington man by birth.'

Polly had no desire to hear the General's reminiscences of his youth.

'I fail to see what that has to do with your sending Major Richards away and disapproving of his plans to marry me.'

The General folded his hands patiently on one knee. 'The Major,' he said compassionately, 'is not like other men.'

'I know that. It is the reason I wish to marry him.'

The General winced. Somewhere between Wilmington and Fort Leavenworth good manners and breeding had been abandoned.

'He is not a white man, but a half breed.'

Polly sat very still. The General now had her full attention.

'He was the result of a rape on a settler's wife in Nebraska. The woman carried the child, but obviously had no desire to rear it. He was left, hours old, outside a Pawnee encampment.'

'The Pawnees being responsible for his birth?' Polly asked in a voice that the General regarded as unnaturally calm.

'Yes.' He had no wish to go into indelicate details with the forthright young lady before him. 'He lived with them for eight years and was then befriended by a fur trapper and his sister. The sister was not without means. Major Richards received a good education and has carved out a very admirable life for himself, considering his handicap.'

'Of course.' Polly's voice was expressionless, but she could imagine the handicaps the General spoke of. The name-calling; never being fully accepted; a tight knot of pain gathered deep within her. She had called him a savage, as so many others must have done.

'Please continue, General.'

The General, glad that she was now composed and listening to sense, continued.

'There was an unfortunate incident some years ago. Richards was a Captain then. A brilliant soldier. There was an infatuation. The sister of a brother officer. To be fair to Richards, I believe the lady in question was not entirely innocent. Still, it was utter folly of him to think it could have become a serious entanglement.'

'What happened?' Polly asked, already knowing and fighting down the waves of anguish that engulfed her.

'Richards formally asked for the young lady's hand in marriage.'

'And was refused?'

'But of course, my dear child. It was explained to him quite tactfully that no young lady could possibly marry a man who was, after all . . .' He hesitated.

'Half Indian,' Polly finished for him politely.

The General swallowed. 'Exactly. He seemed to think

that because of your age and circumstances the situation was now different.'

'He did not.' Polly's voice was vehement. 'He thought it different because he loves me and knows that I love him in return.'

The General coughed and wondered how the Mormons had coped for so many years with such an outspoken young woman. He continued manfully.

'Mr Spencer informed me of your family connections, and, of course, my having grown up with your grandfather . . .'

'I still don't believe he would have changed his mind just because of your opinion,' Polly interrupted and rose to her feet, a dangerous light in the back of her eyes.

'Mr Marriot was called and agreed that his son was eager to marry you. Mr Spencer and Mr Marriot agreed that such a marriage would be most suitable.'

'You sat in here, all three of you, and discussed my future as if my feelings were of no account!'

'It was for your own good, your own happiness.'

'And Major Richards? What did he say?' She was so angry that she was shaking.

'What he said would have court-martialled him if I was not an exceedingly patient and tolerant man,' the General said, his exasperation at last showing through. 'He was adamant that you had no desire to marry elsewhere, but Mr Marriot and Mr Spencer assured him that there could be no happiness for you with him. I also spoke out to him very clearly about the unfortunate attitudes you would meet with from other officers' wives and then, of course, any children . . .'

'You interfering, short-sighted, silly old man!' Polly said furiously. 'Oh, why couldn't you leave well alone? Why can't I live my own life the way I choose? Why does everyone believe they know what is best for me?' She drew in a deep, shuddering breath. 'Goodbye, General. I assume I might have the use of a horse?'

'Of course. I understand you rode with Mr Marriot on your journey here . . .'

The door closed in his face.

She ran to the Captain's quarters and removed the dress so hastily that a button flew off. She pulled on the shift and leggings. If she was to ride hard she had to do so unhampered by skirts. Seizing the cloak she slammed the door behind her.

At the far side of the quadrangle she could see Jared in what appeared to be violent conversation with Nephi and Tom. She ignored them and did not wait to ask for a horse. She fastened her cloak at her throat and mounted the first one that she saw.

Behind her she was aware of a cry of protest from the horse's owner and running footsteps. No doubt Jared and Nephi and Tom were also aware of her dramatic exit. She did not care. They could follow if they wished. It made no difference to her. Her hair streamed unrestrainedly in the wind, the mink skins falling from her shoulders and over the haunches of the horse. Fort Kearney. She knew only that it was on the River Platte and further on from Council Bluffs. How long had she taken to eat her meal and change her clothes? Fifteen minutes? Twenty? She had soaked luxuriously in the tub of hot, soapy water. A half hour could have passed before she had rushed into the General's office. How long had their conversation taken? She had no way of knowing. Time had ceased to exist. Listening to the General she had understood everything: his likeness to Chief Red-Cloud; the agonised parting; the insistence that she had been treated respectfully and that no avenging parties of Mormons or soldiers would seek the Indians out. All his life he had been alone. As she was alone. He did not fit into the society in which he lived and neither did she. They belonged nowhere and with no-one but each other.

'Faster,' she urged the horse, and then her heart leapt and she gave a cry of joy. Ahead of her, shoulders hunched, rode a blue-jacketed figure.

'Dart! Dart!'

He turned. She was too far away to see his face, but she saw his actions: the immediate wheeling around of his horse, the flurry of stones and pebbles and then, as they galloped towards each other, the naked joy on his lean, dark face.

'You've come!'

'Of course I've come,' she cried, slithering from her horse's back as he sprang to the ground. 'I'm your woman! You told Red-Cloud so!'

He seized her in his arms and the dark head and the gold closed together in a long, deep, seemingly endless kiss.

A quarter mile away Jared and Tom and Nephi reined in and watched. 'Emily Merrill for you, Jared my boy,' Tom said at last as the two figures in the distance merged into one.

Jared nodded, silenced by the depth of the love that emanated across the plain.

Neither Polly nor Dart were aware of his presence or departure. They were aware only of each other: of the beginning of a life of joy and companionship and love where loneliness would have no place.

'Where are we going?' she asked, her face turned radiantly to his.

'West,' he said as he lifted her up on to his horse.

She smiled contentedly, leaning her head against his chest. She had found what she had been looking for. A love that defied all convention and was strong enough to overcome all obstacles.

'West,' she repeated happily, and closed her eyes, at peace at last.